REFERENCE

Junior Worldmark Encyclopedia of World Cultures

Junior
Worldmark
Encyclopedia of

World Cultures

VOLUME 8

Rwanda to Syria

AN IMPRINT OF GALE

DETROIT · LONDON

JUNIOR WORLDMARK ENCYCLOPEDIA OF WORLD CULTURES

U•X•L Staff

Jane Hoehner, *U•X•L Senior Editor*
Carol DeKane Nagel, *U•X•L Managing Editor*
Thomas L. Romig, *U•X•L Publisher*
Mary Beth Trimper, *Production Director*
Evi Seoud, *Assistant Production Manager*
Shanna Heilveil, *Production Associate*
Cynthia Baldwin, *Product Design Manager*
Barbara J. Yarrow, *Graphic Services Supervisor*
Pamela A. E. Galbreath, *Senior Art Director*
Margaret Chamberlain, *Permissions Specialist (Pictures)*

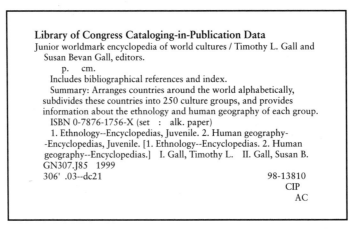

Library of Congress Cataloging-in-Publication Data
Junior worldmark encyclopedia of world cultures / Timothy L. Gall and
Susan Bevan Gall, editors.
    p.   cm.
   Includes bibliographical references and index.
   Summary: Arranges countries around the world alphabetically,
subdivides these countries into 250 culture groups, and provides
information about the ethnology and human geography of each group.
    ISBN 0-7876-1756-X (set : alk. paper)
    1. Ethnology--Encyclopedias, Juvenile. 2. Human geography-
-Encyclopedias, Juvenile. [1. Ethnology--Encyclopedias. 2. Human
geography--Encyclopedias.] I. Gall, Timothy L. II. Gall, Susan B.
GN307.J85 1999
306' .03--dc21   98-13810
                                        CIP
                                        AC

ISBN 0-7876-1756-X (set)
ISBN 0-7876-1757-1 (vol. 1)   ISBN 0-7876-1758-X (vol. 2)   ISBN 0-7876-1759-8 (vol. 3)
ISBN 0-7876-1760-1 (vol. 4)   ISBN 0-7876-1761-X (vol. 5)   ISBN 0-7876-1762-8 (vol. 6)
ISBN 0-7876-1763-6 (vol. 7)   ISBN 0-7876-1764-4 (vol. 8)   ISBN 0-7876-2761-5 (vol. 9)

Printed in the United States of America
10 9 8 7 6 5 4 3 2

Contents
Volume 8

Cumulative Contents

Volume 1

Volume 2

CUMULATIVE CONTENTS

CUMULATIVE CONTENTS

Volume 5

Volume 6

CUMULATIVE CONTENTS

CUMULATIVE CONTENTS

Volume 9

Contributors

Editors: Timothy L. Gall and Susan Bevan Gall

Senior Editor: Daniel M. Lucas

Contributing Editors: Himanee Gupta, Jim Henry, Kira Silverbird, Elaine Trapp, Rosalie Wieder

Copy Editors: Deborah Baron, Janet Fenn, Jim Henry, Patricia M. Mote, Deborah Ring, Kathy Soltis

Typesetting and Graphics: Cheryl Montagna, Brian Rajewski

Cover Photographs: Cory Langley

Data Input: Janis K. Long, Cheryl Montagna, Melody Penfound

Proofreaders: Deborah Baron, Janet Fenn

Editorial Assistants: Katie Baron, Jennifer A. Spencer, Daniel K. Updegraft

Editorial Advisors

P. Boone, Sixth Grade Teacher, Oak Crest Middle School, San Antonio, Texas

Jean Campbell, Foothill Farms Middle School, Sacramento, California

Kathy Englehart, Librarian, Hathaway Brown School, Shaker Heights, Ohio

Catherine Harris, Librarian, Oak Crest Middle School, San Antonio, Texas

Karen James, Children's Services, Louisville Free Public Library, Louisville, Kentucky

Contributors to the Gale Edition

The articles presented in this encyclopedia are based on entries in the *Worldmark Encyclopedia of Cultures and Daily Life* published in 1997 by Gale. The following authors and reviewers contributed to the Gale edition.

ANDREW J. ABALAHIN. Doctoral candidate, Department of History, Cornell University.

JAMAL ABDULLAH. Doctoral candidate, Department of City and Regional Planning, Cornell University.

SANA ABED-KOTOB. Book Review Editor, Middle East Journal, Middle East Institute.

MAMOUD ABOUD. Charge d'Affaires, a.i., Embassy of the Federal and Islamic Republic of the Comoros.

JUDY ALLEN. Editor, Choctaw Nation of Oklahoma.

HIS EXCELLENCY DENIS G. ANTOINE. Ambassador to the United States, Embassy of Grenada.

LESLEY ANN ASHBAUGH. Instructor, Sociology, Seattle University.

HASHEM ATALLAH. Translator, Editor, Teacher; Fairfax, Virginia.

HECTOR AZEVES. Cultural Attaché, Embassy of Uruguay.

VICTORIA J. BAKER. Associate Professor of Anthropology, Anthropology (Collegium of Comparative Cultures), Eckerd College.

POLINE BALA. Doctoral candidate, Asian Studies, Cornell University.

MARJORIE MANDELSTAM BALZER. Research Professor; Coordinator, Social, Regional, and Ethnic Studies Sociology, and Center for Eurasian, Russian, and East European Studies.

JOSHUA BARKER. Doctoral candidate, Department of Anthropology, Cornell University.

IGOR BARSEGIAN. Department of Sociology, George Washington University.

IRAJ BASHIRI. Professor of Central Asian Studies, Department of Slavic and Central Asian Languages and Literatures, University of Minnesota.

DAN F. BAUER. Department of Anthropology, Lafayette College.

JOYCE BEAR. Historic Preservation Officer, Muscogee Nation of Oklahoma.

SVETLANA BELAIA. Byelorussian-American Cultural Center, Strongsville, Ohio.

HIS EXCELLENCY DR. COURTNEY BLACKMAN. Ambassador to the United States, Embassy of Barbados.

BETTY BLAIR. Executive Editor, Azerbaijan International.

ARVIDS BLODNIEKS. Director, Latvian Institute, American Latvian Association in the USA.

ARASH BORMANSHINOV. University of Maryland, College Park.

HARRIET I. BRADY. Cultural Anthropologist (Pyramid Lake Paiute Tribe), Native Studies Program, Pyramid Lake High School.

MARTIN BROKENLEG. Professor of Sociology, Department of Sociology, Augustana College.

REV. RAYMOND A. BUCKO, S.J. Assistant Professor of Anthropology, LeMoyne College.

JOHN W. BURTON. Department of Anthropology, Connecticut College.

DINEANE BUTTRAM. University of North Carolina-Chapel Hill.

RICARDO CABALLERO. Counselor, Embassy of Paraguay.

CHRISTINA CARPADIS. Researcher/Writer, Cleveland, Ohio.

SALVADOR GARCIA CASTANEDA. Department of Spanish and Portuguese, The Ohio State University.

SUSANA CAVALLO. Graduate Program Director and Professor of Spanish, Department of Modern Languages and Literatures, Loyola University, Chicago.

BRIAN P. CAZA. Doctoral candidate, Political Science, University of Chicago.

VAN CHRISTO. President and Executive Director, Frosina Foundation, Boston.

YURI A. CHUMAKOV. Graduate Student, Department of Sociology, University of Notre Dame.

J. COLARUSSO. Professor of Anthropology, McMaster University.

FRANCESCA COLECCHIA. Modern Language Department, Duquesne University.

DIANNE K. DAEG DE MOTT. Researcher/Writer, Tucson, Arizona.

MICHAEL DE JONGH. Professor, Department of Anthropology, University of South Africa.

GEORGI DERLUGUIAN. Senior Fellow, Ph.D., U. S. Institute of Peace.

CHRISTINE DRAKE. Department of Political Science and Geography, Old Dominion University.

ARTURO DUARTE. Guatemalan Mission to the OAS.

CALEB DUBE. Department of Anthropology, Northwestern University.

BRIAN DU TOIT. Professor, Department of Anthropology, University of Florida.

LEAH ERMARTH. Worldspace Foundation, Washington, DC.

NANCY J. FAIRLEY. Associate Professor of Anthropology, Department of Anthropology/Sociology, Davidson College.

GREGORY A. FINNEGAN, Ph.D. Tozzer Library, Harvard University.

ALLEN J. FRANK, Ph.D.

DAVID P. GAMBLE. Professor Emeritus, Department of Anthropology, San Francisco State University.

FREDERICK GAMST. Professor, Department of Anthropology, University of Massachusetts, Harbor Campus.

PAULA GARB. Associate Director of Global Peace and Conflict Studies and Adjunct Professor of Social Ecology, University of California, Irvine.

HAROLD GASKI. Associate Professor of Sami Literature, School of Languages and Literature, University of Tromsø.

STEPHEN J. GENDZIER.

FLORENCE GERDEL.

DON KAVANAUGH. Program Director, Lake of the Woods

ANTHONY P. GLASCOCK. Professor of Anthropology; Department of Anthropology, Psychology, and Sociology; Drexel University.

LUIS GONZALEZ. Researcher/Writer, River Edge, New Jersey.

JENNIFER GRAHAM. Researcher/Writer, Sydney, Australia.

MARIE-CÉCILE GROELSEMA. Doctoral candidate, Comparative Literature, Indiana University.

ROBERT GROELSEMA. MPIA and doctoral candidate, Political Science, Indiana University.

MARIA GROSZ-NGATÉ. Visiting Assistant Professor, Department of Anthropology, Northwestern University.

ELLEN GRUENBAUM. Professor, School of Social Sciences, California State University, Fresno.

N. THOMAS HAKANSSON. University of Kentucky.

ROBERT HALASZ. Researcher/Writer, New York, New York.

MARC HANREZ. Professor, Department of French and Italian, University of Wisconsin-Madison.

ANWAR UL HAQ. Central Asian Studies Department, Indiana University.

LIAM HARTE. Department of Philosophy, Loyola University, Chicago.

FR. VASILE HATEGAN. Author, *Romanian Culture in America*.

BRUCE HEILMAN. Doctoral candidate, Department of Political Science, Indiana University.

JIM HENRY. Researcher/Writer, Cleveland, Ohio.

BARRY HEWLETT. Department of Anthropology, Washington State University.

SUSAN F. HIRSCH. Department of Anthropology, Wesleyan University.

MARIDA HOLLOS. Department of Anthropology, Brown University.

HALYNA HOLUBEC. Researcher/Writer, Cleveland, Ohio.

YVONNE HOOSAVA. Legal Researcher and Cultural Preservation Officer, Hopi Tribal Council.

HUIQIN HUANG, Ph.D. Center for East Asia Studies, University of Montreal.

ASAFA JALATA. Assistant Professor of Sociology and African and African American Studies, Department of Sociology, The University of Tennessee, Knoxville.

STEPHEN F. JONES. Russian Department, Mount Holyoke College.

THOMAS JOVANOVSKI, Ph.D. Lorain County Community College.

A. KEN JULES. Minister Plenipotentiary and Deputy Head of Mission, Embassy of St. Kitts and Nevis.

GENEROSA KAGARUKI-KAKOTI. Economist, Department of Urban and Rural Planning, College of Lands and Architectural Studies, Dar es Salaam, Tanzania.

EZEKIEL KALIPENI. Department of Geography, University of Illinois at Urbana-Champaign.

Ojibwa Cultural Centre.

CONTRIBUTORS

SUSAN M. KENYON. Associate Professor of Anthropology, Department of History and Anthropology, Butler University.

WELILE KHUZWAYO. Department of Anthropology, University of South Africa.

PHILIP L. KILBRIDE. Professor of Anthropology, Mary Hale Chase Chair in the Social Sciences, Department of Anthropology, Bryn Mawr College.

RICHARD O. KISIARA. Doctoral candidate, Department of Anthropology, Washington University in St. Louis.

KAREN KNOWLES. Permanent Mission of Antigua and Barbuda to the United Nations.

IGOR KRUPNIK. Research Anthropologist, Department of Anthropology, Smithsonian Institution.

LEELO LASS. Secretary, Embassy of Estonia.

ROBERT LAUNAY. Professor, Department of Anthropology, Northwestern University.

CHARLES LEBLANC. Professor and Director, Center for East Asia Studies, University of Montreal.

RONALD LEE. Author, *Goddam Gypsy, An Autobiographical Novel.*

PHILIP E. LEIS. Professor and Chair, Department of Anthropology, Brown University.

MARIA JUKIC LESKUR. Croatian Consulate, Cleveland, Ohio.

RICHARD A. LOBBAN, JR. Professor of Anthropology and African Studies, Department of Anthropology, Rhode Island College.

DERYCK O. LODRICK. Visiting Scholar, Center for South Asian Studies, University of California, Berkeley.

NEIL LURSSEN. Intro Communications Inc.

GREGORIO C. MARTIN. Modern Language Department, Duquesne University.

HOWARD J. MARTIN. Independent scholar.

HEITOR MARTINS. Professor, Department of Spanish and Portuguese, Indiana University.

ADELINE MASQUELIER. Assistant Professor, Department of Anthropology, Tulane University.

DOLINA MILLAR.

EDITH MIRANTE. Project Maje, Portland, Oregon.

ROBERT W. MONTGOMERY, Ph.D. Indiana University.

THOMAS D. MORIN. Associate Professor of Hispanic Studies, Department of Modern and Classical Literatures and Languages, University of Rhode Island.

CHARLES MORRILL. Doctoral candidate, Indiana University.

CAROL A. MORTLAND. Crate's Point, The Dalles, Oregon.

FRANCIS A. MOYER. Director, North Carolina Japan Center, North Carolina State University.

MARIE C. MOYER.

NYAGA MWANIKI. Assistant Professor, Department of Anthropology and Sociology, Western Carolina University.

KENNETH NILSON. Celtic Studies Department, Harvard University.

JANE E. ORMROD. Graduate Student, History, University of Chicago.

JUANITA PAHDOPONY. Carl Perkins Program Director, Comanche Tribe of Oklahoma.

TINO PALOTTA. Syracuse University.

ROHAYATI PASENG.

PATRICIA PITCHON. Researcher/Writer, London, England.

STEPHANIE PLATZ. Program Officer, Program on Peace and International Cooperation, The John D. and Catherine T. MacArthur Foundation.

MIHAELA POIATA. Graduate Student, School of Journalism and Mass Communication, University of North Carolina at Chapel Hill.

LEOPOLDINA PRUT-PREGELJ. Author, *Historical Dictionary of Slovenia.*

J. RACKAUSKAS. Director, Lithuanian Research and Studies Center, Chicago.

J. RAKOVICH. Byelorussian-American Cultural Center, Strongsville, Ohio.

HANTA V. RALAY. Promotions, Inc., Montgomery Village, Maryland.

SUSAN J. RASMUSSEN. Associate Professor, Department of Anthropology, University of Houston.

RONALD REMINICK. Department of Anthropology, Cleveland State University.

BRUCE D. ROBERTS. Assistant Professor of Anthropology, Department of Anthropology and Sociology, University of Southern Mississippi.

LAUREL L. ROSE. Philosophy Department, Carnegie-Mellon University.

ROBERT ROTENBERG. Professor of Anthropology, International Studies Program, DePaul University.

CAROLINE SAHLEY, Ph.D. Researcher/Writer, Cleveland, Ohio.

VERONICA SALLES-REESE. Associate Professor, Department of Spanish and Portuguese, Georgetown University.

MAIRA SARYBAEVA. Kazakh-American Studies Center, University of Kentucky.

DEBRA L. SCHINDLER. Institute of Arctic Studies, Dartmouth College.

KYOKO SELDEN, Ph.D. Researcher/Writer, Ithaca, New York.

ENAYATULLAH SHAHRANI. Central Asian Studies Department, Indiana University.

ROBERT SHANAFELT. Adjunct Lecturer, Department of Anthropology, The Florida State University.

TUULIKKI SINKS. Teaching Specialist for Finnish, Department of German, Scandinavian, and Dutch, University of Minnesota.

JAN SJÅVIK. Associate Professor, Scandinavian Studies, University of Washington.

MAGDA SOBALVARRO. Press and Cultural Affairs Director, Embassy of Nicaragua.

CONTRIBUTORS

MICHAEL STAINTON. Researcher, Joint Center for Asia Pacific Studies, York University.

RIANA STEYN. Department of Anthropology, University of South Africa.

PAUL STOLLER. Professor, Department of Anthropology, West Chester University.

CRAIG STRASHOFER. Researcher/Writer, Cleveland, Ohio.

SANDRA B. STRAUBHAAR. Assistant Professor, Nordic Studies, Department of Germanic and Slavic Languages, Brigham Young University.

VUM SON SUANTAK. Author, *Zo History*.

MURAT TAISHIBAEV. Kazakh-American Studies Center, University of Kentucky.

CHRISTOPHER C. TAYLOR. Associate Professor, Anthropology Department, University of Alabama, Birmingham.

EDDIE TSO. Office of Language and Culture, Navajo Division of Education.

DAVID TYSON. Foreign Broadcast Information Service, Washington, D.C.

NICOLAAS G. W. UNLANDT. Assistant Professor of French, Department of French and Italian, Brigham Young University.

GORDON URQUHART. Professor, Department of Economics and Business, Cornell College.

CHRISTOPHER J. VAN VUUREN. Professor, Department of Anthropology, University of South Africa.

DALIA VENTURA-ALCALAY. Journalist, London, England.

CATHERINE VEREECKE. Assistant Director, Center for African Studies, University of Florida.

GREGORY T. WALKER. Associate Director, Office of International Affairs, Duquesne University.

GERHARD WEISS. Department of German, Scandinavian, and Dutch, University of Minnesota.

PATSY WEST. Director, The Seminole/Miccosukee Photographic Archive.

WALTER WHIPPLE. Associate Professor of Polish, Germanic and Slavic Languages, Brigham Young University.

ROSALIE WIEDER. Researcher/Writer, Cleveland, Ohio.

JEFFREY WILLIAMS. Professor, Department of Anthropology, Cleveland State University.

GUANG-HONG YU. Associate Research Fellow, Institute of Ethnology, Academia Sinica.

RUSSELL ZANCA. Department of Anthropology, College of Liberal Arts and Sciences, University of Illinois at Urbana-Champaign.

Reader's Guide

Junior Worldmark Encyclopedia of World Cultures contains articles exploring the ways of life of over 290 culture groups worldwide. Arranged alphabetically by country in nine volumes, this encyclopedia parallels the organization of its sister set, *Junior Worldmark Encyclopedia of the Nations*. Whereas the primary purpose of *Nations* is to provide information on the world's nations, this encyclopedia focuses on the traditions, living conditions, and personalities of many of the world's culture groups.

Defining groups for inclusion was not an easy task. Cultural identity is shaped by such factors as history, geography, nationality, ethnicity, race, language, and religion. Sometimes the distinctions are subtle, but important. Most chapters in this encyclopedia begin with an article on the people of the country as a nationality group. For example, the chapter on Kenya begins with an article entitled "Kenyans." This article explores the national character shared by all people living in Kenya. However, there are separate articles on the Gikuyu, Kalenjin, Luhya, and Luo—four of the largest ethnic groups living in the country. They are all Kenyans, but each group is distinct. Many profiled groups—like the Kazaks—inhabit lands that cross national boundaries. Although profiled in the chapter on Kazakstan, Kazaks are also important minorities in China, Uzbekistan, and Turkmenistan. In such cases, cross-references direct the student to the chapter where the group is profiled.

The photographs that illustrate the articles show a wonderfully diverse world. From the luxury liners docked in the harbor at Monaco to the dwellings made of grass sheltering the inhabitants of the rain forest, people share the struggles and joys of earning a living, bringing children into the world, teaching them to survive, and initiating them into adulthood. Although language, customs, and dress illustrate our differences, the faces of the people pictured in these volumes reinforce our similarities. Whether on the streets of Tokyo or the mountains of Tibet, a smile on the face of a child transcends the boundaries of nationality and cultural identity to reveal something common in us all. Photographer Cory Langley's images on pages 93 and 147 in Volume 6 serve to illustrate this point.

The picture of the world this encyclopedia paints today will certainly differ from the one painted in future editions. Indigenous people like the Jivaro in Ecuador (Volume 3, page 77) are being assimilated into modern society as forest lands are cleared for development and televisions and VCRs are brought to even the most remote villages. As the global economy expands, traditional diets are supplemented with Coke, Pepsi, and fast food; traditional storytellers are replaced by World Cup soccer matches and American television programs; and cultural heroes are overwhelmed by images of Michael Jordan and Michael Jackson. Photographer Cynthia Bassett was fortunate to be among a small group of travelers to visit a part of China only recently opened to Westerners. Her image of Miao dancers (Volume 2, page 161) shows a people far removed from Western culture . . . until one looks a little closer. Behind the dancers, in the upper corner of the photograph, is a basketball hoop and backboard. It turns out that Miao teenagers love basketball!

ORGANIZATION

Within each volume the chapters are arranged alphabetically by country. A cumulative table of contents for all volumes in the set follows the table of contents to each volume.

Each chapter covers a specific country. The contents of the chapter, listing the culture group articles, follows the chapter title. An overview of the composition of the population of the country appears after the contents list. The individual articles follow, and are organized according to a standard twenty-heading outline explained in more detail below. This structure allows for easy comparison between cultures and enhances the accessibility of the information.

Articles begin with the **pronunciation** of the group's name, a listing of **alternate names** by which the group is known, the group's **location** in the world, its **population**, the **languages** spoken, and the **religions** practiced. Articles are illustrated with maps showing the primary location of the group and photographs of the culture group being profiled. The twenty standard headings by which the articles are organized are presented below.

1 ● INTRODUCTION: A description of the group's historical origins provides a useful background for understanding its contemporary affairs. Information relating to migration helps explain how the group arrived at its present location. Political conditions and governmental structure(s) that affect members of the profiled ethnic group are also discussed.

2 ● LOCATION: The population size of the group is listed. This information may include official census data from various countries and/or estimates. Information on the size of a group's population located outside the traditional homeland may also be included, especially for those groups with large scattered populations. A description of the homeland includes information on location, topography, and climate.

3 ● LANGUAGE: Each article lists the name(s) of the primary language(s) spoken by members. Descriptions of linguistic origins, grammar, and similarities to other languages may also be included. Examples of common words, phrases, and proverbs are listed for many of the profiled groups, and some include examples of common personal names and greetings.

4 ● FOLKLORE: Common themes, settings, and characters in the profiled group's traditional oral and/or literary mythology are highlighted. Many entries include a short excerpt or synopsis of one of the group's noteworthy myths, fables, or legends. Some entries describe the accomplishments of famous heroes and heroines or other prominent historical figures.

5 ● RELIGION: The origins of traditional religious beliefs are profiled. Contemporary religious beliefs, customs, and practices are also discussed. Some groups may be closely associated with one particular faith (especially if religious and ethnic identification are interlinked), while others may have members of diverse faiths.

6 ● MAJOR HOLIDAYS: Celebrations and commemorations typically recognized by the group's members are described. These holidays commonly fall into two categories: secular and religious. Secular holidays often include an independence day and/or other days of observance recognizing important dates in history that affected the group as a whole. Religious holidays are typically the same as those honored by people of the same faith worldwide. Some secular and religious holidays are linked to the lunar cycle or to the change of seasons. Some articles describe customs practiced by members of the group on certain holidays.

7 ● RITES OF PASSAGE: Formal and informal events that mark an individual's procession through the stages of life are profiled. These events typically involve rituals, ceremonies, observances, and procedures associated with birth, childhood, the coming of age, milestones in education or religious training, adulthood, and death.

8 ● RELATIONSHIPS: Information on greetings, body language, gestures, visiting customs, and dating practices is included. The extent of formality to which members of a certain ethnic group treat others is also addressed, as some groups may adhere to customs governing interpersonal relationships more or less strictly than others.

9 ● LIVING CONDITIONS: General health conditions typical of the group's members are cited. Such information includes life expectancy, the prevalence of various diseases, and access to medical care. Information on urbanization, housing, and access to utilities is also included. Transportation methods typically utilized by the group's members are also discussed.

10 ● FAMILY LIFE: The size and composition of the family unit is profiled. Gender roles common to the group are also discussed, including the division of rights and responsibilities relegated to male and female group members. The roles that children, adults, and the elderly have within the group as a whole may also be addressed.

11 ● CLOTHING: Many entries include descriptive information (design, color, fabric, etc.) regarding traditional clothing (or national costume) for men and women, and indicate the frequency of its use in contemporary life. A description of typical clothing worn in modern daily life is also provided, especially if traditional clothing is no longer the usual form of dress. Distinctions between formal and work attire and descriptions of clothing preferences of young people are described for many groups as well.

12 ● FOOD: Descriptions of items commonly consumed by members of the group are listed. The frequency and occasion for meals is also described, as are any unique customs regarding eating and drinking, special utensils and furniture, and the role of food and beverages in ritual ceremonies. Many entries include a recipe for a favorite dish.

13 ● EDUCATION: The structure of formal education in the country or countries of residence is discussed, including information on primary, secondary, and higher education. For some groups, the role of informal education is also highlighted. Some articles include information regarding the relevance and importance of education among the group as a whole, along with parental expectations for children.

14 ● CULTURAL HERITAGE: Since many groups express their sense of identity through art, music, literature, and dance, a description of prominent styles is included. Some articles also cite the contributions of famous individual artists, writers, and musicians.

15 ● EMPLOYMENT: The type of labor that typically engages members of the profiled group is discussed. For some groups, the formal wage economy is the primary source of earnings, but for other groups, informal agriculture or trade may be the usual way to earn a living. Working conditions are also highlighted.

16 ● SPORTS: Popular sports that children and adults play are listed, as are typical spectator sports. Some articles include a description and/or rules to a sport or game.

17 ● RECREATION: Listed activities that people enjoy in their leisure time may include structured pastimes (such as public musical and dance performances) or informal get-togethers (such as meeting for conversation). The role of popular culture, movies, theater, and television in everyday life is also discussed where it applies.

18 ● CRAFTS AND HOBBIES: Entries describe arts and crafts commonly fabricated according to traditional methods, materials, and style. Such objects may often have a functional utility for everyday tasks.

19 ● SOCIAL PROBLEMS: Internal and external issues that confront members of the profiled group are described. Such concerns often deal with fundamental problems like war, famine, disease, and poverty. A lack of human rights, civil rights, and political freedom may also adversely affect a group as a whole. Other problems may include crime, unemployment, substance abuse, and domestic violence.

20 ● BIBLIOGRAPHY: References cited include works used to compile the article, benchmark publications often recognized as authoritative by scholars, and other reference sources accessible to middle school researchers. Website addresses are provided for researchers who wish to access the World Wide Web. The website citation includes the author and title of the website (if applicable). The address begins with characters that follow "http://" in the citation; the address ends with the character preceding the comma and date. For example, the citation for the website of the German embassy appears as follows:

German Embassy, Washington, D.C. [Online]
  Available http://www.germany-info.org/, 1998.

To access this site, researchers type:
  www.germany-info.org

A glossary and an index of groups profiled appears at the end of each volume.

ACKNOWLEDGMENTS

The editors express appreciation to the members of the U•X•L staff who were involved in a number of ways at various stages of development of the *Junior Worldmark Encyclopedia of World Cultures.*

SUGGESTIONS ARE WELCOME: We appreciate any suggestions that will enhance future editions. Please send comments to:

Editors
*Junior Worldmark Encyclopedia
of World Cultures*
U•X•L
27500 Drake Road
Farmington Hills, MI 48331-3535
(800) 877-4253

Rwanda

The people of Rwanda are Rwandans. The population of Rwanda is about 85 percent Hutu, who were traditionally farmers. The Tutsi, a warrior people, once made up about 14 percent of the total population, but many have fled into neighboring territories for refuge. To learn more about the Tutsi see the chapter on Burundi in Volume 2. There are also some Twa, a Pygmy tribe of hunters, living in Rwanda, as well as small numbers of Asians and Europeans.

Rwandans

PRONUNCIATION: ruh-WAHN-duhns
LOCATION: Rwanda
POPULATION: 7 million
LANGUAGE: Kinyarwanda; French; Swahili; English
RELIGION: Roman Catholicism; Protestantism; Islam; small numbers of Baha'is

1 ● INTRODUCTION

Rwanda is one of the only African kingdoms to have kept its identity through the colonial era (1890–1962). However, colonial rule harmed Rwanda in ways that helped lead to ethnic warfare in the 1990s.

Rwanda is home to three ethnic groups: the Hutu (about 85–90 percent of the population); the Tutsi (10–15 percent); and the Twa (less than 1 percent). The cultures of these groups have much in common. They have spoken the same language for at least five hundred years.

Rwanda became a German colony in the 1890s. The Germans treated the upper-class Tutsi better than the Hutu. After Germany lost World War I (1914–18), the Belgians took control. Like the Germans, they favored the Tutsi. As a result, some (but not all) Tutsi were better off due to colonial rule. This angered the Hutu majority, and ethnic violence broke out in 1959. Many Tutsis were killed, and many more fled to nearby countries. The Tutsi monarchy was overthrown, and Rwanda became an independent nation in 1962.

For almost thirty years, Hutu political parties held power. In 1990, however, a rebel group composed mostly of Tutsi refugees invaded Rwanda from Uganda. Fighting raged, off and on, for the next four years. In 1994, up to 1 million people were killed. The victims were mostly Tutsi. How-

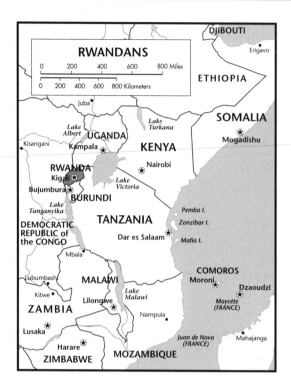

RWANDANS

0   200   400   600   800 Miles
0   200   400   600   800 Kilometers

lion Rwandans fled to refugee camps in Tanzania, Burundi, and the former Zaire (now the Democratic Republic of the Congo). The majority were Hutus. Civil war broke out in Zaire in 1996, and most of the Hutu refugees there returned to Rwanda.

Kigali, the capital, is Rwanda's largest city. It has a population of about 300,000 people.

3 ● LANGUAGE

All Rwandans speak a Bantu language called *Kinyarwanda*. It is a difficult language for outsiders to learn. For example, Kinyarwanda has over twenty different kinds of nouns. In contrast, English has only two: singular and plural.

French is Rwanda's second language. It is spoken by many educated Rwandans. Some Rwandans speak Swahili, a common language of East and Central Africa. English is also spoken, especially in cities.

4 ● FOLKLORE

Rwanda is rich in legends, stories, and poetry. In the past, they were memorized and recited by men who served the king. In the twentieth century much of Rwanda's folklore was written. For this reason Rwanda has a better record of its history and traditions than most neighboring countries.

Rwandan stories and legends are still told to instruct children or to entertain.

5 ● RELIGION

Missionaries have converted many Rwandans to Christianity since the colonial era (1890–1962). Today about 60 percent of

ever, many Hutu who opposed the government also died. In the end, the rebels overthrew the government. The new government vowed to build a society that would not be based on ethnic divisions.

2 ● LOCATION

Rwanda is a tiny country in the Great Lakes region of Central Africa. It is about as large as the state of Massachusetts. To Rwanda's west is the Democratic Republic of the Congo (formerly Zaire). To the east is Tanzania. Uganda is directly to the north, while Burundi is located to the south. Rwanda is very close to the equator. However, it has a temperate climate because of its high altitude.

Rwanda has a total population of close to 7 million people. In 1994 as many as 1 mil-

Rwandans are Roman Catholics. Another 20–30 percent are Protestants. There is also a small Muslim (followers of Islam) minority and some followers of the Baha'i faith.

Rwandans often combine native religions with Christianity. They believe that Imaana, their traditional god, is well-meaning but distant. Imaana is most often contacted through the spirits of deceased family members.

6 ● MAJOR HOLIDAYS

Rwandans celebrate the major Christian holy days such as Christmas (December 25) and Easter (in March or April). They also observe other Roman Catholic festivals, including Ascension Day (forty days after Easter) and All Saints' Day (November 1). Most of the traditional Rwandan festivals are no longer national holidays. However, a harvest ritual called *Umuganura* is still celebrated in August.

7 ● RITES OF PASSAGE

Rwandan rites of passage include birth, marriage, blood brotherhood, and death. Rwandans who practice traditional religions are initiated into the cults of Ryangombe or Nyabingi. Baptism and confirmation are important turning points in the lives of Rwandan Christians.

Birth is the first rite of passage. When a baby is born, the mother and child are left alone for up to eight days. When this period is over, friends and relatives visit and bring gifts. The baby is shown in public for the first time and its name is announced.

Rwandans do not have an initiation rite at puberty. They are not considered adults

Jason Lauré

Rwandan children begin primary school at age seven. By law, all children are ensured at least a sixth-grade education.

until they have married and had a child. Marriage happens in several stages, from the engagement to the wedding. At each stage, the families of the groom and bride exchange gifts. The most important gift is the bride wealth cow that the husband gives his future wife's father.

Most Rwandans have a Christian funeral. However, traditional rituals are often observed as well. It is common to sacrifice a cow or bull, for example.

8 ● RELATIONSHIPS

Rwandans are usually friendly, polite, and helpful. In rural areas, people greet everybody they pass in the fields and pathways.

Cynthia Bassett

Rwandans gather to watch dancers. Ritual occasions such as weddings include traditional music and dance, but there is likely to be modern popular music as well.

In the cities people are expected to greet everyone they know. The warmest greeting is similar to a hug. Each person's left hand touches the other person's hip. The right hand reaches up to touch the other person's shoulder..

Rwandans spend much of their time visiting. Guests are always offered something to drink.

Tutsi and Hutu will often share the same cooking pots and drink containers. However, Twa are not allowed to drink or eat from the same containers. Their dishes are kept separate from those of everyone else.

9 ● LIVING CONDITIONS

Different social classes in Rwanda live very differently. Conditions in the city and the country also vary greatly. In the cities, rich Rwandans may live in brick houses with running water, indoor plumbing, electricity, and telephones. But most urban Rwandans live more simply. Many have small houses with mud walls and iron roofs. Most lack electricity, running water, and indoor plumbing.

In rural areas, the houses vary. Some wealthy people live in brick houses with tile roofs. Wattle-and-daub (rod and clay) houses are more common. The oldest houses are circular. More recently, many Rwandans have built rectangular houses with iron or thatched roofs. These houses usually lack indoor plumbing, electricity, and running water

10 ● FAMILY LIFE

Inzu, the Rwandan word for family, means either "family," "household," or "house." The Rwandan family consists of a husband, one or more wives, and the children. (Only about 10 percent of Rwandan men have more than one wife.) When a man has more than one wife, each one has her own house on the family grounds.

After the inzu, the next largest family unit is the *umuryango*. It consists of several inzus who trace their family line back five or six generations to the same male ancestor. Rwandans must marry someone outside their *umuryango*. A young man goes to see the father of a woman he wishes to marry. His father also pays a visit and brings gifts. Then the two fathers discuss the marriage. The bridegroom and his father have to pay at least one bride wealth cow to the bride's father. This payment grants legal status to any children the couple have.

11 ● CLOTHING

Today Rwandans wear modern Western-style clothing. However, they buy it at used clothing stores. Some Rwandans can afford to buy new clothing made by tailors in Rwanda. The traditional Rwandan costumes made of animal skins and bark cloth is seen only in museums.

12 ● FOOD

The two most common foods are beans and plantains. (Plantains are similar to bananas.) Often they are boiled together. Another food staple is sorghum grain. It is used as a beverage, a porridge, and a type of flour. Rwandan beer is brewed from sorghum and plantains. Other common foods are white potatoes, sweet potatoes, manioc (cassava), and maize (corn).

Only wealthy Rwandans eat meat often. The most common meat is goat. It is usually barbecued over a charcoal burner. Beef is the most valued meat. In most cases it is only eaten if a bull or cow is sacrificed for a ritual. In the past, Rwandans hardly ate any fish. Today, fish farming provides tilapia and catfish.

Only urban Rwandans eat three times a day. Except for a beverage, Rwandan farmers don't eat until about midday. Often they cook food right in the field. They eat again after returning home at night.

13 ● EDUCATION

Rwandan children begin primary school at age seven. By law all children are ensured at least a sixth-grade education. Sometimes, however, parents cannot afford school uniforms, supplies, and other expenses. Only the better students attend secondary school. Rwandans can go to a university, a nursing school, or even a medical school in their own country. Some study in Europe or the United States.

Many Rwandans in rural areas cannot read or write.

Families try hard to educate all their children. However, this is rarely possible because education is so costly.

14 ● CULTURAL HERITAGE

Groups known as *intore* perform traditional ritual dances. The dancers wear headdresses made from dried grasses. They carry small shields on their left arms. There is also dancing at weddings and other special occasions. The Twa people are renowned for their musical skills. Rwanda has its own musical instruments.

15 ● EMPLOYMENT

Rwandans work very hard. Men in rural areas try to find paid employment but also perform farm tasks. The women mostly farm instead of working for wages. In the cities, though, many women have paid jobs.

16 ● SPORTS

The most popular sport in Rwanda is soccer. The country's many soccer clubs compete in organized leagues. Large crowds attend soccer matches, especially when the national team is playing. Running has become very popular. Rwandans begin competing in races at a very young age.

17 ● RECREATION

Almost everyone in Rwanda owns and listens to a radio. In the cities, the wealthier people have televisions and VCRs. There are video stores in large cities. In urban dance clubs, one can hear American rock music, Caribbean reggae, and pop music from Zaire and Kenya. American dances are popular, but the Rwandans do them their own way.

Special occasions such as weddings also provide recreation. Food and beer are served, and there is music and dancing.

18 ● CRAFTS AND HOBBIES

Rwandans are known for weaving baskets and mats with detailed designs. Similar designs are painted on large cooking pots made by Twa potters. In recent years, woodcarving, sculpture, and painting have become important crafts.

19 ● SOCIAL PROBLEMS

The most pressing social problem in Rwanda today is ethnic conflict. Restoring the country after the violence of 1994 has been a difficult task. In the final weeks of 1996, hundreds of thousands of Hutu returned to Rwanda from refugee camps in Tanzania and the Democratic Republic of the Congo (formerly Zaire).

Differences between rich and poor have widened the country's ethnic divisions. Poor rural youths migrate to cities but often cannot find jobs. They then turn to crime or get involved in terrorist activities.

20 ● BIBLIOGRAPHY

Handloff, R., ed. *Rwanda: A Country Study.* Washington, D.C.: U.S. Government Printing Office, 1990.

Prunier, G. *The Rwanda Crisis: History of a Genocide.* New York: Columbia University Press, 1995.

Taylor, C. *Milk, Honey and Money.* Washington: Smithsonian Institution Press, 1992.

WEBSITES

World Travel Guide. Rwanda. [Online] Available http://www.wtgonline.com/country/rw/gen.html, 1998.

Hutu

PRONUNCIATION: HOO-too
LOCATION: Rwanda; Burundi
POPULATION: Approximately 10 million
LANGUAGE: Kinyarwanda; Kirundi; French; Swahili
RELIGION: Christianity combined with traditional beliefs

1 ● INTRODUCTION

The word *Hutu* is the name for the majority of people who live in the countries of Rwanda and Burundi. The Hutu have much in common with the other peoples of these countries, the Tutsi and the Twa. All three groups speak the same Bantu language.

Social relations in Rwanda and Burundi were affected by European rule. Both countries were European colonies between 1890 and 1962. The Germans ruled from 1890 until the end of World War I (1914–18). They favored the upper-class Tutsi. The Belgians who followed the Germans also favored the Tutsi at first. In the 1950s, however, they supported Hutu leaders because the Tutsi were seeking independence.

Rwanda and Burundi took very different paths to independence in 1962. In Rwanda, Hutu leaders overthrew the *mwami* (the Tutsi king) and seized power by force. In Burundi, the change to independence was more peaceful. The mwami helped the Tutsi and Hutu reach an agreement. However, the peace did not last. The Hutu tried to gain power by force, and they were defeated.

At the time of independence, opposite sides controlled the two countries. Burundi is controlled by a branch of the Tutsi. In

Rwanda, the Hutu ruled until 1994. Then Tutsi refugees from Uganda invaded the country. The government was overthrown and thousands of Hutu fled to neighboring countries. Many have returned since 1996.

2 ● LOCATION

Rwanda and Burundi are mountainous countries in east-central Africa. They share a common border. Their total combined area is roughly 20,900 square miles (54,100 square kilometers)—about the combined size of the states of Maryland and New Jersey.

The combined Hutu population of Rwanda and Burundi was about 13 million in 1994. Many Hutu have left the two countries in recent decades. Thousands fled Burundi in 1972. Hundreds of thousands fled Rwanda in 1994. Many ended up living in refugee camps in neighboring countries. They started returning in 1996.

3 ● LANGUAGE

The Hutu, Tutsi, and Twa all speak the same Central Bantu language. It is called *Kinyarwanda* in Rwanda and *Kirundi* in Burundi. The two versions differ slightly in pronunciation. Some words are different, also.

Many Rwandans and Burundians speak French and have French first names. Swahili is also spoken, especially along the Tanzanian border and in the cities.

The Rwandans and Burundians have long names with clear meanings. For example, the name *Mutarambirwa* means "the one who never gets tired."

4 ● FOLKLORE

The Hutu tell proverbs, folktales, riddles, and myths. Samadari is a popular folk hero. He broke the rules everyone else had to follow. He could make fun of the rich and powerful and insult the wealthy cattle owners.

5 ● RELIGION

Today most people in Rwanda and Burundi are Christians. However, they have kept some of their ancient beliefs. The ancient Hutu god, *Imaana*, had many human qualities. Imaana meant well, but he was distant from the people.

The *abazima* were the spirits of the ancestors. They could become angry and bring bad luck to the living. Gifts were offered to the abazima for protection. People contacted them through fortune-tellers.

6 ● MAJOR HOLIDAYS

The Hutu observe the Rwandan and Burundian independence days, May Day (May 1), New Year's Day (January 1), and the major Christian holidays.

7 ● RITES OF PASSAGE

When a baby is born, the baby and mother stay alone in their house for seven days. A naming ceremony is held on the seventh day. Children who live nearby take part, and food is served.

Marriages are legal when the man's family pays the bride wealth to the woman's family. It is paid in cattle, goats, and beer. For the ceremony, the bride's body is covered with herbs and milk to make it pure.

Death is marked by prayers, speeches, and rituals. Close family members do not take part in certain activities. After a death, they do not work in the fields or have sexual relations during the period of mourning. When the family declares that the mourning period is over, they hold a ritual feast.

8 ● RELATIONSHIPS

The Hutu have different greetings for morning, afternoon, and evening. The morning greeting—*Warumutse ho?*—is answered with *Waaramutse*. The afternoon greeting—*Wiiriwe ho?*— is answered with *Wiiriwe*.

Hutu young people meet each other through group activities such as dances and church events. Western-style dating is practiced by wealthier Hutu in the cities.

Cynthia Bassett

A Hutu woman carries produce on her head.

9 ● LIVING CONDITIONS

Almost all Rwandans and Burundians live in rural areas. Traditional Hutu houses are huts made from wood, reeds, and straw and are shaped like beehives. High hedges serve as fences. In recent years, modern houses have been built with modern materials.

10 ● FAMILY LIFE

Women take care of the home. They also plant, hoe, and weed the crops. Men and boys look after the livestock and clear the fields to prepare them for planting.

In the past, the families of the bride and groom decided all marriages. These days most young people choose the person they want to marry.

Marriages between Hutu and Tutsis have always been rare, although Hutu men were allowed to court Tutsi women. Such marriages occur more often today, but they are still uncommon.

11 ● CLOTHING

In the past, Hutus wore skirts of cloth made from tree bark, and cloaks made of animal hides. These have long been replaced by Western-style clothing. However, handmade beaded necklaces and bracelets are still worn.

12 ● FOOD

The staple foods of the Hutu include beans, corn, millet, sorghum, sweet potatoes, and cassava. Milk and beef are important foods. Goat meat and goat milk are eaten by people of low social status. Meals are often planned around a family's work schedule.

An alcoholic drink made from bananas and sorghum grain is saved for special occasions.

13 ● EDUCATION

Only about half the people in Rwanda and Burundi can read and write in their native language. Even fewer can read and write French. There are schools for teachers and at least one university in each country. Well-educated persons speak French. Rwanda's educational system was disrupted by the 1994 conflict.

14 ● CULTURAL HERITAGE

Music, dancing, and drumming are important parts of rural life. Men and women have different dances. The dancers move their arms and bodies quickly. They also stomp their feet in time to the music. People sing alone (solo) or in a chorus. There are many different kinds of songs. They include hunting songs, lullabies, and songs in praise of cattle (*ibicuba*).

Hutu literature consists of myths, legends, and praise poetry.

15 ● EMPLOYMENT

Most Hutu have always been farmers. Raising and herding cattle are ranked more highly than raising crops.

16 ● SPORTS

Both young people and adults enjoy a game called *igisoro* (or called *mancala* in other parts of Africa). Beans are placed in holes in a wooden board. The players line up their own pieces in rows and try to capture those of their opponent.

The main spectator sport in Rwanda and Burundi is soccer.

17 ● RECREATION

Movie theaters in the capitals of Rwanda and Burundi show current European and American films.

18 ● CRAFTS AND HOBBIES

Hutu crafts include pottery, woodwork, jewelry, metal work, and basket weaving.

19 ● SOCIAL PROBLEMS

Thousands of Hutu civilians fled from Rwanda to the Democratic Republic of the Congo (formerly Zaire) in 1994. In 1996 they were caught up in a civil war in that country. Many returned to Rwanda.

20 ● BIBLIOGRAPHY

Lemarchand, Rene. *Burundi: Ethnocide as Discourse and Practice*. New York: Cambridge University Press, 1994.
Malkki, Liisa H. *Purity and Exile: Violence, Memory, and National Cosmology among Hutu Refugees in Tanzania*. Chicago: University of Chicago Press, 1995.
Twagilimana, Aimable. *Hutu and Tutsi*. Heritage Library of African Peoples. New York: Rosen Publishing Group, 1998.

WEBSITES
Weiner, Neil. Background Briefing: Hutu and Tutsi of Rwanda and Burundi. [Online] Available htttp://www.backgroundbriefing.com/hutu-tuts.html, 1994.
World Travel Guide. Rwanda. [Online] Available http://www.wtgonline.com/country/rw/gen.html, 1998.

St. Kitts and Nevis

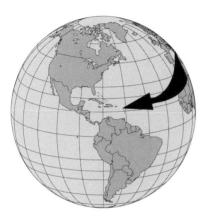

The population of St. Kitts and Nevis is mainly of African descent. About 95 percent of the population is black, about 5 percent is mulatto (mixed race), 3 percent is of Indian or Pakistani descent, and just over 1 percent is of European descent. For more information on Indians, see the chapter on India in Volume 4; on Pakistanis, the chapter on Pakistan in Volume 7.

Kittitians and Nevisians

PRONUNCIATION: Ki-TEE-shuns and ne-VEE-zhuns
LOCATION: St. Kitts and Nevis
POPULATION: 41,000–45,000
LANGUAGE: English; English-based Creole dialect with West African and French elements
RELIGION: Anglicanism; other Protestant sects; Roman Catholicism; Bahaism

1 ● INTRODUCTION

The nation of St. Kitts and Nevis (pronounced NEE-vis) consists of two Caribbean islands separated by a narrow strait of water. The people of the two islands are called Kittitians and Nevisians.

Christopher Columbus sighted St. Kitts and Nevis in 1493. Originally called St. Christopher, St. Kitts is the location of the first British colony established in the West Indies in 1623. For that reason, St. Kitts is sometimes called "the mother colony of the West Indies." Five years later, the British officially settled Nevis. The French were soon competing with the British for control of the islands. The native Carib population was virtually destroyed in the first years of European occupation. Eventually, both St. Kitts and Nevis were turned over to the British under the Treaty of Paris in 1783. Under the British rule, sugarcane plantations flourished on both islands, supported by the labor of slaves imported from West Africa.

St. Kitts, Nevis, together with Anguilla, were united within a larger Leeward Islands Federation in 1882. St. Kitts and Nevis achieved full independence on September 19, 1983. The two-island nation remains a member of the British Commonwealth and retains many British traditions.

2 ● LOCATION

St. Kitts and Nevis belong to the Leeward Islands, in the Lesser Antilles. They are separated from each other by a two-mile strait called The Narrows. The country has a total land area of 104 square miles (269 square kilometers), about one and one-half times the size of Washington, D.C. St. Kitts is the larger of the two islands. The capital city and main port of Basseterre is located on the southwestern coast. St. Kitts has a varied terrain: volcanic peaks, rain forests on the higher mountains, fertile lowlands, and coves with black, brown, and white sand.

The most outstanding feature of the circular island of Nevis is Nevis Peak, rising to 3,232 feet (985 meters) at its center. Like St. Kitts, Nevis has forested mountains in its interior and low-lying areas along the coast. Charlestown is Nevis's only town.

Population estimates for St. Kitts and Nevis range from 41,000 to 45,000. About 10,000 people live on Nevis and the rest on St. Kitts. About 95 percent of the population is of African descent. The remaining 5 percent are of mixed-race, East Indian, or European ancestry.

3 ● LANGUAGE

The official language of St. Kitts and Nevis is English. Standard English, with correct grammar, is spoken in formal situations. Informally, most residents speak a local English-based Creole dialect. It combines elements of West African languages and French. Subject and object pronouns are reversed and past actions are expressed with present-tense verbs. For example, in infor-

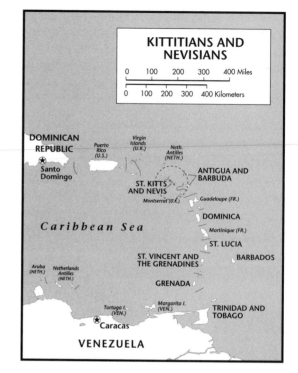

mal conversation, a Kittian might say "I tell she" for "I told her." Also, the African-influenced "de" is used in place of "the."

4 ● FOLKLORE

Kittitians and Nevisians tend to be superstitious. Some still fear the black magic called *obeah* that is common to the Caribbean region.

5 ● RELIGION

Between one-third and one-half of the country's population is Anglican, a Protestant group with roots in England. Other Protestant groups include Methodists, Moravians, Baptists, and Seventh-Day Adventists. About 10 percent of the residents are Roman Catholic. The Baha'i religion is also represented.

6 ● MAJOR HOLIDAYS

Major holidays in St. Kitts and Nevis include New Year's Day (January 1), Good Friday (in March or April), Labor Day (May 1), Whitmonday, Bank Holiday on the first Monday in August, Independence Day (September 19), Prince of Wales's Birthday (November 14), Christmas (December 25), and Boxing Day (December 26).

St. Kitts's annual Carnival celebration is held the last week of the year, from December 25 through January 2. It is a typical Caribbean Carnival, with masquerades, calypso and steel band music, and street dancing. Nevis' Carnival, called Culturama, is held in late July and early August, and includes arts and crafts and talent shows in addition to carnival festivities.

7 ● RITES OF PASSAGE

Major life transitions, such as birth, marriage, and death, are marked by religious celebrations appropriate to each Kittitian's and Nevisian's faith.

8 ● RELATIONSHIPS

There is a local handshake called a "bump." It consists of two people clenching their hands into fists and bumping them gently together. "Liming" is a popular pursuit in St. Kitts and Nevis. This term, which means "hanging out" is used throughout the Caribbean region, and reflects the easygoing lifestyle.

9 ● LIVING CONDITIONS

Until the 1970s, the typical islander's house was wooden with a corrugated metal roof, often painted red. The houses themselves were often painted in pastel colors. By the 1990s, most houses were built from concrete blocks and wood. Roofs are still made of corrugated metal. It is becoming more common for islanders to own the land on which they live. At one time, houses were built on piles of stones in case they had to be moved quickly, but this is no longer the practice.

St. Kitts and Nevis enjoy a healthy climate with almost no tropical diseases. Sanitation conditions are good. The life expectancy is sixty-eight years.

The country has a good system of roads. Following the British way, motorists drive on the left side of the road. Drainage ditches along the side of the roads are called "ghauts." Drivers must be careful not to go off the road into one of these ditches. The phrase "Watch de ghaut" is a common warning to drivers.

10 ● FAMILY LIFE

Family loyalty is strong. It is not uncommon to find households with extended families including members from two or three generations living together.

11 ● CLOTHING

People on St. Kitts and Nevis take great pride in their appearance and wear modern Western-style clothing. Even for casual wear, women wear skirts or dresses. Men wear jeans or casual slacks. For men, business attire usually includes a shirt and tie, or at least a button-down shirt, called a shirt jack. Fashion-consciousness on the islands is especially strong on weekends, when people dress up rather than down. School children wear uniforms.

Recipe

Cassava Bread

Ingredients

½ pound cassava, finely grated (sweet potato may be substituted)
3 to 4 ounces grated coconut
½ cup brown sugar
1 teaspoon salt

Directions

Preheat oven to 350°F.

1. Sprinkle the grated cassava with salt. Wrap it in a clean dish towel or piece of cheesecloth. Twist to wring out liquid.
2. In a 8X8 inch baking pan, spread out half the cassava. Top with brown sugar and grated coconut. Cover with the remaining cassava.
3. Press down firmly on the mixture. Bake 20 minutes.

Cut into squares and serve.

12 ● FOOD

Dietary staples include yams, plantains, rice and peas. Soups are popular, including pumpkin, bean, pepperpot, and fish soups. Lime juice is a common seasoning. Hot pepper sauce made from Scotch Bonnet peppers is a specialty on Nevis. Carib beer is a favorite beverage. Sweet cassava bread is a popular dessert.

13● EDUCATION

St. Kitts and Nevis have traditionally had very high standards for education. Ninety-eight percent of adults are literate (can read and right), among the highest percentages in the Western Hemisphere.

Primary education is free and required between the ages of five and fourteen. There are more than thirty primary schools and eight secondary schools. There is no university on either island. However, post-secondary education is offered at a teachers' training college, a technical college, and a nursing school.

14 ● CULTURAL HERITAGE

An annual St. Kitts Music Festival is held in July. It features music from reggae to gospel. On Nevis, the Drama and Cultural Society sponsors an annual play and other cultural events. St. Kitts' well-known folk dance troupe, Masquerades, performs traditional dances ranging from the French-derived *kwadril* to African war dances. Nevis' best-known artist is Dame Eva Wilkin, who is now more than eighty years old. Her pastels and watercolor artwork portray the island's people and way of life.

15 ● EMPLOYMENT

More than 33 percent of the labor force is engaged in agriculture. The sugar industry is the country's main employer. Many islanders have more than one source of income. These may include fishing, selling garden produce, and working part-time or seasonally in the sugarcane fields or the tourist industry. Working in the sugarcane fields under a tropical sun is very difficult labor. Clumps of sugarcane grow ten feet (three meters) tall. The workers cut the clump at its base with a machete, trim the tops, divide the stalks into smaller lengths then stack them and clear up the debris.

© Catherine Karnow/Woodfin Camp & Assoc.

Two men working in the sugarcane fields. The sugar industry is the country's main employer.

Much of the labor force lacks the employment skills to move from agricultural work to better-paying service-oriented jobs. An estimated 20 percent of the population emigrate each year to the United States, Canada, or Great Britain in search of better-paying jobs. They send money home to the islands and that has been a major source of income on the islands.

16 ● SPORTS

Cricket is the national sport of St. Kitts and Nevis. The whole country practically shuts down for a major cricket match. Other pop-ular sports are horse-racing on Nevis, and soccer on St. Kitts.

17 ● RECREATION

Music is an important form of entertainment on St. Kitts and Nevis. Steel drum, dance, string band, and reggae music are all popu-lar.

18 ● CRAFTS AND HOBBIES

The islands' crafts include batiked (dyed) clothing and wall hangings made from local sea island cotton. Nevisian craftspeople are also known for their fine pottery.

19 ● SOCIAL PROBLEMS

The country's continued economic dependence on the sugar industry has made its economy sensitive to the ups and downs of international sugar prices.

20 ● BIBLIOGRAPHY

Gordon, Joyce. *Nevis: Queen of the Caribees.* London: Macmillan Caribbean, 1990.

Walton, Chelle Koster. *Caribbean Ways: A Cultural Guide.* Westwood, Mass.: Riverdale, 1993.

WEBSITES

Nevis Newsgroup. [Online] Available http://www.interknowledge.com/stkitts-nevis/, 1998.

World Travel Guide, St. Kitts and Nevis. [Online] Available http://www.wtgonline.com/country/kn/gen. html, 1998.

St. Lucia

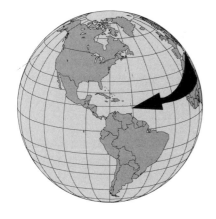

The people of St. Lucia are called St. Lucians. It is estimated, however, that over 90 percent of the population consists of descendants of slaves brought from Africa in the seventeenth and eighteenth centuries. About 5 percent of the population is mulatto (mixed race) and about 3 percent is of Indian descent. For more information on Indians, see the chapter on India in Volume 4.

St. Lucians

PRONUNCIATION: (Saint) LOO-shahns
LOCATION: St. Lucia
POPULATION: 140,000–151,000
LANGUAGE: English; French-based dialect with West African, English, and Spanish influences
RELIGION: Roman Catholicism; small groups of Anglicans, Methodists, Baptists, and Seventh-Day Adventists; Hinduism; Islam

1 ● INTRODUCTION

St. Lucia is a nation in the Windward Islands in the Caribbean Sea. It was believed that Christopher Columbus first saw the island on St. Lucy's Day, December 13. Although historians dispute this, the island, under the name of St. Lucia, can be seen on a Vatican map dated 1502.

The population is descended from West African slaves who worked for both French and British plantation owners. St. Lucia alternated between French and British con-trol fourteen times before it became a British Crown Colony under the Treaty of Paris in 1814. Although the British ruled the island for 165 years without interruption, the cultural influence of the French persists to the present day. It is reflected in the islanders' Catholicism, in their French-based patois (dialect), and in such customs as its Flower Festivals.

In the twentieth century, St. Lucia gradually moved toward self-government. In 1958 it joined the short-lived West Indies Federation. On February 22, 1979, St. Lucia became an independent state within the British Commonwealth. Replacing a dependence on sugar as the basis of its economy, St. Lucia today produces a large banana crop.

2 ● LOCATION

St. Lucia is the second-largest of the Windward Islands. (The Windward Islands are a group of islands in the Caribbean that are situated south of Martinique.) With an area of approximately 239 square miles (620

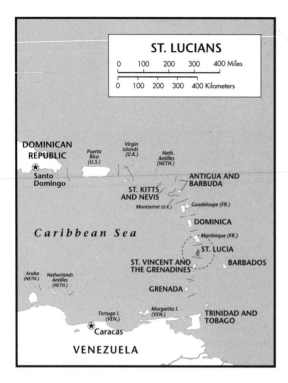

ST. LUCIANS

0   100   200   300   400 Miles

0   100   200   300   400 Kilometers

DOMINICAN
REPUBLIC
★
Santo
Domingo

Puerto
Rico
(U.S.)

Virgin
Islands
(U.K.)

Neth.
Antilles
(NETH.)

ANTIGUA AND
BARBUDA

ST. KITTS
AND NEVIS

Montserrat (U.K.)

Guadeloupe (FR.)

DOMINICA

Caribbean Sea

Martinique (FR.)

ST. LUCIA

ST. VINCENT AND
THE GRENADINES

BARBADOS

Aruba
(NETH.)

Netherlands
Antilles
(NETH.)

GRENADA

Tortuga I.
(VEN.)

Margarita I.
(VEN.)

TRINIDAD AND
TOBAGO

★
Caracas

VENEZUELA

square kilometers), it is between three and four times the size of Washington, D.C.

The island was formed by volcanoes. It has a mountainous interior with lush rain forests. Fertile plains that support the country's banana plantations are located at the base of the central mountains. Many rivers flow from its interior to the Caribbean.

There are still areas where thermal activity from the earth bubbles to the surface. Pools of boiling hot mud—filling the air with the smell of sulfur, similar to rotten eggs—are seen not far from the island's beautiful beaches.

St. Lucia's population is estimated to be about 150,000 people. The capital city of Castries has a population of about 60,000.

3 ● LANGUAGE

Although the official language of St. Lucia is English, most people speak the local patois (dialect). It is based on French and is influenced by the grammar of west African languages. Proper English is the language of the schools, government, and media. Patois is spoken at home, on the streets, and at informal occasions. A written form of patois has been developed for teaching purposes. Examples of patois textbook titles are *Mwen Vin Wakonte Sa Ba'w* (I am going to explain it to you) and *Se'kon Sa I Fèt* (Know how it is done). The name of St. Lucia in patois is "Sent Lisi."

4 ● FOLKLORE

The folk religion of St. Lucia, called *obeah*, is based on practices from Africa. Many of its practices are meant to keep one from being harmed by spirits, devils, and by other human beings. People believe obeah can heal the sick and hurt one's enemies. The preparation of herbal potions is a part of obeah. People often combine obeah with observances of the traditional Christian church.

5 ● RELIGION

About 80 percent of the island's population is Roman Catholic. Smaller groups belong to Protestant groups, including Anglican, Methodist, Baptist, and Seventh-Day Adventist churches. The island's East Indians are either Hindu or Muslim. The Catholic population celebrates various saints' days.

Susan D. Rock

St. Lucia is a volcanic island, the younger part of which is the mountainous southern half. Here, pools of bubbling mud fill the air with the smell of sulfur.

6 ● MAJOR HOLIDAYS

St. Lucia's public holidays include New Year's Day (January 1), Independence Day (February 22), Good Friday and Easter Monday (in March or April), Labor Day (May 1), Queen's Official Birthday (June 5), Corpus Christi (June 6), August Bank Holiday on the first Monday in August, Thanksgiving Day (first Monday in October), St. Lucia Day (December 13), Christmas (December 25), and Boxing Day (December 26).

The annual Carnival celebration is held in the town of Castries right before Shrove Tuesday and Ash Wednesday. It includes parades, a calypso competition, and the naming of a Carnival King and Queen.

St. Lucia has two competing flower festivals held on the feast days of two saints. La Rose, the Feast of St. Rose of Lima, is held on August 30. Its counterpart, La Marguerite, the Feast of St. Margaret Mary Alacoque, occurs on October 17. Each festival includes costumed parades and a "royal court" of kings and queens. In the evening there is feasting and dancing.

The National Day, St. Lucia Day on December 13, is marked by nationwide cultural and sporting events in honor of the island's patron saint.

7 ● RITES OF PASSAGE

Major life transitions are marked by religious ceremonies appropriate to each St. Lucian's particular faith. For instance, Catholics hold funeral wakes on the first and eighth nights after a person's death. Mourners gather at the house of the deceased, and music is performed.

8 ● RELATIONSHIPS

St. Lucians who do not speak English— about 20 percent of the population—are excluded from full participation in the island's social, economic, and political life. However, there has been a revival of respect for patois as a symbol of cultural pride among St. Lucians. Social relations in St. Lucia are strongly influenced by Roman Catholicism.

9 ● LIVING CONDITIONS

St. Lucia has a housing shortage due to overcrowding. It was aggravated by damage from Tropical Storm Debbie in 1994. Most of the country's urban dwellers have access to safe drinking water. Local mass transit is provided by vans and minibuses called "transports." Rural dwellers often reach the nearest town or main road by footpath. The average life expectancy is seventy-two years.

10 ● FAMILY LIFE

Couples in St. Lucia are united in three basic types of relationships. They may be legally married, live together without marriage, or have a "visiting union," where the man and woman live apart and the woman raises the children. The traditional nuclear family is mostly found among the upper classes. Female-headed families are the norm at other levels of society. Children have a strong sense of responsibility toward their families. They are expected to care for their parents as they age.

In rural areas, men and women do the same types of farm work. However, women also take care of the majority of domestic chores and assume primary responsibility for child-rearing.

11 ● CLOTHING

St. Lucians wear modern Western-style clothing. Some older women still wear the traditional national costume. It consists of a madras head-tie and a skirt with lace petticoats draped at the sides. The traditional costumes are worn at festivals.

12 ● FOOD

St. Lucia's cuisine combines the island's French and African heritages. It is based on the local produce and seafood catch, generously spiced and prepared in clay pots heated by coals. Favorite Caribbean dishes enjoyed on St. Lucia include fish soup, callaloo (a type of crabmeat stew), and plantains prepared in many different ways. *Pouile Dudon* is a sweet-and-spicy chicken meal. The national dish is "saltfish and green figs." (Green figs are a type of banana, also known as "bluggoe.")

13 ● EDUCATION

Education on St. Lucia is free and mandatory between the ages of five and fifteen. The literacy rate of the adult population has

Recipe

Saltfish and Green Figs

Ingredients

¼ pound salted codfish
2 Tablespoons vegetable oil
water
3 medium-sized green figs (unripe bananas)
1 small onion, finely chopped

Directions

1. Place the salted codfish into a bowl, breaking it into large chunks. Add water to cover and let soak for 12 hours, replacing the water with fresh water at least twice.
2. Cut the bananas into 1-inch (2.5-centimeter) pieces. Simmer in enough water to cover (about 2 cups) for about 15 minutes.
3. Boil the salted fish in 3 cups of water for 15 minutes, or until tender.
4. Drain thoroughly. Remove any remaining skin or bones, and shred or flake the fish.
5. In a large skillet, sauté the fish with the onion for about 5 minutes.
6. Stir in the drained bananas and cook for 2 more minutes.

Serve with optional garnish of tomato or avocado slices or celery sticks.

been estimated at about 80 percent. There are eighty-three primary schools and thirteen secondary schools, which are like junior high schools. Many young people enter the work force after secondary school. Higher education is offered at Sir Arthur Lewis Community College and at a branch of the University of the West Indies.

14 ● CULTURAL HERITAGE

St. Lucia's traditional music includes work songs that originated during the days of slavery. There are also beach party and game songs and Carnival music. Folk instruments include the *bélè* (or *ka*) drum; a long, hollow tube called the *baha;* a rattle called the *chakchak;* the *zo* (bones); and the *gwaj* (scraper). Various types of banjos and a four-stringed instrument called the *cuatro* are also native to the island.

St. Lucian gospel songs are called *sankeys* in honor of American singer and songwriter Ira D. Sankey. Each year the calypso tunes currently popular on the island appear in a recorded collection called *Lucian Kaiso.* The St. Lucian *kwadril*, a popular traditional dance, reflects the island's French heritage (it is based on the quadrille). It is a complicated dance with five distinct parts.

Nobel-prize-winning poet and playwright Derek Walcott was born in St. Lucia in 1930. He established an international writers' retreat, the Rat Island Foundation, off the coast of his native land. Other St. Lucian writers include Walcott's twin brother, Roderick Walcott, novelist Garth St. Omer, and poet and short-story writer John Robert Lee.

Calypso and reggae music are universally popular in the Caribbean. Two other musical styles—zouk and cadance—are heard on French-influenced islands like St. Lucia.

15 ● EMPLOYMENT

The majority of the work force is engaged in agriculture. Light manufacturing and a growing tourist industry employ most of the rest. Villagers join together in "work parties" to help a neighbor build a new house or organize a family event like a wedding.

16 ● SPORTS

Cricket is very popular on St. Lucia. Its national cricket team competes regularly against the British team.

17 ● RECREATION

Dancing is extremely popular on St. Lucia. Dances are held regularly, even in the smallest towns. Other favorite forms of recreation include beach parties and informally gathering with friends in the evening. The rum shop is the traditional after-hours gathering place for men.

18 ● CRAFTS AND HOBBIES

Traditional crafts on St. Lucia include pottery, woodcarving, and weaving.

19 ● SOCIAL PROBLEMS

In recent years, low banana prices have effected St. Lucia's economy. The situation has been aggravated by farmers' strikes and the damage caused by Tropical Storm Debbie in 1994.

20 ● BIBLIOGRAPHY

Eggleston, Hazel. *Saint Lucia Diary.* Greenwich, Conn.: Devin-Adair, 1977.

Hornbeck, John F. "St. Lucia." In *Islands of the Commonwealth Caribbean: A Regional Study,* edited by Sandra W. Meditz and Dennis M. Hanratty. Washington, D.C.: U.S. Government Printing Office, 1989.

Walcott, Derek. *Another Life.* New York: Farrar Straus & Giroux, 1973.

WEBSITES

St. Lucia Tourist Board. [Online] Available http://www.interknowledge.com/st-lucia/, 1998.

World Away Travel. St. Lucia. [Online] Available http://www.worldaway.com/islands/stlucia/home.html, 1998.

World Travel Guide, St. Lucia. [Online] Available http://www.wtgonline,com/country/lc/gen.html, 1998.

St. Vincent and the Grenadines

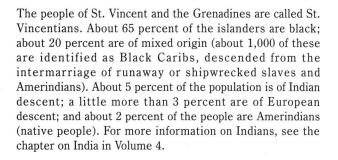

The people of St. Vincent and the Grenadines are called St. Vincentians. About 65 percent of the islanders are black; about 20 percent are of mixed origin (about 1,000 of these are identified as Black Caribs, descended from the intermarriage of runaway or shipwrecked slaves and Amerindians). About 5 percent of the population is of Indian descent; a little more than 3 percent are of European descent; and about 2 percent of the people are Amerindians (native people). For more information on Indians, see the chapter on India in Volume 4.

St. Vincentians

PRONUNCIATION: (Saint) vin-SEN-shuns
LOCATION: St. Vincent and the Grenadines
POPULATION: 107,000
LANGUAGE: English; local dialect with French, West African, Spanish, and English elements
RELIGION: Protestant sects (80–90 percent): Anglican, Methodist, and Seventh-Day Adventist churches; Roman Catholicism; Hinduism; Islam

1 ● INTRODUCTION

In spite of its small size, St. Vincent and the Grenadines had a turbulent early history. Control of its islands was fought over by both Amerindian and European groups for nearly three hundred years. Its heritage includes the unique mingling of Africans and Amerindians that produced the group known as the Black Caribs. The Amerindian (native) population on the island of St. Vincent guarded its homeland so vigorously that it became the last major Caribbean island to be colonized.

St. Vincent's native Carib population resisted European settlement until the eighteenth century. In 1675, however, the Caribs welcomed black Africans who survived the shipwreck of a Dutch ship carrying settlers and slaves. They were allowed to settle on the island and mix with its population. The resulting people became known as the Black Caribs.

St. Vincent is named for the saint's day on which Christopher Columbus first sighted the island on January 22, 1498.

In 1763 the Treaty of Paris granted control of St. Vincent to the British. The French retained control of some of the Grenadines for a number of years. Thus, their cultural

ST. VINCENTIANS

0   100   200   300   400 Miles

0   100   200   300   400 Kilometers

DOMINICAN REPUBLIC

Virgin Islands (U.K.)

Puerto Rico (U.S.)

Neth. Antilles (NETH.)

Santo Domingo

ANTIGUA AND BARBUDA

ST. KITTS AND NEVIS

Montserrat (U.K.)

Guadeloupe (FR.)

DOMINICA

Caribbean Sea

Martinique (FR.)

ST. LUCIA

ST. VINCENT AND THE GRENADINES

BARBADOS

Aruba (NETH.)

Netherlands Antilles (NETH.)

GRENADA

Tortuga I. (VEN.)

Margarita I. (VEN.)

TRINIDAD AND TOBAGO

Caracas

VENEZUELA

of Martinique. The Lesser Antilles include all the islands in the south Caribbean north of Venezuela.) The Grenadines include more than one hundred tiny islands. Thirty-two of the Grenadines are part of St. Vincent and the Grenadines, while the rest belong to Grenada. St. Vincent itself has a total area of 134 square miles (347 square kilometers). The country is slightly less than twice the size of Washington, D.C.

St. Vincent is a volcanic island whose highest point is La Soufrière, an active volcano. The volcano's last major eruption was in 1979. La Soufrière, with elevation of 4,048 feet (1,234 meters), is at the northern end of a mountain range that runs southward to Mount St. Andrew. The mountains are heavily forested, with numerous streams fed by heavy rainfall.

Bequia (pronounced BECK-way), the largest of the Grenadines, could only be reached by sea until the construction of an airport in 1992.

St. Vincent and the Grenadines has an estimated population of 107,000 people. Some 99,000 live on St. Vincent and about 8,000 on the Grenadines. There is a reservation for the native Carib people at Sandy Bay in the northern part of St. Vincent.

influence in the area continued. In the first part of the nineteenth century, East Indian and Portuguese laborers were brought to St. Vincent to work on its sugarcane plantations.

Throughout the nineteenth century and for much of the twentieth century, St. Vincent and the Grenadines remained a British crown colony. It joined the West Indies Federation in 1958 and achieved full independence on October 27, 1979. In 1987 Hurricane Emily destroyed almost 70 percent of the nation's banana crop.

2 ● LOCATION

St. Vincent and the Grenadines is located among the Windward Islands in the Lesser Antilles in the Caribbean Sea. (The Windward Islands are the group of islands south

3 ● LANGUAGE

English is the official language of St. Vincent and the Grenadines. Most people on the islands speak a local dialect, or Creole, that combines elements of West African languages and French. West Indian Creole languages use object pronouns in the subject position. For example, a Vincentian might say, "Me going down town" for "I am going down town."

There are many French names for places in St. Vincent and the Grenadines, including Sans Souci, Petit Vincent, and Mayreau. Carib place names include Bequia (one of the Grenadines) and the Commantawana Bay on St. Vincent.

4 ● FOLKLORE

The folklore of St. Vincent and the Grenadines reflects its combined English, African, and French heritage. There are Creole and West Indian influences as well. Vincentians tend to be superstitious. Some still fear the African-derived black magic called *obeah* that is common in the Caribbean region.

5 ● RELIGION

Between 80 and 90 percent of the population is Protestant, with Anglicans representing the greatest share. Other sects include Methodists and Seventh-Day Adventists. Catholics account for about 10 percent of the population. There are also small Hindu and Muslim (followers of Islam) minorities among the East Indian community.

6 ● MAJOR HOLIDAYS

Public holidays in St. Vincent and the Grenadines include New Year's Day (January 1), St. Vincent and the Grenadines Day (January 22), Good Friday and Easter Monday (in March or April), Labor Day (May 1), Whitmonday (in May), Carnival Tuesday (July 9), CARICOM Day (July 11), Emancipation Day (August 1), Independence Day (October 22), Christmas (December 25), and Boxing Day (December 26). The nation's

Carnival celebration ("Vincy Mas") is held in late June and early July. It features costumed parades, calypso and steel drum bands, and "jump-up" (street dancing).

Union Island, one of the Grenadines, holds sporting and cultural events, including a calypso competition at Eastertime and a Big Drum festival in May.

7 ● RITES OF PASSAGE

Major life transitions, such as birth, marriage, and death, are marked by religious ceremonies appropriate to each St. Vincentian's faith.

8 ● RELATIONSHIPS

"What di' man say?" is a typical greeting. Popular slang among young people on the islands includes "Irie" (an all-purpose phrase that is something like "stay cool" or "see you later") and "Sic too bad" (similar to "awesome").

9 ● LIVING CONDITIONS

St. Vincentians generally own their own homes. Women are more likely to own homes through inheritance. Men usually build their own. It is not uncommon for a family to live in a house owned by the wife. A woman may also acquire a home by having a son or daughter build it for her. A typical rural dwelling is a single-story wooden house with a tin roof, often painted red. Parts of St. Vincent are accessible only by foot or boat.

10 ● FAMILY LIFE

Three common family structures are found on St. Vincent and the Grenadines: legal marriage, unmarried couples living together, and "visiting unions," where the man and woman live apart and the woman raises the children. Even in visiting unions, which are also called "friending," strong ties between father and child are maintained.

Infants receive a great amount of attention and physical affection from all members of the household. The mother takes care of the family's washing and cooking. She also grows its produce and, in many cases, also serves as the household's water carrier. Men are responsible only for those children they have actually fathered, either through present or previous relationships. Thus they may be responsible for children living in different households. The mother is at the center of the household, with obligations to all the members of the household.

Women accounted for 38 percent of the nation's work force in the 1980s. Traditional expectations, however, keep most women from receiving an education equal to that of men.

11 ● CLOTHING

People on St. Vincent and the Grenadines wear modern Western-style clothing. They favor light, brightly colored clothes and are interested in the latest fashions. Some young people enjoy dressing in attention-getting items such as bright orange jeans, the latest in expensive footwear, or shirts with popular designer names. Children wear uniforms to school.

12 ● FOOD

Staple foods include rice, sweet potatoes, and fruits. Especially popular are fruits from the banana family, including plantains and bluggoe ("green figs"). Another widely eaten food is breadfruit. The national dish is "jackfish and breadfruit." Arrowroot, a major cash crop, is used in desserts, including arrowroot sponge cake and arrowroot custard. Also popular are dishes that contain spicy Scotch Bonnet peppers.

13 ● EDUCATION

Primary education is free but not compulsory. Government-run secondary schools are free; government-assisted secondary schools are private and charge tuition. Over three-fourths of children at the primary level attend school, while only about one-fourth of older students enroll in secondary school. St. Vincent has a technical college and a teacher training college affiliated with the University of the West Indies. Most students seeking a higher education study abroad.

14 ● CULTURAL HERITAGE

Big Drum music is popular in St. Vincent and the Grenadines and throughout the Windward Islands. Reflecting an African heritage, this music combines the African "call-and-response" with features of calypso and reggae. The Big Drum is actually a set of three drums. They were originally carved from trees, but are now commonly made from rum kegs. The singers are usually women; the lead singer is called a "chantwell." The songs feature satire and social commentary. Dances are performed by dancers wearing full skirts and headdresses.

© Catherine Karnow/Woodfin Camp & Assoc.

Houses on a hillside. The Grenadines include more than one hundred tiny islands. Thirty-two of the Grenadines are part of St. Vincent and the Grenadines, while the rest belong to Grenada.

15 ● EMPLOYMENT

Many St. Vincentians farm or fish, either for subsistence or for profit. Those who farm small plots take their produce and chickens or fish to market on Saturdays. Bananas are St. Vincent's main commercial crop. Banana growers are paid for their harvest at the stations where bananas are boxed. Hundreds of thousands of dollars are counted into small envelopes every week and distributed to as many as three thousand waiting St. Vincentians.

On the Grenadines, most men are fishermen or boat-builders. The International Whaling Commission has granted the whalers of the island of Bequia with Aboriginal Whaling Status. This classification is reserved for people who traditionally hunt whales for local consumption rather than commercial use. No more than three whales are caught in any one year. A successful catch is considered an important event on Bequia. Much of the island's population flocks to Petit Nevis to see the whale.

16 ● SPORTS

Cricket, the most popular sport, is played throughout the islands on any piece of flat ground and even on the beach. Other sports include soccer, netball, volleyball, and basketball.

17 ● RECREATION

Nighttime gatherings outdoors are a favorite form of recreation. They often include singing, dancing, and the popular pastime of gossiping. With the recent growth of tourism on the islands, it has become common for locals to gather at hotel and restaurant entertainment facilities to eat, drink, dance, and socialize. Men on St. Vincent and the Grenadines enjoy the popular Caribbean pastime of playing dominoes.

18 ● CRAFTS AND HOBBIES

Folk music is played on the four-stringed quatro, as well as the guitar, fiddle, drums, and a variety of percussion instruments. The island of Bequia is known for its skilled model boat builders. They fashion small-scale versions of yachts, whaleboats, and other vessels that are perfect in every detail. Even the island's children make model boats—out of coconut shells—with brightly colored sails.

19 ● SOCIAL PROBLEMS

The low percentage of young people who complete their secondary education has created a shortage of skilled workers on the islands. Better-educated St. Vincentians often emigrate and live abroad until they retire. Drug-related crime is a concern on the islands.

20 ● BIBLIOGRAPHY

Bobrow, Jill, and Dana Jinkins. *St. Vincent and the Grenadines*. Waitsfield, Vt.: Concepts Publishing, 1993.

Cosover, Mary Jo. "St. Vincent and the Grenadines." In *Islands of the Commonwealth Caribbean: A Regional Study,* edited by Sandra W. Meditz and Dennis M. Hanratty. Washington, D.C.: U.S. Government Printing Office, 1989.

Potter, Robert B. *St. Vincent and the Grenadines*. Santa Barbara, Calif.: ABC-Clio, 1992.

Young, Virginia Heyer. *Becoming West Indian: Culture, Self, and Nation in St. Vincent*. Washington, D.C.: Smithsonian Institution Press, 1993.

WEBSITES

World Travel Guide, St. Vincent. [Online] Available http://www.wtgonline.com/country/vc/gen.html, 1998.

San Marino

The people of San Marino are called Sammarinese. The population is almost all of Italian descent.

Sammarinese

PRONUNCIATION: sam-ahr-ehn-EEZ
LOCATION: San Marino
POPULATION: 23,700
LANGUAGE: Italian; Romagna
RELIGION: Roman Catholicism

1 ● INTRODUCTION

The tiny nation of San Marino is located completely within the borders of Italy. It is Europe's third-smallest country and its oldest independent republic. The people of San Marino are called Sammarinese.

San Marino had its beginnings in AD 301, when a Christian stonecutter named Marinus founded a monastery at the top of Mount Titano. He later became known as Saint Marinus *(San Marino* in Italian). For hundreds of years, the tiny country remained independent, aided by its strong walls and towers and its mountaintop location. In 1862, the newly formed Kingdom of Italy signed an agreement guaranteeing its neighbor's independence. The two nations also have a free-trade agreement through an arrangement called a customs union.

2 ● LOCATION

San Marino lies completely within the country of Italy. It is located in the central Apennines, on the summit and lower slopes of Mount Titano. San Marino has an area of 23 square miles (60 square kilometers). It is about one-third the size of Washington, D.C. The tiny republic is only 8 miles (13 kilometers) long, and 5.5 miles (9 kilometers) wide at its widest point.

In 1992, San Marino had a population of 23,700. The Sammarinese are mostly of Italian ancestry, and most new residents of the country come from Italy. The capital city of San Marino is also called San Marino.

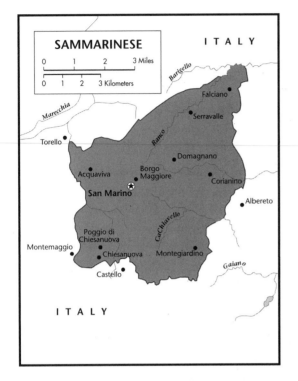

SAMMARINESE

0   1   2   3 Miles
0   1   2   3 Kilometers

ITALY

Bargello
Falciano
Marecchia
Serravalle
Ranco
Torello
Domagnano
Acquaviva
Borgo
Maggiore
Corianino
San Marino
Albereto
CaChiavello
Poggio di
Chiesanuova
Montemaggio
Chiesanuova
Montegiardino
Gaiano
Castello

ITALY

3 ● LANGUAGE

Italian, the official of language of San Marino, is spoken by all its people. However, the Italian of the Sammarinese is distinctive, with certain words and phrases unique to San Marino. Many Sammarinese also speak the regional dialect of Romagna, the part of Italy where San Marino is located.

4 ● FOLKLORE

Mount Titano, on which San Marino is located, is named for the Titans, characters from Roman mythology. They tried to overthrow Jupiter, the supreme god, by piling one mountain on top of another in order to reach the sky.

5 ● RELIGION

Roman Catholicism is San Marino's official religion and the faith of almost all its residents. Ceremonies marking many official occasions are held in the country's churches.

6 ● MAJOR HOLIDAYS

The Sammarinese observe the standard holidays of the Christian calendar, including Epiphany (January 6), Easter and Easter Monday (in March or April), Ascension Day (in May), Assumption Day (August 15), Immaculate Conception (December 8), and Christmas (December 25). Legal holidays in San Marino include New Year's Day (January 1), Labor Day (May 1), an August Bank Holiday (August 14 to 16), and All Saints' Day and Commemoration of the Dead (November 1 and 2).

San Marino also has five national holidays that mark important historical or political events. February 5 marks an important 1740 military victory. The Anniversary of the Arengo, observed on March 25, commemorates the date of the country's first democratic elections. April 1 and October 1 are the two days of the year when San Marino's Captains Regent, its joint heads of government, take office. On September 3, the feast day of its patron saint (Saint Marino), the republic celebrates the anniversary of its founding.

7 ● RITES OF PASSAGE

San Marino is a mainly Catholic country. Many of the rites of passage its young people undergo are religious ceremonies, such as baptism, first communion, confirmation, and marriage. In addition, a student's progress through the education system is marked by many families with graduation parties.

8 ● RELATIONSHIPS

The Sammarinese show the same basic openness and friendliness found among the neighboring Italians. This quality has been important to the success of their nation's busy tourist industry.

Respect toward the elderly is an important social tradition.

9 ● LIVING CONDITIONS

Nearly all dwellings in San Marino have electricity and indoor plumbing. All Sammarinese are covered by a national healthcare plan. In 1992, the average life expectancy (average number of years that people live) was seventy-seven years.

10 ● FAMILY LIFE

San Marino's government provides financial allowances to families with children. Until 1982, Sammarinese women who married citizens of other countries lost their San Marino citizenship. In 1973, women won the right to be elected to any political office in the land.

11 ● CLOTHING

The Sammarinese wear modern Western-style clothing like that worn in the other countries of Western Europe. However, colorful ceremonial costumes are connected with some of their traditions. The young members of the flag-bearers' corps wear brightly colored tights, black boots, and loosely fitting colored shirts with black belts. The honor guards for the nation's leaders, the Captains Regent, wear black uniforms with gold trim, including a gold stripe down their trousers. They wear high, plumed hats with blue and white feathers.

12 ● FOOD

Homemade pasta is one of the most popular foods eaten by the Sammarinese. *Fagioli con le cotiche*—a hearty bean soup with bacon rind—is a special holiday dish traditionally eaten at Christmastime. *Nidi di rondine,* whose name means "swallows' nests," consists of hollow pasta filled with ham, cheese, and a meat-and-tomato sauce, and then baked in a white sauce.

A popular dessert is *zuppa di ciliege,* cherries soaked in red wine and sugar and served with a special bread. Another favorite is *bustrengo,* a traditional holiday dish made with milk, eggs, sugar, raisins, corn flour, and bread crumbs.

San Marino is known for its wines, especially a red wine called *Sangiovese.*

13 ● EDUCATION

San Marino's educational system is based on the system of Italy. School is compulsory (required) between ages six and fourteen. San Marino has no universities of its own. However, its high school graduates may attend colleges and universities in Italy if they pass a qualifying examination.

14 ● CULTURAL HERITAGE

The Valloni Palace houses many of San Marino's cultural treasures. Its famous paintings include *Saint Philip Neri* and *Saint Marino Lifting Up the Republic,* both by Guercino, and *Saint John* by Strozzi. The

SAMMARINESE

fourteenth-century Church of St. Francis, an architectural treasure, houses more historic paintings.

San Marino's national anthem is probably the oldest of any country in the world. It is unusual because it has no words and is played rather than sung. San Marino has a military band that performs at ceremonial events.

15 ● EMPLOYMENT

Farming provides a smaller proportion of San Marino's income than it did in the past. However, many Sammarinese are still farmers, growing barley, corn, vegetables, grapes and other fruits, and raising livestock. Most other jobs are in tourism or manufacturing. San Marino has very low unemployment.

16 ● SPORTS

The traditional national sport of San Marino is archery. Two other favorite sports are pistol and rifle shooting. San Marino's location near Italy's coast on the Adriatic Sea allows its residents to enjoy water sports including swimming, sailing, and deep-sea diving. The Italian sport of *bocce,* lawn bowling with heavy metal balls, is a popular pastime. The Sammarinese also enjoy soccer, baseball, tennis, and basketball.

17 ● RECREATION

The Sammarinese enjoy socializing at cafes and attending movies, concerts, and plays. In addition, they may view painting and sculpture in their museums and churches.

18 ● CRAFTS AND HOBBIES

Pottery is created in a variety of styles. The region's white sandstone has been carved into statues, building stones, and other objects since ancient times. Other traditional crafts include painting, jewelry, wood carving, tile work, leather goods, and textiles.

Like Liechtenstein, another tiny European country, San Marino is famous for its stamps. They are designed by respected artists and provide the republic with an important source of income. They are known for their wide variety of themes: there has even been a Walt Disney series with such cartoon characters as Mickey Mouse, Donald Duck, and Goofy. San Marino's coins show the same artistic creativity as its stamps.

19 ● SOCIAL PROBLEMS

With its small size, low rate of unemployment, and extensive social programs, San Marino has relatively few of the social problems that effect other modern nations.

20 ● BIBLIOGRAPHY

Catling, Christopher. *Umbria, the Marches, and San Marino.* Lincolnwood, Ill.: Passport Books, 1994.

Carrick, Noel. *San Marino.* New York: Chelsea House, 1988.

WEBSITES

Intelcom Fotonica. San Marino Online. [Online] Availabel http://www.smol.sm/1995.

World Travel Guide. San Marino. [Online] Available http://www.wtgonline.com/country/sm/gen.html, 1998.

Saudi Arabia

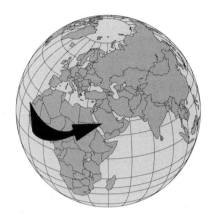

The people of Saudi Arabia are called Saudis. The great majority have a common Arabian ancestry. The Bedu (called Bedoins by Westerners) are people who live in one of the desert areas of the Middle East and raise camels, sheep, or goats.

Saudis

PRONUNCIATION: SOWD-eez
LOCATION: Saudi Arabia
POPULATION: 10 to 16 million
LANGUAGE: Arabic
RELIGION: Islam

1 ● INTRODUCTION

Modern-day Saudis are descended from ancient nomadic desert tribes who were fiercely independent. The country, officially known as the Kingdom of Saudi Arabia, was officially founded on September 23, 1932.

The Islamic religion started in the city of Mecca (or Makkah) in what is now Saudi Arabia sometime around AD 610. Mecca is still the spiritual center of Islam. All Muslims are expected to make a pilgrimage to Mecca at least once. Saudi Arabia hosts these pilgrims, who number in the millions every year. The discovery of oil in the 1930s led to rapid economic growth and development for the entire nation. Saudi Arabia is a founding member and the largest supplier of the Organization of Petroleum Exporting Countries (OPEC), established in 1960. OPEC is an oil cartel (an international monopoly that sets its own production amounts and prices).

2 ● LOCATION

The Kingdom of Saudi Arabia makes up almost four-fifths of the Arabian Peninsula. The Saudi government estimates the size of the country to be 856,350 square miles (2,217,949 square kilometers). The country is about one-third as big as the United States, yet the population is less than that of the state of New York. Population figures are difficult to estimate, with figures ranging from 10 to 16 million (the higher figure includes foreigners living in Saudi Arabia). About 99 percent of the land is barren and harsh, unable to support large numbers of people. The national annual average rainfall is only 4 inches (10 centimeters). The Empty Quarter (Rub al-Khali) is the largest undivided sand desert in the world, and rain may only fall there once every ten years. There are only a few permanent streams and natural lakes in Saudi Arabia. In the desert, summer temperatures can reach as high as 111°F to 122°F (44°C to 50°C). In the mid-winter and early summer, the *shamal*—a north wind carrying sand and dust—blows fiercely.

Saudi Arabia is surrounded on three sides by water: the Persian Gulf and Gulf of Oman to the east, the Arabian Sea and Gulf of Aden to the south, and the Red Sea to the west. Saudi Arabia is bordered on the north by Jordan, Iraq, and Kuwait; on the south by Yemen and Oman; on the east by the United Arab Emirates, Qatar, and Bahrain; and on the west by the Red Sea.

3 ● LANGUAGE

The official language of Saudi Arabia, spoken by virtually all Saudis, is Arabic. Arabic is spoken by 100 million people worldwide and has many distinctive dialects. Written Arabic, on the other hand, is the same for Arabic writers the world over. It is written and read from right to left.

"Hello" in Arabic is *marhaba* or *ahlan*, to which one replies, *marhabtayn* or *ahlayn*. Other common greetings are *As-salam alaykum* (Peace be with you) with the reply of *Walaykum as-salam* (and to you peace). *Ma'assalama* means "goodbye." The numbers one to ten in Arabic are: *wahad, ithnayn, thalatha, arba'a, khamsa, sita, sab'a, thamanya, tis'a,* and *'ashara.*

4 ● FOLKLORE

Much folklore glorifies the city of Mecca, the holiest place in Islam. One such story tells the tale of the creation of Mecca. According to the tale, in creating the earth, Allah (God) first shaped the area around Mecca, laying the rest of the earth around Mecca to make this sacred city the center of the world. He then made the angels from light and the *jinn* (supernatural beings that take human or animal form) from fire. The angels remained in heaven, circling Allah's Sacred House, and the jinn were sent to the earth. When Allah decided to create Adam, the angels objected, making Allah angry. To gain His favor, the angels built on earth a replica of Allah's Sacred House in heaven. This was the *Ka'ba* (the sacred cubic shrine in Mecca), to which all Muslims should go for their pilgrimage.

There are also thousands of proverbs and fables known to Saudis. Some are attributed to an ancient wise man known as Lukman. Two of Lukman's proverbs are: *He who does good has good done unto him;* and *Walk quietly, lower your voice, for the voice of the jackass is the loudest and most ugly of voices.*

5 ● RELIGION

Saudis are Muslims (followers of Islam). Saudi Arabia is an Islamic state and by law no other religious practices are allowed. Non-Muslim religious services were tolerated in Saudi Arabia for a long time. Although they were discouraged, they were not prohibited outright until after the 1991 Persian Gulf War.

© Robert Azzi/Woodfin Camp & Assoc.

A worshiper in the Holy Mosque in Mecca (Makkah), reading the Koran (the sacred text of Islam).

In the eighteenth century, the Muslim preacher Muhammad Ibn Abdul Wahhab advocated strict observance of Islamic practices. He founded the Wahhabi sect of Islam, which is still followed in Saudi Arabia. In the Wahhabi sect, men are required to pray in a ritual manner, music and dancing are at times forbidden, and the type of clothing women are allowed to wear is specified.

Since the early 1990s, Saudi Arabia has experienced a religious revival, reflected in an increase in religious programs on television and radio, and an increase in religious articles in newspapers.

6 ● MAJOR HOLIDAYS

There is one secular (nonreligious) holiday, National Day, on September 23. It commemorates the founding of the modern Kingdom of Saudi Arabia in 1932. The rest of the official holidays are Muslim, which follow the lunar calendar. The main Muslim holidays are: *Eid al-Fitr*, a three-day festival at the end of Ramadan; *Eid al-Adha*, a three-day feast of sacrifice at the end of the month of pilgrimage to Mecca (known as the *hajj*)—families who can afford it slaughter a lamb and share the meat with poorer Muslims; the first of *Muharram*, or the Muslim New Year; *Mawlid An-Nabawi*, the prophet Muhammad's birthday; and *Eid al-Isra wa al-Miraj*, celebrating Muhammad's night visit to heaven from Jerusalem. Most businesses and services are closed on Fridays because it is the Muslim day of rest.

7 ● RITES OF PASSAGE

A Saudi marriage involves a contract, which specifies the amount of the dowry *(mahr)* that the groom pays to the bride. It might also specify a second amount of money known as *muta'akhir* (a postponed dowry), to be paid to the wife in case of divorce. Sometimes the requirement of an advanced dowry makes it difficult for a young man to afford marriage. Some couples, however, set only a token amount for the dowry in order to fulfill the legal requirements. In case of divorce, the woman receives the postponed dowry, and her father and brothers become responsible for her.

8 • RELATIONSHIPS

Arab customs are the norm in Saudi Arabia. An Arab will never ask personal questions, as that is considered rude. A person is expected to say what he or she wishes without being asked. A direct refusal is also considered rude, so one must learn to recognize indirect signals.

Men either shake hands or kiss on the cheeks during a salutation. Women do the same. However, a man and woman who are unrelated do neither.

Chastity and sexual modesty are highly valued, and many of the social restrictions on women in Saudi Arabia are said to be for the purpose of protecting a woman's honor and virtue.

Saudi society is tribal in nature, with a tribe consisting of groups of relatives traced through males. Members of the tribe take an interest in one another's well-being, and the more wealthy come to the aid of the poor if the need arises. Each tribe has a leader known as a *shaykh*, who serves as a mediator in conflicts between tribal members. The shaykhs and their tribes pledge their allegiance to the ruling Al Saud royal family.

Saudis highly value hospitality to guests. Food and drink are always taken with the right hand. Even if a host or hostess has a domestic staff, it is customary for him or her to personally serve guests.

9 • LIVING CONDITIONS

Since the discovery of oil in the 1930s, there have been dramatic improvements in the Saudi standard of living. An extensive network of roadways connects almost every corner of Saudi Arabia, and public transportation is widely available within and between cities. Saudi Arabia has many modern airports, and the national airline, Saudia, is the largest in the Middle East. Telephone, telex, pager, and cellular phone services are available.

Modern health care and education are available free of charge to all Saudi citizens and pilgrims. Social services provide for workers and families in case of disability, retirement, or death. There are also provisions for social security pensions; elderly, orphans, or widows without incomes; home health care; rehabilitation of juvenile delinquents; nursing homes for the elderly; and orphanages for children. Low-income housing is available for public employees and students. The government also offers no-interest, long-term loans for the construction of homes. All adult Saudis, if not independently wealthy, are entitled to a plot of land and a loan to build a home.

The media exercises self-censorship, in keeping with an unwritten censorship code that restricts expressing opposition to the government. Foreign newspapers are heavily censored for political and moral content.

10 • FAMILY LIFE

Extended families often live together in the same house. Marriages are usually arranged by families. Islamic law allows a man to have up to four wives, if he can treat and love them all equally. However, men rarely marry more than one woman at a time. Divorce, easy for men and possible for women, is now commonplace. Women may write their own provisions into the marriage

New public housing.

contract, and they may own and dispose of property freely. A Saudi woman does not take her husband's last name. She keeps her own family name because she is legally considered to belong to her own family for life.

Socially, women are very restricted. They are not permitted to mingle with men who are not close family members, at any time or in any way. They must wear a black veil over their heads, faces, and clothing whenever they are in public. It is illegal for women to drive cars or to travel alone. A woman may not attend a lecture given by a man, but she may watch it on closed-circuit television; in this way, women may now

earn advanced degrees at universities formerly closed to them.

11 ● CLOTHING

Saudis generally wear traditional clothing. Men wear a *thob*, a simple ankle-length robe of wool or cotton, usually in white or earth tones. On their heads they wear a *ghutra*, a large, diagonally folded cotton square worn over a *kufiyyah* (skull-cap) and held in place with an *i'gal*, a double-coiled cord circlet. Sometimes men wear a flowing floor-length outer cloak called a *bisht* over their thob; the bisht is made of wool or camel hair in black, beige, brown, or cream colors.

Women's traditional dress varies by region, but it always covers the body from head to toe. It is often adorned with coins, sequins, metallic thread, or brightly colored fabric appliques. Some women wear a *shayla*, a black gauzy scarf wrapped around the head and held in place by a variety of hats, head circlets, or jewelry. In public, women sometimes wear a black outer cloak called an *'abaya* over their dress. In the southwest district known as the *Asir*, women wear brightly colored, long-waisted dresses and no veils.

12 ● FOOD

Traditionally, dates were the staple food of the Saudis. A typical Saudi dish is lamb (or chicken) on a bed of seasoned rice. Pork is forbidden by Islamic law, as is alcohol. Tea and/or coffee are served at all gatherings, large or small. Buttermilk, camel's milk, and *laban*—a yogurt drink—are favorite beverages. Dessert generally consists of fruit. A unique Saudi food is *arikah*, a bread from the southwest region (the *Asir*) which is broken off and formed into a spoon shape to be dipped into a dish of honey. Locusts, although terribly destructive when swarming, are considered a delicacy in the Saudi diet.

Meals that commemorate religious events, such as the birth of the prophet Muhammad, are served on a white tablecloth on the floor. Forks and knives are not used at these meals; either the right hand or a spoon is used on religious occasions. Everyday meals are served at tables, and forks and knives are commonplace.

13 ● EDUCATION

The emphasis on completing secondary school (high school) includes academic and religious studies. Both boys and girls are educated, but they are educated separately. The purpose of education for girls is to teach them how to serve their families. Training prepares girls for occupations such as teaching and nursing.

Parents are very involved in their children's education. Public education—from preschool through university— is free to all citizens. Government scholarships are also available for study abroad; most students go to the United States. Saudi Arabia has 7 universities, 83 colleges, and more than 18,000 schools. Primary schooling begins at age six and continues for six years. Intermediate schooling begins at age twelve and lasts for three years. High school lasts from age fifteen to eighteen and is geared toward either the arts and sciences or vocational training. Nearly all children attend school until they are twelve years old, but many do not continue beyond that.

Most Saudi Arabian schools are run by the government, which also provides schools for children and adults who are blind, deaf, or physically or mentally challenged. As of 1990, literacy rates among men had reached 73 percent, but those for women had only reached 48 percent.

14 ● CULTURAL HERITAGE

The national dance of Saudi Arabia is the *ardha*, or men's sword dance. Men carrying swords stand shoulder to shoulder, and a poet among them sings verses while drummers beat out a rhythm. The dance consists of a ceremonial procession and symbolizes the unity of the kingdom. *Al-mizmar* is the name of both a folk dance involving skillful stick movements and a musical instrument resembling an oboe.

Islam forbids showing the human body in art, so Saudi art focuses on geometric and abstract shapes. Calligraphy is considered a sacred art, with the Koran (or Qur'an—the sacred text of Islam) being the primary subject matter.

15 ● EMPLOYMENT

The Saudi work week runs from Saturday through Wednesday, with Thursday and Friday as the weekend. Working hours are usually 8:00 AM to 7:00 or 8:00 PM, with a long break in the afternoon. Eight industrial cities have been built near sources of raw materials, with factories and other industrial facilities.

Many jobs are not open to women because women are not allowed to mingle with men who are not close family members, even in the workplace. However, this is slowly changing, and women are begin-

Two Saudi girls.

ning to enter all ranks of employment, from skilled labor to professional positions.

16 ● SPORTS

Soccer is the national sport of Saudi Arabia. Volleyball, basketball, and tennis are also popular modern sports. The traditional sports of horse- and camel-racing are still enjoyed as well. The annual King's Camel Race draws 2,000 competitors and 20,000 to 30,000 spectators each year. Many other horse and camel races are also held throughout the country. Hunting with guns is banned, but traditional hunting (with dogs or falcons) is still popular.

The government promotes sports through physical education in the public schools and the establishment of huge Sports Cities in large urban centers, smaller neighborhood Sports Centers, and Sports Clubs in rural areas. Fifteen Sports Cities already exist; each contains a multipurpose stadium, a small indoor stadium, Olympic-size swimming pools, indoor and outdoor courts and playgrounds, cafeterias, conference facilities, and sports-medicine clinics.

17 ● RECREATION

Entertainment is largely a private matter—there are no public cinemas, for example. Camping is very popular, and there is an extensive network of local and national parks and campgrounds across Saudi Arabia. Water sports are enjoyed in the Arabian Gulf and Red Sea.

The strict Saudi moral standard restricts what can be broadcast on television or radio for entertainment. Programs are screened for scenes that contradict the codes of sexual chastity and religious observance.

18 ● CRAFTS AND HOBBIES

Saudi Arabia is famous for gold and silver handicrafts, particularly jewelry fashioned as both a decorative art and as a status symbol. Jewelry is treasured both for its beauty and for the its monetary value, and is regarded as insurance against hard times. One of the finest examples of gold and silver handicrafts is on the *kiswah*, a black cloth embroidered in gold and silver with verses from the Koran (Qur'an). The kiswah measures approximately 28,500 square feet (2,650 square meters) and covers the four walls of the *Ka'ba* (the sacred cubic shrine in Mecca). The kiswah is replaced every year and made in Mecca.

Pottery is another Saudi craft, and brass and copper crafts are also abundant. Since ancient times, Saudis have crafted goods from leather, including handbags, saddlebags, sandals, and shoes. Wood carving is another prized art. Geometric designs and religious inscriptions are carved with sharp knives to create both artwork and fixtures such as wooden plates and engraved panels for doors. Straw is also used in artwork, with straw hats, mats, containers, and cooking lids.

19 ● SOCIAL PROBLEMS

Violent street crime is rare in Saudi Arabia, although crime rates have risen with the presence of foreign workers. The most common crimes are theft, the possession of alcohol, fighting, and moral offenses. People convicted of murder, abandoning the Islamic faith, adultery, drug smuggling, and sabotage are subject to the death penalty, which is carried out by beheading, firing squad, or stoning. Repeated theft is punishable by amputation of the right hand, and drunkenness and gambling are punishable by flogging with a cane. Saudi Arabia has been criticized by Amnesty International for its human rights record concerning prison conditions. People opposing the government have been arbitrarily arrested, held without trial, and routinely tortured during interrogations.

20 ● BIBLIOGRAPHY

Al-Hariri-Rifai, Wahbi, and Mokhless al-Hariri-Rifai. *The Heritage of the Kingdom of Saudi Arabia.* Washington, D.C.: GDG Publications, 1990.

Al-Saleh, Khairat. *Fabled Cities, Princes and Jinns from Arab Myths and Legends.* New York: Peter Bedrick Books, 1985.

Foster, Leila Merrell. *Enchantment of the World: Saudi Arabia.* Chicago: Childrens Press, 1993.

Metz, Helen Capin. *Saudi Arabia: A Country Study.* Washington, D.C.: Library of Congress, Federal Research Diivision, 1993.

Saudi Arabia, pamphlet series. Washington, D.C.: The Royal Embassy of Saudi Arabia, Information Office, 1994.

The Saudi British Bank Business Profile Series: Saudi Arabia, 5th ed. Hong Kong: Hong Kong and Shanghai Banking Corporation, Ltd., 1991.

Zubaida, Sami, and Richard Tapper, eds. *Culinary Cultures of the Middle East.* London and New York: I. B. Tauris Publishers, 1994.

WEBSITES
ArabNet. Saudi Arabia. [Online Available http://www.arab.net/saudi/saudi_contents.html, 1998.
World Travel Guide. [Online] Available http://travelguide.attistel.co.uk/country/sa/gen.html, 1998.

Bedu

PRONUNCIATION: BEH-doo
ALTERNATE NAMES: Bedouin
LOCATION: Deserts of Israel, Jordan, Lebanon, Syria, Saudi Arabia, Iraq, Kuwait, Yemen, Oman, Qatar, the United Arab Emirates, Bahrain, and Egypt
POPULATION: 4–5 million
LANGUAGE: Arabic
RELIGION: Islam

1 ● INTRODUCTION

The Western term *Bedouin* is actually a double plural; in the Arabic language the people we know as Bedouin refer to themselves as "Bedu" (also plural, but for simplicity it will be used here as both singular and plural). The definition of who is and is not a Bedu has become somewhat confused in recent times, as circumstances change and the traditional nomadic life of the desert herders has had to adapt. Generally speaking, a Bedu is an Arab who lives in one of the desert areas of the Middle East and raises camels, sheep, or goats. The Bedu traditionally believe they are the descendants of Shem, son of Noah, whose ancestor was Adam, the first man (see the book of Genesis, chapter 5, of the Bible).

The Arabian Peninsula historically has been the crossroads for trade as well as war. Bedu tribes often took strangers into their system and offered them the tribes' full protection and identity, thus intermingling with other peoples. Bedu are considered the "most indigenous" of modern Middle Eastern peoples, meaning they lived there before anyone else. The first appearance of nomadic peoples in the Arabian desert can be traced back as far as the third millennium BC.

2 ● LOCATION

Bedu territory covers the Arabian deserts of the Middle East, including parts of the modern states of Israel, Jordan, Lebanon, Syria, Saudi Arabia, Iraq, Kuwait, Yemen, Oman, Qatar, the United Arab Emirates, Bahrain, and Egypt. Their entire range extends almost 1 million square miles (over 2.5 million square kilometers)—about the size of western Europe. The exact number of Bedu living within this huge territory is unknown, but it is probably only about 4 to 5 million (the entire population of the Arab nations combined is about 300 million). It would be as if the population of London or New York City were living scattered all across Europe—the population density is around 2.5 persons per square mile (less than 1 person per square kilometer). Probably no more than 10 percent of all Bedu still live in a purely traditional way: nomadic camel herders who follow the scattered, sporadic rainfall to find grazing for their animals, live off the products of those animals (milk, meat, hair, and skins), and use them as their sole form of transportation. (This article primarily focuses on the nomadic Bedu.) Life for the other 90 percent of the Bedu is similar to that of other urbanized Arab peoples.

The desert environment is harsh and does not lend itself easily to the support of human life. Much of the Bedu territory receives only 4 inches (10 centimeters) of rain per year, and those 4 inches are scattered and unpredictable. Temperatures can go as high as 122°F (50°C) in the shade during the summer months, and as low as 32°F (0°C) during the winter. At night, the temperature drops dramatically, plunging as much as 86°F (30°C) from daytime temperatures. The beginning of summer is often heralded by violent sandstorms and scorching winds.

The Bedu recognize four or five environmental seasons which vary in length depending on the amount of rainfall. In a good, rainy year, spring can last as long as six weeks (during February and March), whereas in a dry year there may be no spring at all, with winter simply shifting right into summer.

Despite these harsh conditions, a great deal of life animal and plant life manages to exist in the desert. The Arabian deserts are not all sand, although they do boast the highest sand dunes in the world (with some as high as 600 meters [2,000 feet]). Within Bedu territory are mountains, rock outcroppings, gravel and stony plains, *wadis* (dry riverbeds, which can become sudden torrents during a heavy rainfall), and stands of scrubby bushes or trees. A few days or weeks after a rainstorm, the desert floor is transformed into a carpet of grasses and brilliantly colored wildflowers. The Bedu travel in search of these green places in the desert.

3 ● LANGUAGE

The Bedu speak Arabic, but it is a very rich, stylized Arabic dialect (regional variety of a language). Bedu Arabic is somewhat comparable to the English of Shakespeare's day. As in all societies, the language is filled with words that pertain to the details of their life, making distinctions that are difficult for others to comprehend. The Bedu have many words for desert, and the differences between them are hard to define in English. A *badiya* is something open and uncovered—country in full view. A *sahra* is a vast open space that is generally level, defined in contrast to a "settled" area. To a non-Bedu, both these terms seem to describe the same sort of terrain. But to a Bedu, the distinction is clear. The Bedu also have many words for water, a scarce resource in the desert.

4 ● FOLKLORE

The two main types of Bedu folktales are realistic stories involving the familiar Bedu way of life, and fantasies that tell of love and include a woman as a main character. These two types of folktales generally fall into three categories: raiding stories, which celebrate heroism, strength, and courage; love stories, which describe the emotional highs and lows of star-crossed lovers and struggles to overcome obstacles to true love; and stories about thieves of the desert, which tell of robbery, murder, and treachery.

Some Bedu are superstitious, putting great stock in amulets and charms, lucky numbers (odd numbers are usually considered lucky), and spirits. Stones and designs in jewelry are believed to have magical qualities. Triangles, which represent hands, called *khamsa*, ward off the evil eye, as do blue stones such as turquoise or lapis lazuli; red stones will stop bleeding or reduce inflammation. Children, especially boys, are protected by charms hung around their necks or ankles and with ear studs containing what they believe are magical stones. Animals that prey on the Bedu's herds (such as wolves and wildcats) are considered the embodiment of evil, and in southern Arabia the camel is believed to be the direct descendant of the spirits of the desert.

5 ● RELIGION

Bedu are now Muslim (followers of Islam). At one time there were Jewish and Christian tribes, but none of them survive today. For the most part, Bedu do not follow Islamic duties and rules strictly. Given the Bedu's desert environment and demanding existence, many Islamic rituals are difficult to practice in the same manner as elsewhere. For example, ritual dry washings are utilized when there is insufficient water. The *hajj* (pilgrimage to Mecca) is an important ritual for the Bedu, and most parents take each of their children on his or her first pilgrimage at the age of seven or eight. Some Bedu construct a place of prayer, called a *masjid* or *mashhad*, shortly after setting up their tents by enclosing a small piece of land with pebbles. The morning and noon prayers are usually considered the most important of the five daily prayers of Islam.

6 ● MAJOR HOLIDAYS

The most highly regarded Islamic festival among Bedu peoples is *Eid al-Adha*, the "feast of sacrifice," when the Bedu sacrifice a camel or sheep from their herd to commemorate Abraham's willingness to sacrifice his son. Since Islam uses a lunar calendar, the dates for Muslim holy days change each year on the Gregorian calendar.

Many Bedu do not fast during the month of Ramadan (the ninth month of the Muslim year, during which Muhammad received his first revelations—celebrated by complete fasting from dawn until dusk each day of the entire month). Therefore, the festival of *Eid Al-Fitr* (a three-day celebration to break the fast at the end of Ramadan) has little meaning. Bedu also do not pay much attention to the celebration commemorating Muhammad's birthday or his flight from Mecca; in fact, some Bedu do not even know the dates for those holy days in any given year.

7 ● RITES OF PASSAGE

Some Bedu tribes require that when girls reach puberty, they must cover their hair and wear a mask or veil over the face when in public (whenever anyone but immediate family is present). Girls look forward to wearing these head and face coverings as a sign of maturity, and many design them so as to be alluring and provocative. They use their masks and veils to flirt.

8 ● RELATIONSHIPS

Two things shape the interactions of Bedu people—the Arab tradition of hospitality, and the Bedu code of honor, or *sharaf*. These customs have been shaped by the extreme conditions of desert nomadism. Survival as small groups of wanderers in the harsh desert required tremendous cooperation. A guest fed in one's own tent today may be the one who can provide food tomorrow. Passersby traditionally exchanged formal greetings with the families in the tents they passed, and were asked for any news. The polite reply was to say one has no news or only good news. The passersby were then invited into the men's side of the tent for coffee and tea, served in a ritual way. (It is still considered polite to drink at least three cups before wobbling your glass to show that you do not want it refilled.) Guests were assured of food and shelter for three and one-third days, and then protection for another three days after leaving the tent, that being considered the length of time it takes for all traces of the host's food to pass through the guest's body. Anyone who even exchanged greetings, whether they came into the tent or not, was considered a guest entitled to the host's protection for the customary three days.

Women are protected in the Bedu code of honor. A man who is not closely related to a woman is not allowed to touch her in any way, not even so much as to brush his fingers against hers while handing her something. To do so is to dishonor her. Likewise, in some tribes, if a woman brings dishonor to herself, she shames her family because honor is held not by individuals but by whole families. The loss of a woman's honor, her *ird*, is extremely serious among the Bedu.

Another important element of Bedu honor is *as-sime,* giving up something so that a weaker person will benefit. Children are trained in the code of honor and tradition of hospitality from a very early age. By the time they are seven or eight years old, boys and girls know well what is expected of them and can behave with adult dignity when called upon.

9 ● LIVING CONDITIONS

The traditional Bedu live either in tents made of woven goat hair, known as a *bait sharar* (house of hair), palm-frond shacks called *barasti,* or in the shelter of a few bushes or trees, on which they may drape blankets for more protection from the wind. Bedu adapted to more modern customs live more settled lives in villages, or take advantage of technological items such as portable cabins.

A tent houses an extended family of around ten people, and it is divided into at least two sections—the men's side, or *al-shigg*; and the women's side, or *al-mahram*. Cooking is done and possessions are stored on the women's side, and guests are entertained on the men's side. The men's and women's sections are divided either by a woven curtain called a *sahah* or *gata'ah*, or by a wooden mat called a *shirb* held together by wool woven around the canes in geometric patterns. These tent dividers are frequently beautiful works of art.

Bedu families stay close to their permanent wells during the dry summer months, then migrate to better grazing areas during the winter. The Bedu can travel as much as 1,600 miles (3,000 kilometers) or more in a year. Traditional Bedu ride camels. Some modern Bedu have acquired trucks and other four-wheel-drive vehicles to replace the camel as transportation. Each tribe has its own territory, or *dirah*, but as modernization encroaches on their range, the Bedu have had to cross over each other's territories. However, each tribe still knows its *dirah* and the boundaries of those of other tribes.

The life of Bedu in oil-rich Arab nations is not quite as extreme, as tanker trucks often bring water to outlying areas. Mobile medical units have made Western medicine more available to the Bedu, but most only turn to them when folk medicine fails. Traditional Bedu beliefs held that physical health is related to the actions of spirits and devils. The Bedu traditionally put red-hot coals to their skin to open a door for an evil spirit to exit the body at a place where it was causing trouble (such as between the eyes in the case of headaches). Herbal medicine (teas, poultices, etc.) is widely used, as are charms and amulets. If all else fails, including folk and Western medicine, the Bedu may turn to *sahar*, practitioners of alternative medicine who have been outlawed by most of the governments in the area but who continue to provide their services.

10 ● FAMILY LIFE

Bedu society is based on complicated lineages that govern the formation of tribes and family clans. Bedu introduce themselves by giving their name, then naming two generations of male ancestors, and then stating their tribe: for example, "Suhail son of Salem son of Muhammad of the Bait Kathir." Women are also known as the daughters of their fathers and grandfathers, and they keep their family names even if they marry into a different tribe.

Bedu live in extended families made up of paternal cousins. A group of families who are related to each other make up a *fakhadh* (literally, "thigh"), which means a clan "of the same root" or "part of the whole." A group of fakhadhs constitutes a tribe, called a *kabila* or *ashira*, though these words may also refer to subsections of a larger tribe. Tribes vary widely in size and are constantly changing through marriage or territorial needs for grazing. A small tribe that has to move into the territory of a larger tribe to feed its herds may become absorbed by the larger tribe. Later, if the original small tribe has gained enough members and/or wealth, it may strike out on its own again.

Every group of Bedu has a *sheikh*, or leader. The sheikh always comes from the same family line within each group, but it is not necessarily the oldest son who takes over when the father dies. The post is given to the male family member most qualified for the job. A sheikh leads by mutual agreement, not by absolute will, so all members of the group must respect the sheikh in order for him to lead them effectively.

Marriage is more of a social contract among the Bedu than a love match. The bride and groom are usually first cousins. Women marry between the ages of sixteen and twenty-two, while men marry between the ages of eighteen and thirty. The wedding is essentially a process of customary negotiations after which the bride is escorted to the groom's tent. Divorce is just as simple: a man simply states in front of witnesses that he wants a divorce. A woman can initiate a divorce by moving back to her parents' tent. If she refuses to return to her husband's tent with him, he will grant her a divorce. Siblings are very close to and protective of one another; brothers fiercely guard their sisters' honor.

11 ● CLOTHING

The primary article of clothing for both Bedu men and women is the *dishdasha*, a long gown worn by most Arabs that covers the body from the base of the neck to the wrists and ankles. Men wear the dishdasha as an outer garment with baggy trousers called *sirwal* underneath (some modern Bedu men now wear sweatpants instead), while women wear the dishdasha as an undergarment beneath a larger, looser dress called a *thob*, which is almost always black. Women also wear baggy trousers, which are tight at the ankle and embroidered, under their dresses. Bedu men wear some sort of headcloth, the design of which varies from tribe to tribe. In most tribes, adult women wear veils over their hair and either veils or masks on their faces. Both men and women use *kuhl* (kohl, a black powder made from lustrous antimony) to accent their eyes. It reduces glare from the harsh desert sun and is believed to help repel flies as well. Bedu traditionally walk barefoot.

Women love jewelry and wear a lot of it; they may also wear the family's wealth as jewelry (which will then be completely safe since, according to the code of honor, women cannot be touched). Older women may have tattoos, which were believed to enhance their beauty, but that tradition is dying out, and very few younger women wear them. (It is considered effeminate for a man to have a tattoo.) Men wear silver or gold belts with elaborate curved daggers called *khanja* strapped to them. Belts designed for carrying bullets are now popular, and nomadic Bedu men are rarely seen without their rifles.

Said Elatab

A Bedu woman and her child. In most tribes, adult women wear veils over their hair.

12 ● FOOD

Bedu cooking emphasizes quantity rather than style. The traditional Bedu diet consisted mainly of camel milk, drunk cold or hot, boiled with bread, or cooked with rice. Meat, usually goat's meat, was an occasional luxury. Bedu along coastal areas also eat fish. A thin, flat bread is cooked over the fire on a curved metal sheet. The Bedu also hunt for meat to supplement their diet. They traditionally used trained falcons captured in the fall and released in the spring to hunt desert hares and foxes or migratory birds. Many Bedu hunt with a Saluki, a breed of dog related to the greyhound. Although herding dogs are considered unclean and are never allowed to enter the living area, Salukis are treated with a great deal of affection and live in the tent with their masters.

13 ● EDUCATION

Traditional Bedu education consists of training in the skills necessary to live the life of the nomadic desert camel herder. It takes years to learn how care for a herd of camels and a family in the harsh desert environment. Although some Bedu parents are beginning to provide a more formal education for their children in schools, this makes it difficult for those children to learn important desert skills, such as hunting, ropeweaving, camel herding, camel riding, camel milking, camel breeding, camel tracking, and the rituals of entertaining guests for Bedu boys; and weaving, embroidery, cooking, cleaning, setting up and taking down camp, tent-making, and herding for Bedu girls.

Reading and writing are not very essential for traditional Bedu society. However, reading the Koran (or Qur'an—the sacred text of Islam) is very important, and there are always some members of the family, including women, who must know how to read and write. Bedu can recite poetry and tell stories by memory, however, and recognize all of the hundreds of *wasm*—camel brands of their own tribe and neighboring tribes. They can also interpret the signs left on the hard desert ground by people and animals who have passed that way.

14 ● CULTURAL HERITAGE

Poetry is considered the highest art in Bedu society; it is the outlet for emotional expressions otherwise restricted by the code of honor. The *rabab*, the one-stringed Bedu violin, is often played to accompany the recitation of poetic verse. Other literary genres, all oral, in the Bedu world are the *qissa* (folk tale), *qasid* (ode), riddles and proverbs, the *murafa'a* (pleading one's case before the magistrate), and the discussions of the *majalis* sessions (gatherings of family to pass on wisdom and traditions to the younger members).

15 ● EMPLOYMENT

Herding camels during the winter migration is a full-time job for at least two family members, and usually requires two others part-time. Men and boys do most of the herding, but if there are not enough sons to do the job, teenage girls will help. In a family with no sons, daughters take on all the work, including herding, entertaining guests, and driving the vehicles (if they have any). Setting up and taking down camp is the women's job, along with cooking, cleaning, weaving, and sewing. Pregnant women generally work right up to the time of delivery, and then go back to work as soon as possible after giving birth. Nomadic Bedu life is full of chores: collecting firewood, filling water drums, obtaining and preparing food, taking camels to pasture in the morning and bringing them back to camp at night, milking the camels, moving camp, and making and repairing tents and clothing.

Many Bedu have given up full-time nomadic herding to take on wage-earning jobs. In many Middle Eastern countries, Bedu men are an important part of the military and are well paid. In Jordan and Saudi Arabia, the armed forces are composed almost entirely of Bedu. In Israel, they serve as trackers and game wardens to protect endangered desert species.

16 ● SPORTS

Nomadic Bedu do not have much time for sports, but they do enjoy camel-racing. They train their camels to trot (run by picking up alternate feet, rather than both feet on the same side). This makes them easier to ride at high speeds. Hunting is done purely for sport by wealthier Bedu, though it is a necessity for poorer families.

17 ● RECREATION

Their harsh nomadic way of life prevents the Bedu from having much time for recreation. Winter is the most sociable time for the Bedu, with many clans and tribes gathered in good grazing areas, rather than stuck by their isolated wells in the dry summer. At night, they gather to recite stories in verse around the campfire. Other times, the women may sing to the men in an informal performance called a *summejr*.

18 ● CRAFTS AND HOBBIES

Bedu women weave sheep's wool, goat or camel hair, or cotton into textiles with geometric designs, sometimes including stylized representations of everyday objects such as coffee pots, scissors, or camels. The Bedu traditionally put no border on their designs. They let the design go all the way to the edge of the cloth to represent the infinite horizon of the desert. Natural dyes were traditionally used, producing muted earth tones, reds, and blues. They are difficult and time-consuming to make, so many Bedu women now purchase commercial dyes that create brighter colors.

19 ● SOCIAL PROBLEMS

The modern creation of national borders and the sprawl of cities and cultivated areas into the desert has reduced the Bedu's range and forced many to become only semi-nomadic, settling in villages for part of the year and returning to their herds in the desert for only a few months. The Bedu lost their biggest vocation and source of much of their wealth and power when trucks and airplanes replaced camels as the main transport in the Middle East. Bedu parents often settle near villages to take advantage of available public education for their children. The children then are separated from their ancestors' traditional lifestyle and can no longer survive in the desert, so they must take wage-earning jobs.

These changes have altered the traditional Bedu way of life and threaten their existence as a distinct people.

20 ● BIBLIOGRAPHY

Jabbur, Jibrail S. *The Bedouins and the Desert: Aspects of Nomadic Life in the Arab East.* Albany, N.Y.: State University of New York Press, 1995.

Keohane, Alan. *Bedouin: Nomads of the Desert.* London: Kyle Cathie Ltd., 1994.

WEBSITES

ArabNet. Saudi Arabia. [Online Available http://www.arab.net/saudi/saudi_contents.html, 1998.

World Travel Guide. [Online] Available http://www.wtgonline.com/country/sa/gen.html, 1998.

Senegal

The people of Senegal are called Senegalese. The largest ethnic group is the Wolof, who make about 40 percent of the total population. For information on the Fulani, who make up about 17 percent of the population, see the chapter on Guinea in Volume 4.

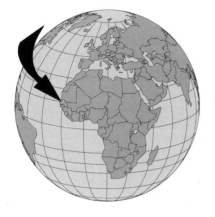

Senegalese

PRONUNCIATION: sen-uh-guh-LEEZ
LOCATION: Senegal
POPULATION: 9 million
LANGUAGE: French; Wolof; thirty-eight African languages
RELIGION: Islam (Sunni, with traditional aspects); Roman Catholicism

1 ● INTRODUCTION

Senegal has an important precolonial history. The lands now comprising Senegal once were part of three empires: Ghana, Mali (which brought Islam to the area), and the Songhai. Senegalese culture strongly reflects influences from these Islamic rulers and conquerors.

In 1444, Portuguese sailors became the first Europeans to visit the Senegalese coast. The French later founded the Senegal colony in 1637, making it the oldest and longest-lasting French colony in Africa. The slave trade, which flourished from the 1600s until 1848, devastated this area. Today one sees remnants of this tragic period in the island fortress of Gorée off the coast from the capital, Dakar. Gorée had served as one of West Africa's main slavery depots.

As the French advanced their colonial claims eastward, areas occupied by the Wolof ethnic group resisted them in the 1880s. Eventually, however, they yielded to superior military force. Dakar became an important city when the French made it the capital of their west African territories in 1902. Under Léopold Senghor (b.1906), who was a French parliamentarian, Senegal declared its independence in 1960.

2 ● LOCATION

Senegal is located at the westernmost point of Africa. It is slightly smaller than the state of South Dakota. Senegal shares borders with Mauritania, Mali, Guinea, Guinea-Bis-

SENEGALESE

0   200   400   600   800 Miles

0   200   400   600   800 Kilometers

MOROCCO
Rabat
Oran

Canary Is.
(SPAIN)

ALGERIA

Semara

WESTERN
SAHARA
(Occupied by
Morocco)

Chegga

MAURITANIA

MALI

Nouakchott

Néma

Tombouctou

CAPE VERDE

Praia

Dakar
SENEGAL

Niger

THE
GAMBIA
Banjul
Bamako
BURKINA
FASO

Bissau

GUINEA-
BISSAU
GUINEA
Yagaba

Conakry
Freetown
CÔTE
D'IVOIRE

SIERRA LEONE
Yamoussoukro
Abidjan

ATLANTIC
OCEAN
Monrovia
LIBERIA

sau, and Gambia. Much of Senegal is very arid with scattered trees and scrub.

The climate varies greatly from north to south, but rains fall throughout the country from December to April. Hot, dry winds blow from the Sahara Desert during the summer. Natural resources include phosphates, iron ore, manganese, salt, and oil. Seasonal flooding, overgrazing, and tree cutting contribute to environmental erosion and desertification.

In 1996, estimates placed Senegal's population at 9 million. Senegalese are members of more than twenty ethnic groups, of which the largest is Wolof (about 40 percent), followed by Fulani (17 percent). Large numbers of Lebanese traders live in the cities, as well.

3 ● LANGUAGE

French is the official language of Senegal, but most people speak Wolof. Besides French and Wolof, people speak the language of their ethnic group, such as Pulaar, Serer, and thirty-eight other African languages.

4 ● FOLKLORE

In Senegalese society, there are professional storytellers, known as *griots*. They are historians, poets, musicians, and entertainers all in one person. Griots use props, flutes, harps, and break into song as they perform. No ceremony or celebration of importance is held without them.

5 ● RELIGION

The Senegalese are overwhelmingly Muslim. Some 90 percent of the population belong to the Sunni branch of Islam. The remaining 10 percent are Roman Catholic. *Marabouts* play a unique role in Senegalese society: in orthodox Muslim communities, marabouts are teachers of the faith. In Senegal, marabouts became intermediaries between Allah (God) and the faithful. Under the French, they became leaders of administrative units *(cantons)*, replacing traditional ethnic chiefs. The marabouts' political influence remains strong, particularly in determining the outcomes of elections in remote areas.

6 ● MAJOR HOLIDAYS

Independence Day is April 4. Muslims celebrate the end of the holy month of Ramadan by feasting for three days. Catholics celebrate Easter and Christmas.

David Johnson

Some 90 percent of Senegalese belong to the Sunni branch of Islam. The remaining 10 percent are Roman Catholic.

Each region has its own secular and traditional folk feasts according to its own calendar. In the Casamance region, the town of Oussouye hosts an annual royal feast day. It is held at the end of the agricultural season and before the beginning of the school year. The highlight of the feast is a fight featuring young women. One of these may be chosen by the king to spend the night in the sacred woods in the heart of the forest.

7 ● RITES OF PASSAGE

Most Senegalese today follow Islamic custom in their rites of passage, including baptism, circumcision, marriage, and death. Each passage marks a part of the cycle that ends in passage to the spirit world. To this end, people and communities constantly celebrate life events. Griots (storytellers) are an integral part of these occasions.

In ancient times, Senegalese celebrated the arrival of puberty with initiation rites. The minority populations in the south still do. The purpose of initiation is to build courage and endurance, communicate traditional and practical knowledge of life, and transfer responsibility to a younger generation.

Some of the knowledge is known only to males. It cannot be shared with females or with the uninitiated. The initiation begins with circumcision, binding the boys by blood. Elders initiate boys of the same age, dividing them into age sets or groups. These sets become "fraternities" for life. Members have both the duty to help each other and the right to reprimand each other for improper behavior. Girls pass through similar processes, and many also are circumcised. However, for girls, this practice is increasingly questioned for reasons of health and sexual fulfillment.

Initiation rites often mark occasions of great community celebration. The Bassari, for example, bring down sacred masks from the mountains that represent supernatural powers. Dancers wearing these masks engage the newly circumcised adolescents in a mock battle, which becomes dance, song, and feasting.

8 ● RELATIONSHIPS

Greeting is an extremely important custom. It can actually last ten to fifteen minutes. It is quite possible that if you do not greet someone properly, he or she will not talk to you. In the village, people do not practice the French custom of kissing three times on the cheeks, as is common in Dakar and in the towns. Handshaking is the preferred way of greeting among traditional people. Men and women, however, do not shake each other's hands.

A common Wolof exchange (with five to ten additional inquiries) would be as follows. Praise for Allah would be interspersed throughout the greetings:

Nanga def? (How does it go?)

Mangi fii rekk. (I am here only.)

Nunga Fe. (They are there.)

Mbaa sa yaram jamm. (I hope your body is at peace.)

Jamm rekk. (Peace only.)

Alhumdullilah. (Praise be to Allah.)

9 ● LIVING CONDITIONS

The government recently made sweeping reforms in the economy and public sector. These changes were meant to counter threats from environmental damage and high population growth. While Senegalese would be considered poor in comparison to people in industrialized countries, they have a relatively comfortable standard of living for an African people. One indication of this is Senegal's gross domestic product per person of $1,600. This far surpasses that of neighboring Guinea ($600).

In the south, houses are made of mud brick and thatch roofs. In the north, walls are made of millet stalks or reeds, and roofs are typically corrugated tin. Dirt floors are common, but are swept daily. As families acquire the means, they build more durable structures of concrete and galvanized iron. Partially finished houses are a common sight because people build them in stages as they have the money.

10 ● FAMILY LIFE

Traditional Senegalese live in compounds with their extended families, although individual families live in their own huts. Elders are highly respected. Besides hauling water, women gather firewood and cook the meals. Few women work outside the home, unless it is to cultivate family gardens and fields, or to sell goods at the market. Men increasingly leave their villages and homes during the dry season to look for work in the cities.

Cynthia Bassett

On festive and traditional occasions, people wear boubous, *loose-fitting cotton tunics with large openings under the arms. Women tie matching headscarfs or turbans to complement their boubous.*

11 ● CLOTHING

In Senegalese society, personal appearance is very important. In the cities, most men and women wear Western-style clothing. Men typically wear shirts and trousers, and suits for dress occasions. Women wear dresses. One rarely sees women in jeans or pants. Shorts are reserved for children, unless they are worn for sports. In more traditional settings, people wear *boubous,* loose-fitting cotton tunics with large openings under the arms.

With much imagination, women tie matching headscarfs or turbans to complement their boubous. For men, footwear includes open leather sandals or closed, pointed ones, according to the occasion. Women have a greater variety of footwear

including colorful, decorated sandals. Depending on the purpose of the boubou, it may be elaborately embroidered and could cost two to three hundred dollars.

12 ● FOOD

Senegal's staple foods include rice, corn, millet, sorghum, peanuts, and beans. Milk and sugar also form an important part of the diet for some people. The Senegalese generally eat three meals a day. The main meal is at about 1:00 PM. The evening meal is served late. In traditional households, men, women, and children usually eat separately. It is not polite to make eye contact while eating. Senegalese eat from a communal platter or large bowl with the right hand, as is the Muslim custom. Muslim adults, and children aged twelve and older, do not eat or drink from sunrise to sunset during the holy month of Ramadan.

Senegal is famous for its national dish, *Tiébou Dienn* (pronounced CHEB-oo JEN). The dish can be made as simply or as elaborately as desired. Basically, it is a fish stew mixed with squash, sweet potatoes, okra, tamarind, and different kinds of peppers. People eat this on rice, which has been cooked in fish broth.

13 ● EDUCATION

Senegal faces great challenges in literacy. Only 30 percent of Senegalese can read and write in French. Only 18 percent of females are literate. School is mandatory and is based on the French system. However, attendance is not enforced. The majority of children attend Koranic (Muslim) school in the afternoons or evenings. Technical schools offer training in dyeing, hotel management, secretarial work, and other trades.

14 ● CULTURAL HERITAGE

Senegal has one of the richest bodies of written literature and film in all of Africa. Léopold Senghor was a leading poet and philosopher, as well as leader of the independence movement. Senegalese filmmakers such as Ousmane Sembene and Safi Faye are internationally famous.

Besides literature and film, the title of Senegal's national anthem offers a clue to Senegalese musical culture: "Pluck your *Koras*, Strike the *Balafons*." The traditional *kora,* a stringed calabash (gourd) instrument, symbolizes the singing poet tradition in the country. A unique percussion sound is made with a small drum held under the arm. It can be pressed against the body to pro-

Cynthia Bassett

Senegalese musicians perform traditional and contemporary music using a variety of drums.

duce different pitches. The goatskin drumhead is hit by a wooden stick with a curved end.

Senegalese musicians have adapted traditional music to contemporary music by using electric and acoustic guitars, keyboards, and a variety of drums. More than a dozen Senegalese rap groups in Dakar have evolved from the special blend of Western and African musical traditions. Griots (storytellers) perform traditional Senegalese rap songs that tell stories about society, much like ancient griots narrated the lives of ancient kings.

15 ● EMPLOYMENT

Senegal may be west Africa's cultural capital, but countries like Cote d'Ivoire and Nigeria have more robust economies. With a small industrial sector (less than 10 percent), and limited amounts of land capable of growing crops (27 percent), Senegal depends heavily on its service sector. Some 56 percent of Senegal's work force provide services. Tourism is important in this respect, accounting for about 65 percent of the gross domestic product.

Unlike many African countries, only 35 percent of Senegalese work in growing food for themselves. Many Senegalese work in peanut farming and in the seafood industry, which together account for the bulk of Senegal's export.

16 ● SPORTS

Soccer, basketball, track and field, and jogging all are popular sports in Senegal. However, an indigenous sport that has existed for centuries is traditional wrestling, called *Laamb* in Wolof. In ancient times, wrestlers competed before the king and queen in village squares. Singers, dancers, and storytellers embellished the match. Wrestlers wore amulets to ward off evil spirits and black magic from their opponents. Nowadays, the tradition remains strong. As in former times, griots praise the victors in song and dance.

17 ● RECREATION

Dakar offers a variety of recreation including television, movies, video rentals, discos, and sporting events. Foreign and national films are enjoyed, especially in the towns. Dakar's popular music is enjoyed and danced to throughout the country. Young people enjoy discos, some of which are very elaborate, with moving dance floors, electronically controlled backdrops, and special effects including smoke, mirrors, and sophisticated light shows. *M'balax* is the Senegalese pop music.

A major pastime is visiting people in their homes. Older men enjoy playing checkers. In many rural areas, religious leaders frown on dancing and sometimes do not allow drumming or dancing in their villages. Griots (storytellers) entertain at ceremonies such as baptisms and marriages. Cultural events such as folk ballets, theater productions, or local dance troupes provide recreational outlets.

18 ● CRAFTS AND HOBBIES

Each region of Senegal has its own traditional crafts. Senegal's many tourists have given a boost to the folk art and crafts cottage industry. One finds jewelry, baskets, pottery, handwoven fabrics, glass paintings, and woodcarvings. Handcrafted jewelry includes gold, silver, and bronze. Bead and amber necklaces are also popular. Tourist items such as handbags, clothing, and footwear are made from locally printed fabrics and leather. Craftspeople fashion animal skins, such as iguana and crocodile, into belts and shoes.

19 ● SOCIAL PROBLEMS

There is widespread use of marijuana among young men. There is a separatist struggle in the Casamance River region, which has an ethnic dimension to it. The fighting there has led to allegations by the human rights group Amnesty International of atrocities on both sides.

A stronger, more balanced economy will not solve all of Senegal's social and political problems. However, it will slow urbanization, and the emigration of Senegalese young men to Europe and the United States.

20 ● BIBLIOGRAPHY

Clark, Andrew Francis. *Historical Dictionary of Senegal*. 2d ed. Metuchen, N.J.: Scarecrow Press, 1994.

Senegal in Pictures. Minneapolis, Minn.: Lerner Publications Co., 1988.

Vaillant, Janet G. *Black, French, and African: A Life of Leopold Sedar Senghor*. Cambridge, Mass.: Harvard University Press, 1990.

WEBSITES

Internet Africa Ltd. [Online] Available http://www.africanet.com/africanet/country/senegal/, 1998.

World Travel Guide, Senegal. [Online] Available http://www.wtgonline.com/country/sn/gen.html, 1998.

Wolof

PRONUNCIATION: WOE-loff
LOCATION: Senegal
POPULATION: About 3 million
LANGUAGE: Wolof
RELIGION: Islam (Sunni Muslim); Roman Catholicism; Protestantism

1 ● INTRODUCTION

The Wolof are the major ethnic group in Senegal. They are very influential culturally and politically. The earliest Portuguese explorers in the fifteenth century observed that the Wolof and Sereer groups were well established along the Senegalese coast at that time. The Wolof had probably occupied that area for centuries.

From the 1600s to the mid-1800s, slave trading caused much dislocation. It did not deplete the Wolof to the same degree as other west Africans, however.

Since the first political reforms in 1946, the Wolof have played a leading role politically, culturally, and economically in Senegal. Despite the country's weak economy, the Wolof have built a reputation for international commerce and trading. Wolof businesspeople are found throughout Africa, Europe, and even on the streets of New York City and Washington, D.C.

2 ● LOCATION

The Wolof presently occupy the westernmost point of Africa. From the Atlantic Ocean on the west, the Wolof extend to the Ferlo Desert, some 185 miles (300 kilometers) east. The Wolof make up about 40 percent of the 9 million Senegalese.

3 ● LANGUAGE

Wolof is Senegal's dominant language, although French is the country's official language. Most Senegalese radio and television broadcasts are in French, but some are in Wolof. About 2.5 million Senegalese speak Wolof, and native Wolof speakers account for a third of the population. Besides Senegal, Wolof is also spoken in other West African countries. There are significant numbers of speakers in Mauritania and Mali. Including second-language speakers, some 7 million people worldwide speak Wolof. About 40 percent of Wolof speakers are literate (can read and write).

4 ● FOLKLORE

In Wolof and Senegalese society, there are professional storytellers, known as *griots*. They are historians, poets, musicians, and entertainers.

5 ● RELIGION

The overwhelming majority of Wolof are Muslim, belonging to the Malikite branch of the Sunni group. The remaining 10 percent are Roman Catholic. Less than 1 percent are Protestant.

6 ● MAJOR HOLIDAYS

The Wolof observe Senegal's secular (non-religious) holidays such as Independence Day on April 4. They also celebrate Christmas, although it has no religious significance for them. The most important holiday for the Wolof is *Tabaski*, or the "feast of the lamb." This feast commemorates Allah's (God's) provision of a lamb for Abraham to sacrifice in the wilderness instead of his son. In the morning, prayers are offered at the mosque, and then a lamb is slaughtered. People get together with family to eat, and then visit their friends later in the day. Typically, children receive new clothing and money. Families often go into debt for the occasion.

7 ● RITES OF PASSAGE

The most important Wolof rites of passage are naming ceremonies, circumcisions, and funerals. Much significance is attached to names. Parents carefully choose a name for their children, usually the name of a family member or friend who has influenced them and who will provide a model for their child. The decision may take up to a year.

At age seven to eight, boys are taken from their homes and circumcised in the bush, where they wear white gowns and caps. When they return, they are looked after by a big brother, or *Selbe*, until they are fully healed. The *Selbe* educates them about Wolof heroes and legends. After this rite, the community regards them as men.

8 ● RELATIONSHIPS

Wolof respect both age and status. It is considered impolite for a woman to look a man directly in the eye. Women and girls traditionally curtsy to their elders. As in other Muslim societies, only the right hand is used to shake hands.

Wolof are accustomed to visiting each other unannounced, even as late as midnight. Impromptu visits are not considered rude or inconvenient. A visitor must share a meal, have tea, or spend the night. This traditional hospitality is called *Terranga*.

Greetings among the Wolof are the same as those practiced by all Senegalese people. See the article on "Senegalese" in this volume.

9 ● LIVING CONDITIONS

Living conditions vary greatly from the city to the countryside. In the cities of Dakar, Saint Louis, and Diourbel, homes have electricity and indoor plumbing, although the water supply is unpredictable. Houses are made of concrete with tin roofs. People who can afford it cook with bottled gas. However, most people use charcoal.

Health care is available from the government for a small fee, though people must pay for their medicine. Many Wolof prefer to consult traditional healers first. While their spells have no known scientific basis, their other treatments involve the use of local herbs, bark, and roots that have medicinal properties.

Outside the cities, life is rustic. People live in huts made of millet stalks and thatched roofs. They sleep on traditional beds of wooden sticks with one end raised, and draw water from wells or rivers. With no electricity, the only modern appliance to be found in some villages is a radio.

10 ● FAMILY LIFE

The nuclear family (father, mother, and children) is the pillar of Wolof life. Whatever misfortune may befall them, family members are there to support each other. The man of the family may officially make the decisions, but the wife and mother runs the household. She takes care of the children, does the marketing and cooking, draws water, and finds firewood.

A Wolof father blames the mother if the children make mistakes ("Look what your son did!"), but enjoys taking credit for a child's accomplishments. A typical family has as many as ten or eleven children. Polygamy (the taking of several spouses) is still practiced in the countryside.

Traditionally, when a child comes of age, the mother looks for an appropriate spouse of equal or higher social status. For example, members of the *Guer* (noble) caste, generally do not marry into the *Griot* (artist) caste. Similarly, members of the Griot caste do not marry *Jam* (serfs), whose ancestors were servants. The father waits for the mother's selection of a prospective spouse for their child and then usually approves it.

11 ● CLOTHING

Wolof dress is the same as all people of Senegal. See the article on "Senegalese" in this volume.

12 ● FOOD

Wolof usually eat three meals a day. Townspeople with money drink cacao and eat French bread with butter or mayonnaise, jam, and processed cheese imported from France. The traditional breakfast consists of a paste-like dough made of millet with milk poured over it *(lakh),* or *sombee* (boiled rice covered with curdled milk, sugar, and raisins).

The Wolof people also are known for their *Mbaxal-u-Saloum*, a spicy tomato, peanut, and dried-fish sauce with rice. Another popular dish, *Mafé*, is made with peanut sauce, meat, and potatoes, sweet potatoes, or cassava, with a bit of dried fish to flavor it. The favorite drink of the Wolof is *bissap*. It is red and tastes somewhat like cranberry juice. It is considered a purgative, or a drink to help digestion.

People eat together on a large floor mat. They kneel on one knee and eat the food directly in front of them, using only the right hand. After finishing their portions, they wait for their neighbors to push some food their way. The goal is to get to the center of the food tray.

13 ● EDUCATION

As with other Senegalese, only about 30 percent of Wolof can read and write in French. Only about 20 percent of women are literate (can read and write). School is mandatory, but attendance is not enforced.

At the age of four or five, the majority of children attend Koranic (Muslim) schools.

A small percentage of high school graduates continue at the University of Dakar. Those who can afford it prefer studying abroad in France or in other French-speaking countries like Belgium, Switzerland, and Morocco.

14 ● CULTURAL HERITAGE

An internationally known filmmaker from Senegal, Djibril Mambeti Diop, is Wolof. Another Wolof, writer Alioune Diop, founded *Presence Africaine*, a prominent African publishing house in Europe.

Wolof are accomplished musicians and have pioneered modern forms of traditional griot music. Modern griot "rap" performed in the Wolof language tells stories about society, much like ancient griots narrated the lives of ancient kings.

The internationally acclaimed singer Youssou N'Dour performs and records in his native Wolof and in several other languages, including English. He has collaborated with Western musicians including Paul Simon *(Graceland),* Peter Gabriel *(So),* and Branford Marsalis.

Traditional Wolof instruments include a small drum held under the arm, which can be pressed against the body to produce different pitches. The goatskin drum head is hit by a wooden stick with a curved end. The Wolof have skillfully adapted such instruments for pop music.

15 ● EMPLOYMENT

Many Wolof farm and keep herds. Although Wolof generally do not fish, a Wolof-speak-

Cynthia Bassett

Wolof-speaking people, the Lebu, are fisherfolk on the coast of Senegal.

ing people, the Lebu, are fisherfolk on the coast of Senegal. If the Wolof have an international reputation, it is mainly for their tailoring, woodcarving, and business ability. They have traded with Arabs for centuries, and specialize in import-export trading. According to a popular Wolof joke, when U.S. astronaut Neil Armstrong stepped foot on the moon, a Wolof tapped him on the shoulder and asked, *"Gorgui* (sir), would you like to buy this product?"

16 ● SPORTS

The Wolof participate in soccer, basketball, track and field, and jogging. Their traditional sport, however, is an ancient form of wrestling. Called *Laamb,* it has been played for centuries. Each year, champions are crowned and praised in traditional songs.

17 ● RECREATION

City residents have access to videos, video games, radio, and television. It is cheaper, however, and more enjoyable for many people to create their own fun. For example, in Dakar, as the day cools late in the afternoon, griots play drums in the streets, often accompanied by dancing. The griot can speed up the beat to dizzying levels.

Older people find enjoyment in quieter pursuits, such as socializing at mosques or playing checkers. For excitement, they go to wrestling matches, traditional dugout canoe racing, and horse racing on weekends. However, betting is frowned on.

18 ● CRAFTS AND HOBBIES

The Wolof are known for their woodcarvings. They fashion statues, figurines, and masks, mainly for the tourist market. Wolof are also fine tailors. Men prefer silver bracelets and rings, while women wear gold necklaces, chains, and rings. Some Wolof are traditional weavers. For hobbies, children enjoy soccer and storytelling. Checkers are a popular pastime.

19 ● SOCIAL PROBLEMS

Wolof society is undergoing rapid change from a rural to an urban style of living. This places stress on social structures, family relationships, and traditional values. Many Wolof migrate to the cities hoping to find white-collar jobs. Children and young people often find it difficult to adjust. This is a factor in the rising abuse of alcohol and drugs by the Wolof.

Unemployment is also a major problem. Poverty and idleness have led to an increase in burglary, prostitution, and mugging. Pickpockets are common in downtown Dakar. Beggars frequently knock on doors for food, and people often cook extra food, in preparation for these visits. Nevertheless, serious crimes such as murder and armed robbery are still very rare.

20 ● BIBLIOGRAPHY.

Africa South of the Sahara. "Senegal." London: Europa Publishers, 1997.

Clark, Andrew Francis. *Historical Dictionary of Senegal.* 2d ed. Metuchen, N.J.: Scarecrow Press, 1994.

Gellar, Sheldon. *Senegal: An African Nation between Islam and the West.* London: Gower, 1983.

Senegal in Pictures. Minneapolis, Minn.: Lerner Publications Co., 1988.

WEBSITES

Internet Africa Ltd. [Online] Available http://www.africanet.com/africanet/country/senegal/, 1998.

NiiCanada Ltd. The Wolof (Djolof) People. [Online] Available http://www.niica.on.ca/gambia/wolof.htm, 1998.

World Travel Guide, Senegal. [Online] Available http://www.wtgonline.com/country/sn/gen.html, 1998.

Seychelles

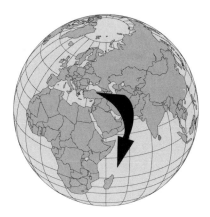

The people of the Seychelles are called Seychellois. The people represent intermarriage of African, French, and Asian ancestors.

Seychellois

PRONUNCIATION: say-shel-WAH
LOCATION: Seychelles Islands
POPULATION: About 72,000
LANGUAGE: Creole, English, and French (official languages); Gurijati; Chinese; other European and Oriental languages
RELIGION: Christianity (Roman Catholicism)

1 ● INTRODUCTION

The Seychelles Islands were a French possession until 1814. They were then under British rule until they gained their independence in 1976. The Seychellois are of African, European, Indian, and Chinese ancestry. The majority have black ancestors who arrived from Africa in the eighteenth and nineteenth centuries. Over time, the different ethnic groups have intermarried. Thus, there is a great degree of racial diversity among the Seychellois.

2 ● LOCATION

The Republic of Seychelles is one of the world's smallest nations in size and population. It is located in the Indian Ocean, east of Tanzania. It has a total land area of only 171 square miles (444 square kilometers), about two-and-a-half times the size of Washington, D.C. The population of Seychelles is only 72,113 people (1994 estimate). The exact number of islands is unknown but has been estimated at 115. Hills up to 3,084 feet high (940 meters) characterize the granite islands. There are also coral islands and reefs.

Mahé, the main island, is home to about 90 percent of all Seychellois. It contains the capital and only city, Victoria, and the only port.

3 ● LANGUAGE

Seychellois have three official languages: Creole, English, and French. Creole devel-

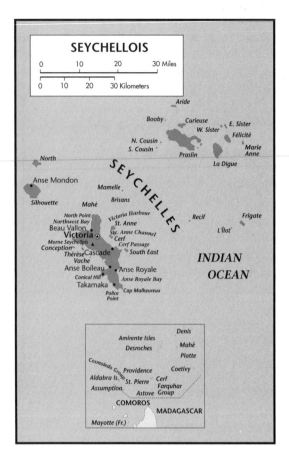

oped from the French dialects of the original settlers. Its vocabulary is mostly French, with a few Malagasy, Bantu, English, and Hindi words.

Most Seychellois can speak and understand French. Most younger Seychellois read English, the language of government and commerce. French is the language of the Roman Catholic Church in the Seychelles Islands.

The following is a Seychellois proverb in the Creole language: *Sak vid pa kapab debout* (meaning "One doesn't work on an empty stomach"). Its literal translation is "an empty bag will not stand up on its own."

4 ● FOLKLORE

Accomplished storytellers and singers pass on Seychellois culture and social customs through fables, songs, and proverbs.

Storytelling is at the center of the traditional *moutia* performance. The *moutia* began during the days of slavery. Two men told stories about the hard labors of the day. Women then joined in to dance, accompanied by singing and chanting. Modern performances still involve dancing to typical African rhythms. Performers often use satire to entertain and teach people of all ages.

5 ● RELIGION

Almost all the inhabitants of Seychelles are Christian. More than 90 percent are Roman Catholic. Sunday masses are well attended. Religious holidays are celebrated as religious and social events.

Like other Africans, many Seychellois Christians still follow tradional religious practices. These may include magic, witchcraft, and sorcery. It is common to consult a local fortune-teller known as a *bonhomme de bois* or a *bonne femme de bois*. Charms known as *gris-gris* are used to harm one's enemies.

6 ● MAJOR HOLIDAYS

The Seychellois have ten public holidays: New Year's Day, January 1–2; Good Friday and Easter Sunday, in March or April; the Fête Dieu (Corpus Christi), in May or June; Assumption Day, August 15; All Saints' Day, November 1; the Day of the Immacu-

Susan D. Rock

Secluded beach cove at Victoria, Seychelles. Seychellois consume an average of 176 pounds (80 kilograms) of fish each year.

late Conception, December 8; Christmas Day, December 25; and the Queen's official birthday.

Families often take advantage of public holidays to picnic at the beach and swim. They may also attend a traditional dance and storytelling performance called a *moutia.*

7 ● RITES OF PASSAGE.

Weddings and funerals are occasions for lavish spending. A family might spend half a year's income on a child's wedding. Sometimes both the bride's and the groom's families pay for the event.

On Mahé, the most elaborate Catholic funerals include three rounds of bell ringing. There is also singing, organ music, and a sermon. The loud tolling makes the death known to everyone. Less expensive funerals involve a more modest ceremony with less bell ringing. At the simplest funeral, a single bell is rung eleven times.

8 ● RELATIONSHIPS

Skin color figures importantly in social relationships and career opportunities. Designations for whites include the *Grand Blanc* (a white person with property or a good job); the *Blanc Coco,* or "white chocolate" (a working-class white who works for

Seychellois artisans have transformed traditional folk art and crafts into livelihoods. Batik-dyed cloth is becoming fashionable and is in high demand by tourists.

a *grand blanc);* and the *Blanc Rouille,* or "rusted white" (an uneducated plantation owner who needs an educated black person to do the accounting). Landless poor people, mostly of African origin, are at the bottom of the social ladder. They are called *Rouge* (red) or *Noir* (black), depending on the darkness of their skin.

It is said, jokingly, that after giving birth, a Seychellois mother asks first what color her child is, and second whether it is a boy or girl.

Western-style dating is fairly common in the capital city, Victoria, but in the outer islands traditional forms of recreation usu-ally bring couples together with other young people.

9 ● LIVING CONDITIONS

Traditional houses rise on stilts above the ground. The main room is used for eating and sleeping. The kitchen is separate to maintain cleanliness. Woven coconut leaves make naturally cool walls and roofs. However, galvanized iron is gradually replacing them for roofing.

10 ● FAMILY LIFE

Mothers are dominant in the household. They control most daily expenses and look after the children. Family size is relatively small by African standards.

Sexual relationships without formal marriage are common among the Seychellois. Most family units take the form of informal unions known as living *en ménage* (by household). Nearly three-fourths of all children born in the islands are born out of wedlock. However, many are legally acknowledged by their fathers. The Church and civil authorities disapprove of unmarried couples living together. However, such unions are usually stable and carry little social shame for either partner or for their children.

Women enjoy the same legal, political, economic, and social rights as men.

11 ● CLOTHING

Generally, the Seychellois wear modern, Western-style clothing. Women go to market in cotton smocks and sandals. They wear locally made straw hats for sun protection. They may also wear African sarongs. Men wear hats, also, and loose-fitting, short-sleeved shirts and trousers. For casual dress, both men and women wear shorts. Some uniformed public servants, such as traffic police, also wear shorts.

12 ● FOOD

The Seychellois Creole cuisine combines a wide variety of cooking styles, including English, French, Chinese, and Indian. Creole cooking is rich, hot, and spicy. It blends fruit, fish, fresh vegetables, and spices. Basic ingredients include pork, chicken, fish, octopus, and shellfish. Coconut milk makes a good sauce for seafood meals. Fish is served in many ways: grilled on firewood,

curried, in boullions or soups, and as steak. Turtle meat is called "Seychelles beef." People also enjoy salads and fruit desserts of mango, papaya, breadfruit, and pineapple.

Locally made alcoholic beverages include palm wine *(calou)*. *Bacca* is a powerful sugarcane liquor drunk on ceremonial occasions.

13 ● EDUCATION

Since 1981, a system of free education has been in effect, requiring attendance by all children in grades one to nine, beginning at age five. Students complete six years of primary school and three years of secondary school. Those who wish to continue their education attend a National Youth Service (NYS) program. In addition to academic instruction, the students receive practical training in gardening, cooking, housekeeping, and livestock-raising. They produce much of their own food, cook their own meals, and do their own laundry.

Students may attend Seychelles Polytechnic, a technical trade school. They may also study abroad through British, U.S., and French scholarship programs.

14 ● CULTURAL HERITAGE

African, European, and Asian influences are present in Seychellois music, dance, literature, and visual art. African rhythms are apparent in the *moutia* and *séga* dances. The *sokoué* dance resembles masked African dancing. Dancers portray birds, animals, and trees. The *contredanse* is a French import, with origins in the court of King Louis XIV (1638–1715). Traditionally, Seychellois performed their music on drums, violins, accordions, and the triangle. Nowadays, the acoustic guitar is usually used as well.

Two young performers, Patrick Victor and David Filoé, have adapted the traditional *moutia* and *séga* dances in a modern setting. Seychelles' most celebrated poet is Antoine Abe.

15 ● EMPLOYMENT

The tourist industry directly employs some 15 percent of the population. In addition, it creates jobs in construction, banking, and other fields. Many households supplement their income from family garden plots and by raising pigs.

An unusual profession on the islands is *calou* (palm wine) tapping. Tappers must climb a tree twice daily. Using a special tap, they collect the sap in a bamboo or plastic container.

16 ● SPORTS

Seychellois play a variety of sports. The most popular participant and spectator sport is soccer. Basketball is also popular.

17 ● RECREATION

Seychellois are fond of singing. They often perform informally together at night when visiting with friends. Families and friends gather on their verandas in the evening for friendly games of checkers and cards.

Seychellois radio and television broadcasts offer programs in Creole, English, and French. Videos and movies are also popular.

18 ● CRAFTS AND HOBBIES

Seychellois are accomplished painters, drawing inspiration from their environment. Sculptors and carvers fashion teakwood goblets, cigar and jewelry boxes, and board games such as dominoes and backgammon. Jewelers make coral and shell bracelets, necklaces, and earrings. Batik-dyed cloth is becoming fashionable.

19 ● SOCIAL PROBLEMS

Juvenile delinquency, resulting from boredom and isolation, is a growing problem. Many adults suffer from alcoholism. In addition, an alarming number of young people are beginning to use marijuana and heroin. Sexually transmitted diseases are widespread. Efforts to contain them have been ineffective. Domestic abuse remains a problem.

20 ● BIBLIOGRAPHY

Bennett, George. *Seychelles*. Denver, Colo.: Clio Press, 1993.

Doubilet, David. "Journey to Aldabra." *National Geographic* (March 1995): 90–113.

Franda, Marcus. *The Seychelles: Unquiet Islands*. Boulder, Colo.: Westview Press, 1982.

Mancham, R. James. *Paradise Raped: Life, Love and Power in the Seychelles*. London: Methuen, 1983.

Vine, Peter. *Seychelles*. London: Immel Publishing, 1989.

WEBSITES

Internet Africa Ltd. [Online] Available http://www.africanet.com/africanet/country/seychell/, 1998.

World Travel Guide, Seychelles.[Online] Available http://www.wtgonline.com/country/sc/gen.html, 1998.

Sierra Leone

The people of Sierra Leone are called Sierra Leoneans. The population is composed of about eighteen ethnic groups. The largest is the Mende (Malinke—about 34 percent of the population). There are also 40,000–80,000 Creoles, descendants of slaves freed from Europe, the West Indies, and other regions. For more information on the Mende, see the article on Malinke in the chapter on Liberia in Volume 5.

Creoles of Sierra Leone

PRONUNCIATION: CREE-uhls of see-AIR-a lee-OWN

LOCATION: Sierra Leone

POPULATION: Approximately 40,000–80,000

LANGUAGE: Krio

RELIGION: Christianity with remnants of traditional African religion

1 ● INTRODUCTION

The Creoles are a culturally distinct people of Sierra Leone. Their ancestors were freed slaves brought to the region as immigrants from London, Nova Scotia, Jamaica, and other parts of west Africa. Britain established a safe place for freed slaves there in 1787 and a colony in 1807. From 1808 to 1863 thousands of liberated Africans came to Freetown.

By the late 1800s, the Creoles had become prosperous through trade. In 1895, the British and French signed a treaty establishing the current boundaries of present-day Sierra Leone. The following year it became a British protectorate. Sierra Leone gained its independence in 1961.

In the twentieth century, racial discrimination in the British Empire hurt the Creoles. Many were restricted to low-level civil service posts. However, political reform in 1951 gave the Creoles new opportunities. In 1967, a Creole, Dr. Siaka Stevens (1905–88), was elected prime minister, a post he held until 1985. A new military government took over in 1992 and loosely held power until it was overthrown in 1996. The country has remained in a state of unrest since then.

2 ● LOCATION

The Creole homeland is a mountainous, narrow peninsula on the coast of west Africa.

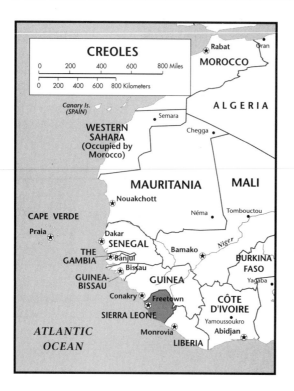

CREOLES

| 0 | 200 | 400 | 600 | 800 Miles |

| 0 | 200 | 400 | 600 | 800 Kilometers |

Rabat
Oran
MOROCCO

Canary Is.
(SPAIN)

ALGERIA

Semara

Chegga

WESTERN
SAHARA
(Occupied by
Morocco)

MAURITANIA

MALI

Nouakchott

CAPE VERDE

Néma

Tombouctou

Praia

Dakar
SENEGAL
Banjul
Bamako

Niger

THE
GAMBIA
Bissau
GUINEA-
BISSAU
GUINEA

BURKINA
FASO

Yadaba

Conakry
Freetown
SIERRA LEONE

CÔTE
D'IVOIRE
Yamoussoukro
Abidjan

ATLANTIC
OCEAN

Monrovia
LIBERIA

The whole of Sierra Leone covers some 28,000 square miles (72,500 square kilometers), roughly the size of South Carolina. At its northern tip lies Freetown, the Sierra Leonean capital. The peninsula's mountain range is covered by tropical rain forests split by deep valleys and adorned with impressive waterfalls. White sand beaches line the Atlantic coast.

3 • LANGUAGE

Krio is the mother tongue of the Creoles. It is spoken in schools, at the markets, and in the workplace. It is based on English, but incorporates elements of west African languages. Native speakers number about 472,000. People who speak it as a second language number perhaps 4 million.

4 • FOLKLORE

Creoles have inherited a wide range of tales from their ancestors. They entertain and provide instruction in Creole values and traditions. Among the best loved are stories about the spider. The following is a typical spider tale:

> Once the spider was fat. He loved eating, but detested work and had not planted or fished all season. One day the villagers were preparing a feast. From his forest web, he could smell the mouth-watering cooking. He knew that if he visited friends, they would feed him as was the custom. So he called his two sons and told both of them to tie a rope around his waist and set off in opposite directions for the two closest villages, each holding one end of the rope. They were to pull on the rope when the food was ready. But both villages began eating at the same time, and when the sons began pulling the rope, it grew tighter and tighter, squeezing the greedy spider. When the feasting was over and the sons came to look for him, they found a big head, a big body, and a very thin waist!

5 • RELIGION

Most Sierra Leoneans (60 percent) follow Islam. However, the majority of Creoles embrace Christianity, combined with some practices from traditional African religion.

6 • MAJOR HOLIDAYS

Creoles celebrate Christmas and Easter with much feasting. On these occasions children receive new clothes and gifts of money. One popular holiday in Freetown is the end of the Muslim Ramadan fast. On this night, young boys parade carrying thin paper lanterns attached to wooden frames. Parties with singing and dancing are held throughout the night. Secular holidays, such as Independence Day, are also celebrated by the Creoles. However, political and economic problems in Sierra Leone have reduced enthusiasm for these holidays.

7 ● RITES OF PASSAGE

Creoles practice certain African rituals in connection with rites of passage. One such ceremony is the *awujoh* feast, intended to win the protection of ancestral spirits. Awujoh feasts are held for newborns and newlyweds, and on other occasions.

When someone dies, pictures in the house are turned toward the wall. At the wake held before the burial, people clap loudly to make sure the corpse is not merely in a trance. The next day the body is washed, placed in shrouds (burial cloths), and laid on a bed for a final viewing. Then it is placed in a coffin and taken to the church for the service, and then to the cemetery for burial.

The mourning period lasts one year. On the third, seventh, and fortieth day after death, *awujoh* feasts are held. The feast on the fortieth day marks the spirit's last day on earth. The family and guests eat a big meal. Portions of the meal are placed into a hole for the dead. The *pull mohning* day—the end of mourning—occurs at the end of one year. The mourners wear white, visit the cemetery, and then return home for refreshments.

8 ● RELATIONSHIPS

The Creoles are a sociable people, given to joking and teasing. Common gestures include handslapping and handshaking.

The Creoles still observe traditional dating and marriage customs. Marriage is still viewed as a contract between two families. Relatives seek out prospective mates for their kin from desirable families. When a mate has been chosen, the groom's parents set a "put stop" day. After this day the girl can no longer entertain other suitors. On the evening before the wedding, the groom's friends treat him to "bachelor's eve," a rowdy last fling before marriage.

9 ● LIVING CONDITIONS

Creole families typically live in two-story wooden houses reminiscent of those found in the West Indies or Louisiana. Despite their dilapidated appearance, they have a distinctive air, with dormers, box windows, shutters, glass panes, and balconies. The elite live in attractive neighborhoods like Hill Station, above Freetown. A large dam in the mountains provides a reliable supply of water and electricity.

At rush hour, downtown Freetown is congested with Landcruisers, Volkswagens, and Japanese cars. Broken-down cars are abandoned and left to rust in the "car cemeteries" of Freetown's back streets. Most people travel by taxi. Fares are negotiated before the ride, with the passenger usually offering half of what the driver demands. Pickup trucks (lorries) with wooden benches in the back provide rural transportation. These are efficient but overcrowded and carry rice bags, cassava, bushels of fruit, and chickens, as well as people, and sport a variety of colorful graffiti. Buses ply the main roads between provincial cities but are more expensive.

Freetown once had a reputation for being the "white man's grave" because of its endemic malaria. Large, deep drainage canals now carry off much of the monsoon rain, reducing the number of flies and mosquitoes. Health care is still not available to many Sierra Leoneans, and this is reflected in the country's low life expectancy of 49 years.

10 ● FAMILY LIFE

Creoles live in nuclear families (father, mother, and their children), but the extended family is important to them. Family members who do well are expected to help those who are less fortunate. They assist poorer relatives with school fees and job opportunities. Women typically shoulder the greatest domestic burdens. In most families, women care for the children, clean house, do the marketing, cook meals, wash dishes and clothes, and carry wood and water.

11 ● CLOTHING

Today, pop fashions—jeans, T-shirts, and sneakers—are very much in style among young people. However, older Creoles still dress conservatively in Western-style suits and dresses. On Sunday mornings, Anglicans and Catholics in Freetown wear their Sunday finery to church. For everyday, women wear simpler dresses, skirts and blouses, or the *lappa* (traditional wraparound) with an African blouse.

12 ● FOOD

Creoles typically eat three meals a day, the largest in the morning or near midday. The staple noonday meal is *foo-foo,* a dough-like paste made of cassava pounded into flour. Foo-foo is always eaten with a "palaver sauce" or "plassas." This is a spicy dish consisting of leafy greens with tripe (sheep or goat stomach), fish, beef, salt pork, and chicken. A west African one-pot meal, jollof rice, is also popular. Other favorites include rice with various sauces, rice bread, and salad. Creoles enjoy alcoholic drinks such as beer, gin, and palm wine.

13 ● EDUCATION

Even under British rule, the Creoles had a strong tradition of education. Creoles sent their children to Fourah Bay College or to a British university. They supplied the colony with lawyers, doctors, clergy, and businessmen. In the twentieth century, schooling in Sierra Leone has become even more universal. In 1987, tuition fees were abolished for government-funded primary and secondary schools.

14 ● CULTURAL HERITAGE

During the colonial period, educated Creoles valued European culture above their own. In the late 1800s, the Creole upper class was more interested in literary societies, public lectures, and piano recitals than in African drumming and dancing. Today Creole attitudes toward their own culture have changed. Creoles participate in Sierra Leone's internationally famous National Dance Troupe.

Creole authors have pioneered a growing literature in the Krio language. The following stanza from a poem by Thomas Decker offers a glimpse into this body of work:

Slip Gud

Slip gud, o, bedi-gial!
opin yai lilibit
en luk mi wan minit
bifo you slip.

(Translation)

Sleep Well

Sleep well, my "baby-girl!"
Open your eyes a little bit
Look, just for one minute
Ere you fall asleep.

15 ● EMPLOYMENT

Creoles are found in all occupations. They farm, fish, trade, and teach. Many have left manual jobs for office work and other higher-status jobs. Often, however, these jobs do not pay enough to support large families. Both men and women operate small businesses, such as food stands and restaurants.

16 ● SPORTS

The favorite Sierra Leonean sport is soccer, called football in West Africa. Schools of all sizes have teams. Even in the smallest villages, games are played every evening. Although children may play without soccer shoes, they usually have uniforms.

17 ● RECREATION

Creoles enjoy going to movies, watching television, and listening to the radio. Transistor radios are found in even the smallest villages. Most programs come from the United States and England.

A favorite traditional pastime for girls is hair braiding. Boys enjoy checkers and other games. Adults like to exchange visits with their friends and socialize at the market. In addition to buying and selling, people come to dress up and exchange the latest gossip.

18 ● CRAFTS AND HOBBIES

Small-scale arts and crafts centers flourish in Freetown, selling mainly to foreign tourists. Miranda Burney Nicol (Olayinka) and Phoebe Ageh Jones are two artists whose works have been distributed internationally. Cloth dyeing (*batik*) is a traditional craft that has recently been revived.

19 ● SOCIAL PROBLEMS

The Creoles' problems are inseparable from those of other Sierra Leoneans. Migration to Freetown has led to overcrowding, pollution, and high crime levels. Most Sierra Leoneans are illiterate (cannot read and write) and have few job choices. In addition, the Creoles and their neighbors find themselves in a period of political instability, and they are vulnerable to changes in the world economy.

20 ● BIBLIOGRAPHY

Alie, Joe A. D. *A New History of Sierra Leone.* New York: St. Martin's Press, 1990.

Binns, Margaret. *Sierra Leone.* Oxford, England; Santa Barbara, Calif.: Clio Press, 1992.

Carpenter, Allan, and Susan L. Eckert. *Sierra Leone.* Enchantment of Africa Series. Chicago: Children's Press, 1974.

Davies, Clarice et al., ed. *Women of Sierra Leone: Traditional Voices.* Freetown: Partners in Adult Education, Women's Commission, 1992.

Foray, Cyril P. *Historical Dictionary of Sierra Leone.* Metuchen, N.J.: Scarecrow, 1977.

Fyfe, Christopher. *A Short History of Sierra Leone.*

New York: Longman, 1979.

Milsome, John. *Sierra Leone.* New York: Chelsea House, 1989.

The President's 27th April Celebrations Committee. *Sierra Leonean Heroes: Thirty Great Men and Women who Helped to Build Our Nation.* N.p.: 1987.

Wyse, Akintola. *The Krio of Sierra Leone: An Interpretive History.* London, England: C. Hurst and Company, 1989.

WEBSITES

World Travel Guide, Sierra Leone. [Online] Available http://www.wtgonline.com/country/sl/gen.html, 1998.

Slovakia

The people of Slovakia are called Slovaks. The people who trace their descent to Slovakia make up 85 percent of the population. Hungarians, concentrated in the south near the border with Hungary, totaled about 12 percent. For more information on Hungarians, see the chapter on Hungary in Volume 4.

Slovaks

PRONUNCIATION: SLOW-vox

LOCATION: Slovakia

POPULATION: 4.7 million

LANGUAGE: Slovak

RELIGION: Roman Catholicism; Protestantism; Greek Catholicism

1 ● INTRODUCTION

Slavic peoples first settled in present-day Slovakia in the fifth century AD, eventually forming the short-lived Moravian Empire. Throughout much of history, Slovakia was dominated by the Magyars (Hungarians). In 1919, political union of the Czechs and Slovaks created the independent state of Czechoslovakia. Slovakia accounted for about 40 percent of the country's total area. Throughout the union of the two ethnic groups, the more numerous and powerful Czechs have had more political power than the Slovaks.

After World War II (1939–45) the communists seized control of the country. Under communist rule, the Slovaks were once again less powerful than the Czechs. In 1989, the communist empire in Eastern Europe collapsed. After the first democratic elections and the departure of the Soviet troops, old ethnic problems resurfaced. The Slovaks demanded separation from the Czechs. On January 1, 1993, the Slovaks declared their independence, establishing their own parliament in Bratislava, capital of the new country, Slovakia.

2 ● LOCATION

Slovakia is a small, landlocked country in Central Europe. It is about the size of Vermont and New Hampshire combined. Slovakia's neighbors are Poland (to the north), the Czech Republic (to the northwest), Austria (to the southwest), and Hungary (to the

SLOVAKS

largest ethnic minority, account for 11 percent of Slovakia's population. According to official figures, the Romany (Gypsies) account for 1.5 percent of the population. The true figure may be higher.

3 ● LANGUAGE

Slovak is a member of the Western Slavic language group. Of all other languages, it has the greatest similarity to Czech, although the two languages are clearly different. The Slovak alphabet, which has forty-three letters, is written using Western-style letters.

Like those of other Eastern European languages, Slovak words feature clusters of consonants; some words have practically no vowels at all. Examples of such words include *smrt'* (death), *srdce* (heart), *slnko* (sun), and *yrt* (to drill, or bore).

4 ● FOLKLORE

Almost every ruined castle in Slovakia has its legend. Sometimes these legends are bloodcurdling. One such legend is the story of Csejte. In this tale, a ruthless countess murders three young girls and bathes in their blood, thinking it will renew her youthfulness. Janosik is a well-known folk hero whose adventures date back to the Turkish invasions of the sixteenth and seventeenth centuries.

Belief in witches, ghosts, and other supernatural beings persist in some areas. Morena, a goddess of death, is the object of a springtime custom. In it, young girls ritually "drown" a straw doll in waters that flow from the first thaw.

south). It also shares a short eastern border with Ukraine.

Much of Slovakia consists of unspoiled mountains and forests. The High Tatras are the second-highest mountain range in Europe after the Alps. Sloping down from this high mountain range are the fertile river valleys. These small rivers drain into the Danube River. The Danube forms part of the southern boundary of the country. Slovakia has fertile farmland. Its winters are severe, and its summers warm.

The population of Slovakia is almost 5.5 million. Forty-three percent of the people live in rural areas. The largest cities are the capital city of Bratislava and Kosice. Ethnic Slovaks make up about 86 percent, or 4.7 million, of the population. Hungarians, the

In rural areas, some Slovaks still believe that illnesses can be caused by witches or by the "evil eye." They seek the services of traditional healers who use folk remedies and rituals.

5 ● RELIGION

Most Slovaks (about 60 percent of the population) belong to the Roman Catholic Church. They have close ties to their church community. Slovak Catholicism is generally more traditional than the more liberal Czech version.

Besides Catholicism, there are also a number of other Christian faiths in Slovakia. The largest denominations are Evangelical Lutherans and Greek Catholics. Others include Calvinist Reformed, Eastern Orthodox, and Baptist. Slovakia's once populous Jewish community was destroyed in the Nazi Holocaust. Close to 10 percent of Slovaks are declared atheists.

6 ● MAJOR HOLIDAYS

National holidays in Slovakia include New Year's Day (January 1), Easter Monday (in March or April), Liberation Day (May 8), Cyril and Methodius Day (July 5), Slovak National Uprising Day (August 29), Constitution Day (September 1), Independence Day (October 28), and Christmas (December 24, 25, and 26).

Christmas has the largest celebrations. On Christmas Eve, Slovaks attend church services. Christmas trees are decorated, gifts are exchanged, and there is a traditional Christmas Eve dinner called *vilija*, consisting of mushroom soup, fish, peas, prunes, and pastries. Slovaks usually celebrate birthdays with their families, and celebrate name days (days dedicated to the saint for which one is named) with friends and co-workers.

Helene Cincebeaux

Slovak woman with rosary and Bible. Most Slovaks (about 60 percent of the population) belong to the Roman Catholic Church and have close ties to their church community.

In late October, Slovakia hosts the Bratislava music festival. Musicians from around the world perform. Many towns and villages host annual folklore festivals in the late summer or fall, with plentiful singing, dancing, and drinking.

7 ● RITES OF PASSAGE

Most Slovaks observe major life events such as birth, marriage, and death within the religious traditions of the Catholic Church.

8 ● RELATIONSHIPS

Shaking hands is a standard form of greeting. Men generally wait for women to extend their hands. Upon parting, a man may hug a woman or kiss her on both cheeks.

Standard greetings include *Dobrý den* (good day), *Velmi ma tesi* (pleased to meet you), and the more informal *Ahoj* (the equivalent of "hi"). *Dovidenia* means "good-bye," and the more casual terms *Ciao* and *Servus* mean either "hello" or "good-bye."

In rural areas, some older people greet each other with *S Bohom* (God be with you). When not among family or close friends, Slovak forms of address are very formal and courteous, including both *Pán* (Mr.) or *Pani* (Mrs.) and any professional title, such as doctor, professor, or engineer.

Slovaks enjoy entertaining at home. Upon entering a Slovak home, guests generally remove their shoes. Their hosts often provide them with slippers. Fresh flowers are always presented unwrapped and in odd numbers. It is the custom to bring even numbers of flowers to funerals. The gesture for wishing someone good luck (the equivalent of crossing one's fingers in the United States) is to fold the thumb inward and close the other fingers around it.

9 ● LIVING CONDITIONS

Life expectancy for Slovaks averages seventy-one years of age. The rate of infant mortality is eleven deaths for every one thousand live births. Almost everyone has access to medical care, and there is a high rate of immunization for infants during their first year.

There is a serious housing shortage in Slovakia. In 1992, approximately 80,000 people were on waiting lists for new apartments. The government plans to build 200,000 new units by the year 2000. Most city dwellers live in modest-sized apartments built during the communist era. Varied types of housing are found in rural Slovakia. These range from two-room detached dwellings to two-story apartment buildings with up to six units.

Indoor plumbing has been standard in rural areas for the past thirty years. Common building materials are concrete blocks and bricks. Most Slovak families own a car, but public transportation, including buses, trolleys, and trains, is widely used due to the high price of gasoline. There are rail links between major cities, and major highway expansion is planned.

10 ● FAMILY LIFE

The most common family unit in Slovakia is the nuclear family (father, mother, and children). Extended families can still be found in rural areas, however, where houses may have extra rooms to house the family of a grown son. The average Slovak family has two or three children. Women receive paid maternity leave and a cash allowance when each child is born. Most women work outside the home (women account for 47 percent of the Slovak labor force). Women and men have equal rights under the law, including property and inheritance rights.

Helene Cincebeaux

A bride from the town of Detva, in central Slovakia. On special occasions, people in the hill country still wear traditional dress, including dark woolen suits and knitted hats for men and full skirts, aprons, blouses, and scarves for women.

11 ● CLOTHING

City and town people in Slovakia wear modern Western-style clothing, including business attire for work, and jeans and T-shirts for casual wear. On special occasions, peasants in the hill country still wear traditional dress. Such outfits include dark woolen suits and knitted hats for men and full skirts, aprons, blouses, and scarves for women.

12 ● FOOD

The Slovak national dish is *bryndzové halusky*, dumplings made with potatoes, flour, water, eggs, and salt, and served with processed sheep's cheese. However, this dish is not often eaten at home. A recipe for kolác follows.

Another favorite is *Kapustnics*, or cabbage soup. *Rezen* (breaded steak) and potatoes is common. A variety of meat served with dumplings, rice, potatoes, or pasta and sauce are also regulars. Fresh fish and wild game are often served in Slovak homes. Fresh-baked bread and soup are dinnertime staples.

Favorite desserts include *tortes* (frosted, multilayered cakes) and *kolác* (rolls with nut or poppy seed filling). Dry, white wine is a popular drink, especially wine from the Male Karpaty region near Hungary. As in the Czech Republic, *slivovice* (plum brandy) is also popular.

13 ● EDUCATION

Nearly all Slovakians are literate. Schooling is compulsory for ten years, from age six through sixteen. There is no charge to attend a university. Admission is limited and highly competitive, however. There are thirteen universities, of which the oldest is Comenius University in Bratislava.

Although Slovak parents and children take education very seriously, once a year it has its comic side. Every spring, high school seniors play hooky on Wenceslas Square, dressing in pajamas to symbolize a

---

Recipe

Bryndzové Halusky

(Dumplings with Cheese)

Ingredients

1½ pounds uncooked potatoes, grated
3 cups whole wheat flour
1 teaspoon salt
8 ounces feta cheese, crumbled
¼ pound cooked bacon, crumbled

Directions

1. Mix together grated potatoes, whole wheat flour, and salt
2. Form into small, walnut-sized dumplings using a teaspoon.
3. Bring a large pan of salted water to a boil.
4. Sprinkle dumplings with cold water and smooth surface. Drop into gently boiling water.
5. Dumplings are done when they float to the surface. Remove them from the pot with a slotted spoon.
6. Transfer to a bowl and mix with crumbled feta cheese. Sprinkle with crumbled bacon and serve.

Adapted from recipe provided by Slovak Heritage Council and Cultural Society of British Columbia.

---

popular lateness excuse—oversleeping. Others wrap their heads in bandages to represent toothaches, and still others make signs saying that they have stomach aches.

14 ● CULTURAL HERITAGE

Slovakia is rich in folk music. The Slovaks' pride in their musical tradition is expressed in the saying *Kde Slovák, tam spev* (Wherever there is a Slovak, there is a song). Villages have amateur musical groups that perform at school graduations and harvest festivals.

Characteristic Slovak folk instruments include the bagpipes (*gajdy*), pipes (*píst'ala*), and the *fujara*, a large shepherd's flute held vertically in front of the body. The *Janosik* songs are based on the exploits of a well-known folk hero. Immigrants from Romania, Germany, and Hungary have also brought their music to Slovakia. More recently, composers have been incorporating Slovak folk melodies into their works.

The Slovaks also have a strong folk-dance tradition, with dances including the *Kolo, Hajduch, Verbunk, Cardas,* polka, a shepherd's dance called the *Odzemok,* and the *Chorodový,* a communal women's dance. There is a major folk festival every year in July.

Until the eighteenth century, there was no attempt to establish a literary language based on the the Slovak dialects. In the early nineteenth century, literary Slovak was established and this "new" language was used by such talented poets as Andrej Sladkovic ("Marina") and Janko Kral, a poet and revolutionary. Kral's ballads, epics, and lyrics are among the most original of Slovak literature. Another famous poet was Ivan Krasko. After 1918, Slovak literature was at its peak, but during the four decades of communist rule after World War II Slovak writing underwent a general decline.

15 ● WORK

Like other Eastern European countries, Slovakia became highly industrialized during the communist era. There are manufacturing jobs in steel, chemicals, glass, cement, and textiles.

In 1994, the country had an unemployment rate of nearly 15 percent. This was caused mainly by the change from communism to capitalism. Employees commonly receive four weeks of paid vacation and retire between the ages of fifty-three and sixty. About 80 percent of Slovak workers belong to a labor union.

16 ● SPORTS

Popular sports include soccer, tennis, skiing, and ice hockey.

17 ● RECREATION

In their leisure time, Slovaks enjoy attending movies, local festivals, and cultural events. They also enjoy participating in outdoor activities including hiking, swimming, and camping. Slovakia also has over one thousand mineral and hot springs. In rural villages, men meet after work at the local bar to drink, play cards, and socialize.

18 ● CRAFTS AND HOBBIES

Slovak artists are well known for their pottery works. They also make small porcelain figurines. Throughout Slovakia there are artists selling painted Easter eggs, cornhusk figures, hand-knit sweaters, wood carvings, walking sticks, cuckoo clocks, and toys of many varieties. Popular hobbies for women are sewing, embroidering, and lacemaking. Most embroidery work is done in the winter, and many designs have special names: the "lover's eye" or the "little widow." Sewing skills are also used for making traditional Slovak costumes. Other crafts include metalworking and woodcarving.

19 ● SOCIAL PROBLEMS

Slovakia is struggling with the challenges of changing from a centrally planned economy run by the government to one based on free markets. Many government-owned companies have yet to be transfered to private ownership. In addition, unemployment and inflation continue to cause economic problems.

20 ● BIBLIOGRAPHY

Mikus, Joseph A. *Slovakia and the Slovaks.* Washington, D.C.: Three Continents Press, 1977.

Momatiuk, Yva, and John Eastcott. "Slovakia's Spirit of Survival." *National Geographic* (January 1987): 120–146.

Palickar, Stephen Joseph. *Slovakian Culture in the Light of History, Ancient, Medieval and Modern.* Cambridge, Mass.: Hampshire Press, 1954.

Pollak, Janet. "Slovaks." *Encyclopedia of World Cultures.* Boston: G. K. Hall, 1992.

Skalnik, Carol. *The Czech and Slovak Republics: Nation vs. State.* Boulder, Colo.: Westview Press, 1997.

WEBSITES

Embassy of Slovakia, Washington, D.C. [Online] Available http://www.slovakemb.com/, 1998.

World Travel Guide, Slovakia. [Online] Available http://www.wtgonline.com/country/sk/gen.html, 1998.

Slovenia

The people of Slovenia are called Slovenes. Almost 90 percent of the the population trace their heritage to Slovenia. Among minority groups, Croats comprise 3 percent and Serbs, 2 percent.

Slovenes

PRONUNCIATION: SLOW-veenz
ALTERNATE NAMES: Slovenci; Slovenians [both forms, *Slovene* and *Slovenian,* are used as noun and adjective]
LOCATION: Slovenia and regions of Austria, Italy, and Hungary along their Slovenian borders
POPULATION: 1.7 million
LANGUAGE: Slovenian
RELIGION: Roman Catholicism

1 ● INTRODUCTION

The Slovenes originally lived in the area northeast of the Carpathian Mountains. They settled in the eastern Alpine region of Central Europe in the sixth and seventh centuries AD. They formed a short-lived country called Karantania in the eighth century. They didn't have their own independent state in modern times until 1991.

For over a thousand years, Slovenes lived under mostly German rule as part of the Holy Roman (962–1806), Austrian (1804–1867), and Austro-Hungarian (1867–1918) empires. The region where the Slovenes live became part of Yugoslavia after World War I ended in 1918.

During centuries of foreign rule, the Slovenes preserved their language. Over the last 200 years, they formed a modern nation with a rich culture and aspirations for political independence, which they achieved when Yugoslavia fell apart in June 1991, after two of its republics, Croatia and Slovenia, proclaimed their independence.

2 ● LOCATION

The Republic of Slovenia borders Italy in the west, Austria in the north, Hungary in the northeast, and Croatia in the east and south. It is about the size of the state of New Jersey. Slovenia's climate varies with its geographical makeup.

About 50 percent of Slovenes live in cities. Ljubljana, the capital, has approxi-

SLOVENES

0   100   200   300 Miles

0   100   200   300 Kilometers

GERMANY   POLAND   • Warsaw   BELARUS

• Leipzig   • Wrocław   Rivne

• Prague   • Kraków   UKRAINE

CZECH   SLOVAKIA

Munich •   Vienna ✪   • Bratislava

AUSTRIA   ✪ Budapest   Cluj-Napoca •

Graz •   HUNGARY

SLOVENIA

Ljubljana ✪   Pécs •   ROMANIA

✪ Zagreb

Venice •   CROATIA   Danube

SAN   BOSNIA-   ✪ Belgrade

MARINO   HERZEGOVINA   BULGARIA

• Florence   ✪   Sofia

Sarajevo   YUGOSLAVIA   ✪

ITALY   Pristina •

✪ Rome   Skopje

MACEDONIA ✪

ALBANIA

Adriatic Sea

mately 330,000 inhabitants. Before World War II (1939–45), over 50 percent of Slovenes made their living from farming. In the 1990s, the number of peasant farmers had dwindled to 7 percent. After World War II, Yugoslavia industrialized quickly but did not become urbanized. In independent Slovenia, many Slovenes still live in the country and commute to work in the cities.

Most of Slovenia's population of 2 million are Slovene—1.7 million, or 88 percent.

3 ● LANGUAGE

The language of Slovenes is Slovenian, which is the official language of the Republic of Slovenia. Slovenian is a South Slavic language, closely related to Croatian and similar to other Slavic languages, such as Czech. It is spoken by approximately two million people in the Slovene ethnic territory, and by emigrants around the world.

At present, slang, especially of youth, and technical language of professional groups are heavily influenced by English. In teenagers' talk, the English words "full" and "cool" are common expressions of emphasis. For examples, *To je ful dober!* (This is very good!) is often heard. Another often-used English expression is "OK."

People are most often named after Catholic saints such as Ann, Andrew, Joseph, Maria, and Matthew (*Ana, Andrej, Jože, Marija, Matevž*). Also popular are old Slavic personal names, such as *Iztok* or *Vesna*. Family names are derived from people's occupations. Examples include *Kmet* (farmer), or *Kovač* (blacksmith). Locations also become family or given names. For examples, *Dolinar* (one who lives in a valley), or *Hribar* (one who lives on a mountain). Names derived from animals are also popular: *Medved* (bear), *Petelin* (rooster), or *Volk* (wolf).

4 ● FOLKLORE

Many Slovene folk traditions are associated with seasonal celebrations. Adults and children enjoy the spring Carnival season, called *pust* (Mardi Gras). Celebrations include parades, carnivals, and masquerade balls. *Kurentovanje* in the city of Ptuj (in northeastern Slovenia) is the most famous tourist attraction. The central figure in the event is the *kurent,* who has fur clothing and unusual masks with horns. These represent human and animals traits. They are meant to evoke images of another planet. Always happy, the kurent is considered to forecast spring, fertility, and new life. Accompanied by a ceremonial plowman, he visits farms and wishes their owners a prosperous year.

Also for Carnival season, the traditional pastries *krofi* and *flancati* (similar to doughnuts) are prepared. Costumed children, wearing masks, go from house to house, asking: "Do you have anything for Pusta, Hrusta?" People give them sweets and fruits. Adults attend masquerade balls.

Slovene heroes are usually optimistic, wise, and cheerful. The story about Kralj Matjaž (King Mathias) dates to difficult times in Slovene history. People imagined a good king, who would protect them from danger and never die. Instead, he and his army are said to be sleeping under Mount Peca. When needed, the king and his soldiers will awaken and protect their people.

5 ● RELIGION

Although 90 percent of Slovenes claim to be Catholic, many fewer practice their religion by attending mass regularly or receiving the sacraments. But Slovene culture is inseparable from Catholicism. Small numbers of people belong to other religious groups. Besides the Roman Catholic Church, the Evangelical Protestant Church (Lutheran) is the oldest.

6 ● MAJOR HOLIDAYS

Religious holidays, such as Christmas, Easter, Assumption Day (August 15), and All Saints' Day (November 1) are recognized as national holidays. A few nonreligious holidays are also observed. Since gaining independence in 1991, Slovenes celebrate

Statehood Day (June 25), and Independence Day (December 26).

Although the majority of Slovenes are Catholic, Reformation Day is also observed as a national holiday on October 31 to recognize the important role the Protestants played in establishing the identity of the Slovene nation. In 1550, is was the Protestants who published the first book in the Slovene language.

7 ● RITES OF PASSAGE

Major life transitions are marked with religious ceremonies and celebrations appropriate to the Roman Catholic tradition followed by the majority of Slovenes. Such events as baptism, first communion, and confirmation are considered important rites of passage in a child's life.

8 ● RELATIONSHIPS

When meeting, Slovenes exchange various greetings, depending on the time of day. Until 10 AM, they say *dobro jutro* (good morning). During the day it is *dober dan* (good day). After dark one says *dober vecer* (good evening). The reply to all of the above is *Bogdaj* (May God grant you).

Slovenes, especially the young, often say *zivijo* (long life) when meeting friends and acquaintances. At parting, various phrases are used. The most common are *nasvidenje* (so long), *adijo* (goodbye) and, in the evening, *lahko noc* (good night). When Slovenes meet or part, they often shake hands.

Slovenes are courteous visitors and when invited to dinner will always bring small gifts. *Hvala* (thanks) is the word used to express gratitude, to which *prosim* (please) is the polite response. *Prosim* is also used when a request is put forward, or when a listener did not hear or understand what was said.

9 ● LIVING CONDITIONS

Statistics show that the quality of life in Slovenia is good. Life expectancy for men is seventy years and for women seventy-six years. Mothers are entitled to one year's maternity leave so that they can stay with their babies and nurse them. Maternity leave is actually "parental" leave, as half of it can be used by fathers.

There is a shortage of housing. Apartments are small and modest. Very few children have their own rooms. Most share them with other siblings, sometimes even with parents. However, many people living in cities have small cottages, called *vikendi,* in the country, in the mountains, along rivers, or in spas where they spend their weekends.

Every family has at least one radio and television, while telephones and computers are somewhat less common.

10 ● FAMILY LIFE

The majority of young people get married in their twenties and establish a family with one or two children. Families with three or more children are rare.

Slovenes maintain close relations with their parents, siblings, and extended families. In recent decades, younger husbands have begun to share responsibility for housework and the education of children. About half of all marriages end in divorce,

and most children are left with their mothers. In general, divorce is easily obtained.

11 ● CLOTHING

Slovenes wear modern, Western-style clothing. Young people love blue jeans and T-shirts. Women are mostly elegantly dressed and like Italian fashions, while men dress informally, even at the office.

12 ● FOOD

Slovenes love breads and potatoes. Potatoes are served boiled, sautéed, deep-fried, or roasted, and are used in various dishes. Breakfast consists of coffee, tea, or hot chocolate, and rolls with butter and jam. *Zemlja,* a special kind of hard roll, is especially popular. Some people skip breakfast and drink only strong coffee.

For lunch, the main meal of the day, people eat soup, meat, a main-course starch, vegetables, and a salad. Lunch is prepared by working mothers after returning from work and is eaten in the midafternoon. Supper is a light meal with salads, yogurt, and leftovers from lunch.

Slovenes have many traditional dishes, often prepared for celebrations. One of the most genuine festive Slovene foods is a rolled yeast cake, called *potica,* with sweet (walnuts, tarragon, raisins) or salty (cracklings or crisp pork fat) fillings. Potica is served at Christmas and Easter. Among traditional meat dishes, *kranjske klobase* (sausages, similar to Polish kielbasa) are well known, as are pork dishes *(koline)* in winter.

13 ● EDUCATION

The Slovene literacy rate (ability to read and write) is almost 100 percent. Compulsory eight-year elementary education has been a legal requirement since 1869. About 90 percent of students who finish elementary school continue their education at the secondary level. Some go to four-year schools to prepare for higher studies, but many enter two- and three-year vocational schools. A school year lasts 190 days. Not all students graduate.

Those who finish take the upper-level comprehensive exam *(velika matura),* which enables them to enroll in university. There is no tuition in the public school system at any level for full-time students, but parents have to pay for the students' textbooks and other supplies. Since 1991, the law allows home-schooling and private schools, though there are few private schools.

14 ● CULTURAL HERITAGE

Music has always been an important part of the Slovene culture. Vocal and instrumental music has ritual and entertainment functions. Folk songs are simple in form, lyrics, and music, and deal with love, patriotism, war, work traditions, changes of season, and religious and family holidays. In the past, folk singing was part of everyday life.

Slovenes have built hundreds of churches and numerous art galleries, which are testimony to a rich cultural heritage. Although influenced by particularly Slovene cultural characteristics, the literature, music, visual arts, architecture, and theater in Slovenia have been part of larger art movements in Central Europe. Slovene artists worked in the European art centers, and European masters came to Slovenia. The same is true today.

15 ● EMPLOYMENT

Most employed people work a forty-hour week. Some industrious Slovenes work much longer. Besides holding jobs in factories and offices, many work second jobs, run their own businesses, or work on small, family-owned farms. Switching from a communist to a capitalist economy has been difficult.

16 ● SPORTS

Slovenes like hiking, mountain climbing, biking, swimming, rafting and rowing, tennis, horseback riding, fishing, and many other sports. In winter, they ski and skate. Almost every child and adult owns a bike, and many ride bikes to school or the office every day. Skiing has a long history in this part of the world and is probably the most popular sport in Slovenia. Skis were invented in Slovenia at the same time as in Scandinavia. They were once a major means of transportation. Today, there are a few hundred thousand recreational skiers, from whose ranks competitive skiers are recruited. They compete internationally.

17 ● RECREATION

Many schools organize dances for their students on weekends. Proms *(maturitetni plesi)* are traditional in elementary and secondary schools and are organized for graduates every year in the spring. Adults dance on various occasions. The polka and waltz are very popular, but Slovenes dance all major dances from the tango to the macarena.

Slovenes enjoy strolling, often in attractive old town centers, meeting people, chatting, and having a drink in small coffee shops, or *kavarnas*. Weekend trips to the mountains are also very popular. Slovenes enjoy walking in the woods and picking mushrooms to prepare them as culinary specialties.

Movies, concerts, and theater performances are enjoyed by many people. In Slovenia, concerts have greater attendance than soccer games. Young people enjoy listening to various jazz, rock, and pop groups. Although there are several local rock groups, young people listen mostly to popular American, English, and German groups. The Beatles, The Rolling Stones, and Bob Marley are known to every Slovene teenager. Television viewing has increased in the last decade. Besides Slovene television programs, Slovenes can also watch Italian, Austrian, English, and American television shows, including news on CNN.

18 ● CRAFTS AND HOBBIES

Folk arts were mostly associated with crafts and decorating peasants' or, later, workers' homes. Painters often decorated furniture (for example chests, bed headboards, and cribs). Painting on glass was popular in the nineteenth century. Talented but unschooled folk artists often portrayed religious images and geometric patterns. Traditional Slovene crafts include pottery, woodenware, embroidery, lace making, candle making, gingerbread pastries, glass making, wrought iron, and clock making. Potters produce many useful objects such as pots, baking and roasting dishes, jars, pitchers, and goblets.

Woodenware (spoons, various kitchen utensils, toothpicks, and sieves) was produced in several centers. The best known of these, Ribnica Valley, is still active.

19 ● SOCIAL PROBLEMS

Alcoholism is an old, persistent, and serious problem among Slovenes of all ages and both sexes. Consumption of alcohol has increased by about 25 percent during the last decade. Drug use has also increased, especially among young people.

Unemployment has always been a problem for Slovenes. At most times, it was solved by emigration. In the late nineteenth and early twentieth centuries, thousands of Slovenes emigrated to industrialized Europe and the United States. Economic emigration continued after World War II. Many emigrants returned home in the 1980s. Today, about 14 percent of Slovenes are out of work.

20 ● BIBLIOGRAPHY

Benderly, Jill, and Evan Kraft. *Independent Slovenia*. New York: St. Martin's Press, 1994.
Glenny, Michael. *The Fall of Yugoslavia: The Third Balkan War.* New York: Penguin, 1992.
Plut-Pregelj, Leopoldina, and Carole Rogel. *Historical Dictionary of Slovenia*. Lanham, Md.: Scarecrow Press, Inc., 1996.
Stanič, Stane. *Slovenia*. London, England: Flint River Press, 1994.

WEBSITES
Embassy of Slovenia in Washington, D.C. [online] Available http://www.ijs.si, 1998.
National Supercomputing Center in Ljubljana. [Online] Available http://www.ijs.si/slo/, 1998.
Slovenia Travel, Inc. (New York). [Online] Available http://www.sloveniatravel.com/, 1998.
World Travel Guide, Slovenia. [Online] Available http://www.wtgonline.com/country/si/gen.html, 1998.

Somalia

The people of Somalia are called Somalis. About 98 percent of the population trace their descent to Somalia. The nonnative population consists primarily of immigrants.

Somalis

PRONUNCIATION: suh-MAH-leez
ALTERNATE NAMES: Somalians
LOCATION: Somalia
POPULATION: More than 7 million
LANGUAGE: Maxaad tiri; Arabic
RELIGION: Islam (Sunni)

1 ● INTRODUCTION

In the late nineteenth century, the northern half of Somalia became a British protectorate. The southern half of Somalia was an Italian colony until 1960. In that year, it was united with the northern half to become an independent republic. Since the early 1990s, Somalia has suffered from a civil war between rival clans.

Unlike most African nations, Somalia has only one ethnic group, divided into various clans. However, the Somalis are all united by a common language and a reliance on raising animals. They also have a shared Islamic heritage. In addition, they believe they are descended from a common ancestor. Somali-speakers living in parts of Kenya, Ethiopia, and Djibouti, as well as Somalia, are all considered to be part of one Somali nation.

2 ● LOCATION

Somalia is located on what is commonly called the Horn of Africa. Two long, sandy plains dominate the coastal areas along the Indian Ocean to the east. The interior includes a series of moderate mountain ranges in the north, and a large rugged plateau in the south. The total area of the country is about 250,000 square miles (647,500 square kilometers).

3 ● LANGUAGE

The language spoken by the vast majority of the Somali people is referred to as *Maxaad tiri*. However, various dialects are spoken

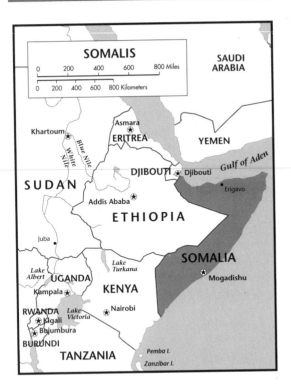

associated with Islam. They pray five times a day and do not eat pork products or drink alcohol. Men may have up to four wives at one time. However, Somalis are not as traditionally religious as Muslims in many other cultures. For example, women do not practice *purdah,* or seclusion. They do not wear veils or cover their entire bodies when outside the home.

Somalis incorporate a belief in a spirit world into their religious system. These spirits, or *jinns,* can be either good or evil. They are believed to cause illness, loss of property, marital problems, infertility, and even death. There are specialists who "fight" *jinns* through special ceremonies resembling exorcisms.

6 ● MAJOR HOLIDAYS

Ramadan is a month-long fast during which Muslims do not eat or drink during daylight hours. Ramadan ends with the feast of *Eid al-Adha.* Believers are expected, at least once in their lives, to make a *hajj,* or pilgrimage to Mecca during the month of Ramadan. Muhammad's birthday, *Mowluud,* is celebrated with feasting.

7 ● RITES OF PASSAGE

Life events among the Somali are celebrated by feasting. Birth is always an important event. Sheep or goats are killed to celebrate the birth of either a boy or girl. Death is also marked by feasting. The status of the deceased dictates the type and number of animals killed (a goat for a young child, one or more camels for the death of an old, wealthy male).

Marriage is viewed as a bond between two families, rather than between two indi-

by different clans. Maxaad tiri and Arabic are the official languages of Somalia. Many older people in the south also speak Italian. Government officials in the cities often speak English.

4 ● FOLKLORE

Ceremonial feasts among the Somali people always include the telling of heroic tales of ancestors. Much Somali folklore revolves around ancestors on the father's side of the family. They are regarded as "family heroes."

5 ● RELIGION

The official state religion of Somalia is Islam. Almost 100 percent of the Somali population is Sunni Muslim (branch of Islam). The Somali follow the practices viduals. It is marked by a series of exchanges and ceremonies. A bride price *(meher)* of camels, cattle, sheep, or goats is given to the family of the bride. The bride's family supplies items for everyday life: the *aqal* (a portable house), a bed, cooking utensils, mats, ropes, and skins.

8 ● RELATIONSHIPS

There is a strong tradition of hospitality that obligates individuals to welcome close kinfolk, clan members, and even strangers with tea and food. The most common greetings are *Maalin wanaagsan* (Good day) and *Nabad myah?* (How are you?). For men, these greetings are followed by an extended shaking of hands. Women greet each other less formally.

There is nothing resembling dating in the rural areas of Somalia. Even in urban areas, the contact between unmarried men and women is limited. Unmarried men in their twenties will flirt with women by dancing together as a group.

9 ● LIVING CONDITIONS

The vast majority (90 percent) of the Somali people live in small villages scattered throughout the rural areas of the country. Few of them have electricity, clean running water, paved roads, or public services. There are two types of rural housing: *mundals* and *aqals. Mundals* are permanent structures made of a mud and dung mixture. It is spread over a wooden frame and then topped with a thatched roof. These houses are occupied by a husband and wife, with their children. An *aqal* is a mobile house made of wooden sticks and hides. It can be transported on the back of a camel. Every

married woman owns an aqal. She is responsible for setting up and dismantling it as nomadic camps are moved.

The standard of living in urban areas has declined since the civil war of the early 1990s. Before the war, the residents of the capital city of Mogadishu, Hargeysa, and other cities had access to electricity, running water, and paved roads. Most urban dwellers lived in single-family houses.

10 ● FAMILY LIFE

Family structure is based on descent through the father's lineage (patrilineal descent). Men belong to their father's clans, and inheritance *(wahaad)* passes from father to son. As Muslims, men are allowed as many as four wives at one time. Divorce is easy and common. Thus, some men may have had ten or more wives in the course of a lifetime. After marriage, women live in the village or camp of their husband.

11 ● CLOTHING

Somalis dress for comfort in the hot, dry climate. Men have traditionally worn a long piece of lightweight cloth *(mawhees)* as a wraparound skirt. A lightweight shirt is usually worn, as well. Women traditionally wear a dress that covers their entire body from shoulders to ankles. They generally wear a shawl for covering their heads when in the presence of nonfamily males.

Young girls usually wear a simple dress made of a lightweight fabric. Young boys wear shorts and, most recently, imported T-shirts with logos of American and European sports teams.

12 ● FOOD

Meat is the most valued food among the Somalis. Camel meat is the most popular. Cattle, goats, sheep, and chickens are also killed and eaten. Grains and vegetables are the everyday staple, with sorghum the most common grain. Maize (corn) and rice are available in urban areas. All grains are cooked as a porridge and traditionally eaten from a common bowl.

Food delicacies include camel's hump, sheep's tail, goat's liver, and camel's milk.

13 ● EDUCATION

The civil war of the 1990s virtually destroyed the educational system. Almost all government-run schools closed. Koran schools (where teaching is based on the Muslim holy scriptures, the Koran) provide the only schooling available for the majority of children. These schools are usually attended only by boys and traditionally emphasize memorization of the Koran. However, many are now providing a broader education.

14 ● CULTURAL HERITAGE

At feasts, men tell heroic tales about their ancestors, and recite passages from the Koran. They also recall past events that affected themselves and their animals. Dancing, accompanied by singing, is usually only performed by unmarried males in their twenties. These dances are intended mostly to attract a mate. In the course of the dance, the men prove their bravery by slashing their arms and legs with large knives.

15 ● EMPLOYMENT

Raising animals (animal husbandry) is the most common activity in Somalia. Somalis do this to feed themselves, and earning just enough money from their animals to get by. The main animals kept are camels, cattle, sheep, and goats. Agriculture is practiced between the country's two major rivers. Sorghum, maize (corn), and other crops are raised.

Somalis practice a clear division of labor based on gender. Men and boys tend to the animals. Women and girls prepare meals and undertake other domestic tasks. In areas where crops can be grown, women and children are largely responsible for tending, weeding, and harvesting them.

16 ● SPORTS

Soccer is the most popular and widely played sport in Somalia. However, it is played primarily in the cities and larger towns.

In rural areas, children take on responsibilities at an early age. Boys, especially, have little time for organized sport.

17 ● RECREATION

Most entertainment among rural Somalis occurs in ceremonies associated with major life transitions. It includes storytelling and recounting the exploits of one's kinfolk and ancestors.

Television is nonexistent in Somalia, although before the civil war the government did provide a radio service. Many urban and rural Somalis listen regularly to BBC radio broadcasts. Before the civil war of the 1990s, movie theaters also operated

Jason Laure

Somali women dressed in traditional costumes perform in the capital city of Mogadishu. Women traditionally wear dresses that cover their entire body from shoulders to ankles. It is also customary for women to wear shawls that they can use to cover their heads when in the presence of nonfamily males.

in all major cities and towns, before the outbreak of widespread fighting

18 ● CRAFTS AND HOBBIES

The Somali produce fine wooden utensils, leather goods, woven mats and ropes, knife blades, and arrow points. Much of the craft work is done by ordinary villagers for their own use.

19 ● SOCIAL PROBLEMS

The complete breakdown of the government since the early 1990s has brought public services to a halt. Civil warfare began in late 1991 and lasted for over two years. Agriculture and livestock-raising were disrupted. Approximately 400,000 people died of starvation. Another 50,000 people died in the fighting. As of the late 1990s, United Nations' efforts to reestablish a stable central government had failed.

20 ● BIBLIOGRAPHY

Burton, Richard F. *First Footsteps in East Africa.* London, England: Routledge & K. Paul, 1966.

Cassanelli, L. V. *The Shaping of Somali Society.* Philadelphia: The University of Pennsylvania Press, 1982.

Hassig, Susan M. *Somalia,* Cultures of the World. New York: Marshall Cavendish, 1997.

Jardine, D. *The Mad Mullah of Somaliland.* Westport, Conn.: Negro Universities Press, 1969 (orig. 1924).

Loughran, Katheryne S. et al., eds. *Somalia in Word and Image.* Bloomington: Indiana University Press, 1986.

Metz, Helen Chapin, ed. *Somalia, A Country Study,* 4th ed. Washington, D.C.: Headquarters, Dept. of the Army, 1993.

WEBSITES

ArabNet. [Online] Available http://www.arab.net/somalia/somalia_contents.html, 1998.

World Travel Guide, Somalia. [Online] Available http://www.wtgonline.com/country/so/gen.html, 1998.

South Africa

The people of South Africa are called South Africans. The population has a complex ethnic makeup. For most of the twentieth century, government policy required the separation of racial communities by a system called apartheid. Although apartheid was ended in 1991, the division of the population into racial communities remained. Blacks form the largest segment of the population, constituting almost 75 percent of the total. The black population includes a large number of groups. Among the largest are the Xhosa numbering 5.6 million, the Zulu (5.3 million), and the Sotho (4.2 million). To learn more about the Sotho, see the chapter on Lesotho in Volume 5. Whites account for about 14 percent of the total population. About 60 percent of these are Afrikaners, and 40 percent are English. Cape Coloreds (persons of mixed race) represent about 11 percent of the total population.

Afrikaners

PRONUNCIATION: ahf-rih-KAHN-ers
ALTERNATE NAMES: Boers
LOCATION: Republic of South Africa
POPULATION: About 3.3 million
LANGUAGE: Afrikaans
RELIGION: Protestantism

1 ● INTRODUCTION

South Africa is located at the southern point of Africa. During the seventeenth century, Dutch colonists from the Netherlands (known as Boers) settled there. Over the next 200 years, British, French, and German settlers joined them. At first, they settled along the coast, but eventually settlers moved inland. These settlers developed a unique cultural identity and language and became known as Afrikaners. Their language, Afrikaans, began as a spoken dialect, but developed into a written language, too.

Over the next 300 years, the Afrikaners battled indigenous (native) African peoples, established independent republics in the interior, and fought the British in two wars

AFRIKANERS

Lake Tanganyika

TANZANIA

ANGOLA

MALAWI

ZAMBIA

ZIMBABWE

NAMIBIA

BOTSWANA

MOZAMBIQUE

SWAZILAND

SOUTH AFRICA

LESOTHO

the 1980s, there were many Afrikaners who joined the effort to do away with apartheid.

2 ● LOCATION

The Afrikaners are concentrated in the Republic of South Africa, located at the southern tip of the African continent. The country consists of four plateaus: the coastal zone, averaging 500 feet (150 meters) above sea level; the Little Karoo, averaging 1,500 feet (450 meters) above sea level; the Great Karoo, averaging 2,500 feet (760 meters) above sea level; and the High Veld, which averages 4,000 feet (1,200 meters) above sea level and rises to 6,000 feet (1,800 meters) above sea level in the northeast. South Aftrica's capital, Johannesburg, has an annual mean temperature of 60°F (15.6°C). This temperature range is typical for the entire country. Rainfall (which is so critical for farming and ranching) decreases as one moves from east to west. South Africa's eastern coastal zone has relatively high rainfall, but the western veld (open grassland) tapers into the Kalahari desert. About 75 percent of the country receives less than 25 inches (63.5 centimeters) of rain per year. The country's average rainfall is only 17.5 inches (44.5 centimeters) because so much of the country is extremely dry. The highest rainfall is in the mountain region of the southern region— about 200 inches (508 centimeters) per year.

Of South Africa's 42 million people, about 3.3 million are Afrikaners.

3 ● LANGUAGE

Afrikaans, the language spoken by Afrikaners, evolved as a dialect of Dutch spoken by settlers on the frontier during the eighteenth

known as the Anglo-Boer Wars. All territories were finally united on May 31, 1910, to become the Union of South Africa. (The Republic of South Africa was established fifty years later on May 31, 1960.) In 1910, there was a clear division between the Afrikaners (who belonged to Afrikaner political parties, spoke Afrikaans, supported Afrikaner cultural and linguistic endeavors, and belonged to one of the Dutch Reformed Churches) and British-oriented, English-speaking South Africans. In 1948 the Afrikaner-based National Party came to power. Under a strong religious philosophy and racist social policy, the National Party started to implement the system of apartheid. Apartheid separated the people of South Africa by law along color lines. By and nineteenth centuries. As various groups—French, German, and English speakers—settled in South Africa, they contributed to the emerging language. Also contributing to the language and culture were slaves brought by the Dutch from their holdings in southeast Asia (especially Malaysians). Settlers also took vocabulary and cultural practices from the native Africa people. Afrikaans first appeared in print during the early nineteenth century. Among the unique features of the language is the double negative: *Hy wil nie speel nie* (literally, "He does not want to play not").

In 1910, the Constitution of the Union of South Africa recognized Afrikaans and English as official languages. Since then, most Afrikaners have been bilingual. In 1991, when apartheid was eliminated, eleven official languages were recognized.

There are also some 13,000 persons of Asian descent in South Africa who speak Afrikaans as their native language.

4 ● FOLKLORE

Early Afrikaner beliefs and traditions come from three major sources: European colonists, native people, and immigrants from Malaysia and India. Heroes and myths from these groups became intertwined as stories were passed down orally.

Much folklore revolved around *Oom* (Uncle) Paul Kruger (1925–1904, the former president of the Afrikaner republic).

5 ● RELIGION

Afrikaner religion comes from Protestant practices of the seventeenth-century Reformed Church of Holland. The British brought English-speaking ministers to South Africa in the early 1800s. Next, French settlers brought the ideas of Swiss reformer John Calvin (1509–1564) to South Africa. Calvin believed the church should influence government policy, and that races should remain pure and separate. This led to the development of a unique brand of Protestantism in South Africa. Government policies on apartheid (separation of the races) were supported by Afrikaners' religious doctrines.

6 ● MAJOR HOLIDAYS

Religious holidays include Christmas (December 25), Good Friday (and the secular Easter Monday, in March or April), and Ascension Day (in April or May). Secular (nonreligious) holidays include New Year's Day and Boxing Day (also known as Goodwill Day, December 26). Political holidays include Founder's Day commemorating the arrival of Jan van Riebeeck (the first governor of the Cape) on April 6, 1652; Republic Day commemorating the establishment of the Union of South Africa on May 31, 1910 (and later the Republic of South Africa on May 31, 1960); Kruger Day, commemorating the birthday of Paul Kruger (1825–1904, former president) on October 10; and the Day of the Vow, commemorating the day when Afrikaners resisted an attack by Zulu warriors on December 16, 1838.

Traditionally, Afrikaners observed Sunday as a day of rest. Stores and movie theaters were closed, organized sports were not permitted, and very little activity took place. People were expected to attend church services. By the late 1990s, this had changed somewhat, although there is still

Jason Lauré

Days and dates of special significance to Afrikaners are those which are associated with their religion and their national history. Many of these are no longer recognized in the new constitutional dispensation, while new holidays have been added to recognize the cultures of other ethnic groups in South Africa. The Afrikaners shown here at Voortrekker Monument are celebrating the Day of the Covenant, which commemorates the day when Afrikaner pioneers beat back an attack of Zulu warriors on December 16, 1838.

less activity on Sunday than on other days of the week.

7 ● RITES OF PASSAGE

It is the custom for Afrikaner married couples to name their first son after the husband's father and their first daughter after the wife's mother.

Birthdays are celebrated with a party accompanied by the giving of gifts. Almost all infants are baptized. Afrikaner children attend Sunday school where they are required to memorize verses from the Bible. At about age sixteen, young people must take catechism, where they learn the basis of Calvinistic Protestantism. Upon completion of catechism, the young person is confirmed as a church member and takes his or her first communion. In many families, sixteen is also the age when the young person is allowed to begin dating. The twenty-first birthday is a major celebration. The family often presents the son or daughter at age twenty-one with a key that symbolizes adulthood.

Adults celebrate birthdays, frequently with a *braai*—the equivalent of the American barbecue. Death is marked at the family level by mourning and the wearing of black dresses by women, and black ties or a black arm band by men. At church services on New Year's Eve, the front pew is draped in black or purple to remember those who have died during the year, and their names are read aloud.

8 ● RELATIONSHIPS

It is customary to greet each person, including children, with a handshake. Friends and relatives of both genders greet each other with a kiss on the lips. (This practice does not generally apply to males greeting males.) Taking leave involves the same actions and the expression, *Totsiens* (Till we see [each other] again). In the past, Afrikaners practiced informal gender separation. After a meal, men would visit with each other, smoking and discussing such topics as national affairs or sports. Women talked about homemaking and the children. By the late 1990s, opportunities for women in education and employment had improved, and this practice of separate social conversation had declined.

9 ● LIVING CONDITIONS

When Afrikaners controlled the government, most white people lived in luxury, with the best housing (many with swimming pools), schools, and hospitals available to them. Afrikaners controlled the best civil service and other jobs, earned dependable salaries, owned automobiles, and had electricity and telephones in their homes. After apartheid (separation of the races) ended in 1991, this lifestyle was legally available to everyone, regardless of race.

10 ● FAMILY LIFE

In rural communities, Afrikaner families were large because children represented wealth. Some Afrikaner politicians advocated a policy of large families to assure the position of whites in South Africa. Today Afrikaner families average two or three children. Dogs and cats are favored as pets. Dogs are also bred to protect home and property.

Traditional Afrikaner dating and marriage practices involved a young man courting his girlfriend, and then formally requesting permission from her parents (especially her father) to become engaged. For three Sundays prior to the wedding, the couples' names were read in church. If there were no objections raised (for example, that one was already married to someone else), the marriage was performed in church, with a reception afterward. This practice had become less formal by the 1990s.

11 ● CLOTHING

Afrikaners dress in modern Western clothing. On holidays and special occasions, traditional clothing may be seen. Boys and men wear shorts with knee socks. Women wear long dresses and bonnets for formal folk dancing called *volkspele*. Male folk dancing partners wear shirts with vests and long pants.

12 ● FOOD

The everyday meal of the Afrikaner is characterized by an emphasis on meat, starch, and cooked vegetables. Green or fresh salads are rare. Breakfast features some kind of porridge. Away from the coast, Afrikaners learned from the native peoples to make a gruel called *stywe pap* or *putu pap* (stiff porridge or putu porridge). It is common to have this porridge for breakfast with milk and sugar, and also to eat it with meat or *boerewors* (boer sausage, made of beef and pork) at a *braai* (barbecue). Venison has always formed part of Afrikaner dishes, as grazing animals could be hunted or culled from national parks.

Sosaties (skewered marinated meat similar to shish kebab) is frequently included in a *braai*. A recipe for *bobotie*, another favorite dish accompanies this article. Fish has become popular for those living near the ocean. Two foods from pioneer days are still popular among Afrikaners: *beskuit* and *biltong*. Beskuit (rusks) are biscuits that have been oven-dried. They are served with coffee. Biltong are strips of dried meat (traditionally, beef or venison; more recently, elephant and ostrich). The biltong are treated with salt, pepper, and spices prior to drying.

13 ● EDUCATION

Children are required to attend school from age six through age sixteen. Each school has its own colors, and girls and boys wear blazers that display the crest of the school. For girls, the uniform is dress or skirt in the color with a white or matching blouse. Boys wear the same color shirt and pants. During most of the year, boys wear shorts with knee socks. Among Afrikaners, almost everyone attends school and is literate (can read and write). Most Afrikaner students who have completed high school (by passing the

Recipe

Bobotie

Ingredients

2 slices of white bread, torn into pieces
1¼ cups milk
1 cup onions, chopped
1 tart apple, peeled and chopped
3 Tablespoons fresh lemon juice
3 Tablespoons golden raisins
3 Tablespoons slivered, blanched almonds
2 Tablespoons curry powder
1½ pounds ground lamb
2 bay leaves
2 egg yolks

Directions

1. Place ground lamb in a frying pan. Cook over medium heat until browned, stirring frequently.
2. Combine bread and milk; set aside.
3. Add onions to the lamb and cook, stirring frequently, for about 2 minutes. Add apples and cook for 1 minute.
4. Remove bread pieces from milk and add to frying pan. (Save the milk for use in step 7.) Add lemon juice, raisins, almonds, and curry powder.
5. Preheat oven to 325°F. Transfer lamb mixture to a baking dish.
6. Insert bay leaves into mixture, and pat the mixture down in the center. Bake for 20 minutes. Remove from oven but do not turn oven off.
7. Beat eggs yolks and milk (from step 4) together. Pour milk mixture slowly over meat mixture in casserole. Return to oven and bake 25 minutes more.

Adapted from Hillman, Howard. *Great Peasant Dishes of the World.* Boston: Houghton Mifflin, 1983.

national examination) continue their education. They go to a university or to a "technicon," an institute that offers technical training.

14 ● CULTURAL HERITAGE

Much of Afrikaners' heritage is derived from European cultural traditions. The performing arts all follow the western European model. Some South African themes have been depicted, especially in visual arts.

15 ● EMPLOYMENT

Most Afrikaners are employed in fields ranging from civil service and education to mining, industry, and business. Afrikaners are the majority of whites in rural areas. Afrikaners believe in hard, industrious work, and their religion reinforces that value. Children are raised with statements such as "Idleness is Satan's pillow," implying that idleness is where temptation to get into trouble can be found.

16 ● SPORTS

Television was not permitted in South Africa until the 1960s, so the emphasis was on participating in, rather than watching, sports. Afrikaner children play organized sports starting at an young age. Boys play rugby, cricket, or athletics (track and field). Girls play netball (basketball), field hockey, and also participate in athletics. It is common to see a group of boys on an open field with a tennis or rubber ball playing informal cricket or tossing a ball in a variation of touch football. Girls are more likely to participate only in school or club sports.

Older adults engage in *jukskei,* a competition from pioneer days. Carved pieces of wood, resembling the yoke pin used on draft animals, are tossed in an attempt to knock over a stake. This resembles the American game of horseshoes.

17 ● RECREATION

In the past, Afrikaner young people entertained themselves in folk dances, church-sponsored youth activities, and the bioscope (movies). By the 1990s, it was common for a group of young people to rent videos, gather at a bar or a dance, or go to a disco. It had also become acceptable to socialize with English-speaking persons and members of other ethnic groups.

18 ● CRAFTS AND HOBBIES

There has been a clear division of labor based on gender among Afrikaners that carries over to the present. Women are known for quilting, crocheting, and knitting. A beautiful doily with a circle of shells or beads covers every jug of milk. Men are known for woodworking, delicate leather-working, and the making of chairs with seats of interwoven strips of leather.

19 ● SOCIAL PROBLEMS

After the end of apartheid in 1991, Afrikaners still bore a heavy burden for the actions of their ancestors who developed the philosophy that led to apartheid. Not all Afrikaners agreed with the apartheid policy of their government and not all Afrikaners were racist. Yet, Afrikaners bear the stereotype or label. Their challenge in the late 1990s is to find a role for themselves in the new South Africa, known as the Rainbow Nation.

20 ● BIBLIOGRAPHY

De Klerk, W. A. *The Puritans in Africa: A Story of Afrikanerdom*. London, England: R. Collins, 1975.

Drury, Allen. *A Very Strange Society: A Journey to the Heart of South Africa*. New York: Trident, 1967.

Hillman, Howard. *Great Peasant Dishes of the World*. Boston: Houghton Mifflin, 1983.

WEBSITES

Embassy of South Africa, Washington, D.C. [Online] Available http://www.southafrica.net/, 1998.

Government of South Africa. [Online] http://www.polity.org.za/gnu.html, 1998.

Interknowledge Corp. South Africa. [Online] Available http://www.geographia.com/south-africa/, 1998.

Southern African Development Community. South Africa. [Online] Available http://www.sadc-usa.net/members/safrica/, 1998.

Cape Coloreds

ALTERNATE NAMES: Coloureds, Coloreds
LOCATION: South Africa
POPULATION: 3.6 million
LANGUAGE: Afrikaans; English
RELIGION: Christianity; Islam

1 ● INTRODUCTION

South Africa's 3.6 million mixed-race people are referred to as Cape Coloreds or Coloreds. In other places in the world, the word *colored* used to describe race is considered disparaging (negative or critical). In South Africa, it is used to describe an important segment of the population.

South Africa's Coloreds are descended from the intermarriage of white settlers, African natives, and Asian slaves who were brought to South Africa from the Dutch colonies of Asia in the eighteenth and nineteenth centuries. Most Coloreds worked as domestic servants, farm laborers, and fisherfolk, but large numbers were also involved in the skilled trades. Colored masons and engineers are responsible for nearly all of the beautiful buildings in Cape Town, and colored seamstresses and tailors are well-known for their craftsmanship.

Coloreds were always closely associated with whites. They spoke the same languages (English and Afrikaans), worshiped in the same churches (mostly Christian Protestant, but also some Catholic), enjoyed the same foods, wore the same kind of clothes, and—especially in latter years—enjoyed the same sports and pastimes. In spite of this common heritage, Coloreds were never fully integrated into white society.

There is still a sense among Coloreds that they continue to be victims of discrimination in South Africa, but this time at the hands of the black majority government.

2 ● LOCATION

Most of South Africa's 3.6 million Coloreds live in both the urban and rural areas around Cape Town, where they make up influential political and cultural groups. However, they have also migrated to other major centers, and significant concentrations can be found around the cities of Johannesburg, Pretoria, Port Elizabeth, East London, and Durban. There are also important groups in the neighboring nations of Namibia and Zimbabwe.

The region around Cape Town is known as the western Cape. It is regarded as the traditional homeland of the Coloreds. Coloreds play a vital role in the agriculture industry (fruit, wine, wheat, and dairy products), not only as farm laborers but also as managers, skilled artisans, and increasingly as property-owning entrepreneurs. They also dominate the fishing industry that has grown up in the rich cold waters of the country's west coast. In the cities, many Coloreds work in trades such as carpentry, plumbing, auto repair, and construction, and in professions like health care, accounting, law, and education.

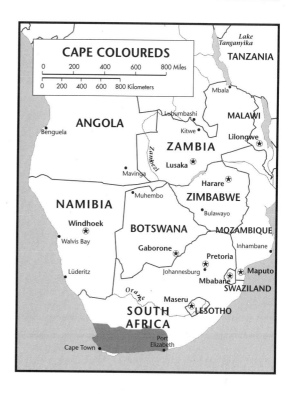

3 ● LANGUAGE

Coloreds speak two languages, English and Afrikaans. At one stage during the struggle against apartheid, many Coloreds chose to avoid speaking Afrikaans because of its association with white domination. It is not unusual for Coloreds to combine the two languages in a distinctive, informal local dialect. It is especially heard in humor and in light-hearted songs known as *moppies*. In formal settings, however, Coloreds use either formal English or Afrikaans.

4 ● FOLKLORE

Most folklore is shared by Afrikaners and Coloreds. There are *goel* or ghost stories, which are frequently as amusing as they are alarming, that can be traced to the stories of slaves from India and Malaysia. A popular time to tell goel stories is in Cape Town in summer when the strong southeast wind, known as the "Cape Doctor," blows. Sometimes it blows so hard that people can hardly walk in the city and the harbor is closed to shipping. Cape Doctor time, when windows are rattling and doors are creaking, is ideal for the telling of goel stories.

Folk music features traditional ballads and *moppies* (joke songs). An especially delightful moppie tells the story of a baboon trying to learn how to swim. He learns very quickly when he sees a crocodile in front of him and a shark behind.

5 ● RELIGION

The Coloreds of Cape Town observe two main religions—Christianity (mostly Protestantism, but also some Catholicism) and Islam, which plays an influential role in a large sector of the population. In urban areas where Coloreds live in large numbers, it is common to hear the faithful Muslims (observers of Islam) being summoned to prayer from mosques. Muslim Coloreds take an intense interest in events in the Mid-

Cynthia Bassett

School children on a walk with their teacher. Education is viewed as the road to self-improvement by South Africa's Coloreds. As a result, families will save and sacrifice to send their children to the best schools and colleges available.

dle East and other parts of the Muslim world. Religious beliefs are seen as a factor in the emergence of a strong conservative element among Coloreds.

6 ● MAJOR HOLIDAYS

For more than one hundred years, Cape Town's Coloreds were associated with a New Year's Day parade. Neighborhoods formed troops that dressed in colorful satin costumes and marched or danced behind guitar and banjo bands. Each troop had its own combination of colors. When they all arrived at central sports fields, they com-

peted for trophies in front of large crowds of spectators. This tradition was largely abandoned during the latter days of apartheid because many members of the community felt the name it had been given by the white population was racist. When apartheid was eliminated in the 1990s, the citizens of Cape Town revived the parade.

A traditional song performed in the parade is "January, February." The words consist simply of the months of the year sung to a catchy tune and rhythm. Everybody knows this song, and spectators often join in when the band marches by.

7 ● RITES OF PASSAGE

Birthdays are celebrated by parties where the guests bring gifts. Baptism of infants, confirmation, and first communion are celebrated among Christian Coloreds. On their twenty-first birthday, many young adults in South Africa receive a symbolic key to adulthood.

8 ● RELATIONSHIPS

Although separation of the races was the norm in South Africa for most of the twentieth century, there were always close contacts between whites and Coloreds. They met in the workplace, stores, and the street. Until 1986, it was illegal for members of different race groups to have sexual relations, and people were prosecuted for breaking this law.

Whites and colored adjusted easily to the elimination of apartheid laws. Relations between Coloreds and members of the majority black groups are still evolving, and there has been tension because many Coloreds feel that the government does not always consider the interests of Coloreds.

9 ● LIVING CONDITIONS

When most of the apartheid laws were introduced after 1948, many Coloreds were forcibly moved from their traditional residential areas to segregated suburbs and townships. This relocation was bitterly resented and resisted, and it remains one of the worst memories of South African history.

District Six, an area in Cape Town, was the traditional home of many Colored families. Under apartheid laws, it was renewed, but for whites. The Colored residents were forced to move to the sandy Cape Flats, where crime, alcoholism, and other social problems soon developed. As of the late 1990s, Coloreds can live wherever their economic status allows. Some have moved into gracious homes, but the problems of forced removal created a legacy which will take a long time to eradicate.

10 ● FAMILY LIFE

Colored families tend to be conservative and mutually supportive. It was largely these qualities that enabled the community to survive the treatment it received during the apartheid years.

11 ● CLOTHING

Colored South Africans wear both formal and casual clothing, similar to that worn by people in major industrial nations anywhere in the world. Young people wear jeans, sneakers, and T-shirts, and baseball caps have become popular. Jackets and ties are becoming less common everywhere, even in the workplace. This is a result of the example set by President Nelson Mandela and other leaders, who wear comfortable casual clothes rather than Western-style business attire.

12 ● FOOD

Coloreds are famous for *bredies* (stews) made with mutton (lamb), tomatoes, cabbage, or local plants known as *water-blom-metjies*. Also popular are small, triangular pies known as *samoesas* that contain a ground meat mixture seasoned with curry. Samoesas are ideal for snacks or lunch and are often served as appetizers or at cocktail parties. Working men often carry a lunch consisting of a hollowed-out loaf of bread filled with a bredie.

13 ● EDUCATION

Education is viewed as the road to self-improvement among Coloreds. As a result, families save and sacrifice to send their children to the best available schools and colleges. In the past, Coloreds were allowed to attend only those institutions designated for them. While these schools were better equipped than those allocated to black Africans, they were nevertheless inferior to the schools for whites. When the transition from apartheid to non-racial democracy took place in 1994, the student-to-teacher ratio in white schools was eighteen to one; in Colored schools, it was twenty-two to one; and in black schools, it was fifty to one.

14 ● CULTURAL HERITAGE

The Colored schools produced notable figures in the fields of medicine, law, government, diplomacy, the arts, engineering, commerce and industry, and education itself. Some of South Africa's finest writers and poets—such as the internationally acclaimed Adam Small—are Colored.

15 ● EMPLOYMENT

During apartheid, Coloreds were kept by law out of the best jobs and the best schools. Because they were restricted in where they could live, Coloreds had to travel long distances each day to low-paying jobs. The result was a high incidence of crime, alcoholism, and other social ills. When apartheid ended in 1991 and the black majority assumed power in government, many Col-

oreds feared that the government would create programs that gave strong education, economic, and employment advantages to blacks. This would leave the Coloreds on the sidelines. They did not want to lose what they have gained in economic and educational opportunities.

16 ● SPORTS

The most popular sports are soccer, cricket, rugby, and track and field. After 1991, there was increasing interest in tennis, swimming, golf, yachting, and wind- and wave-surfing, sports not open to Coloreds under apartheid. Hiking and mountaineering are popular, especially in the western part of the country.

17 ● RECREATION

Coloreds enjoy the same entertainment as most people in industrialized society—pop and classical music, the movies, dances and nightclubs, and radio and television.

18 ● CRAFTS AND HOBBIES

Coloreds enjoy varied hobbies typical of citizens of an industrialized society.

19 ● SOCIAL PROBLEMS

Until the mid-1990s, South Africa was governed by apartheid. The result was a relatively poor education for Coloreds because their schools had poor facilities, and many Coloreds abandoned schooling early to help support their families. When people were forced to move into townships and suburbs defined by the race, social problems such as alcoholism, poor health care, and a rising crime rate resulted. Not all of these negative factors have been eliminated under the new democratic system. Colored leaders want to ensure that their people will not be abandoned by the black majority.

20 ● BIBLIOGRAPHY

Green, Lawrence G. *Tavern of the Seas.* Cape Town: Timmins, 1953.

Picard, Hymen W. J. *Grand Parade, the Birth of Greater Cape Town, 1850–1913.* Cape Town: Struik, 1969.

Reader's Digest Illustrated History of South Africa. Cape Town: Reader's Digest Association, 1994.

Suzman, Helen. *In No Uncertain Terms, A South African Memoir.* New York: Knopf, 1993

Wilson, Monica, and Leonard Thompson, eds. *The Oxford History of South Africa II (1870–1966).* Oxford: Clarendon, 1971.

WEBSITES

Embassy of South Africa, Washington, D.C. [Online] Available http://www.southafrica.net/, 1998.

Government of South Africa. [Online] http://www.polity.org.za/gnu.html, 1998.

Interknowledge Corp. South Africa. [Online] Available http://www.geographia.com/south-africa/, 1998.

Southern African Development Community. South Africa. [Online] Available http://www.sadc-usa.net/members/safrica/, 1998.

English

LOCATION: South Africa
ALTERNATE NAMES: Whites (a generic term that includes Afrikaners)
POPULATION: About 3.1 million
LANGUAGE: English
RELIGION: Christianity

1 ● INTRODUCTION

About 14 percent, or 6.3 million, of the population of South Africa is white. English South Africans make up just under half of that group, or about 6 percent. Despite their small numbers, English culture and language are powerful influences. English is the principal language of business and tourism, English-language newspapers are published daily in the urban centers, and public signs and notices are posted in English. A visitor to South Africa who speaks only English would have no difficulty getting about and being understood.

Throughout most of the twentieth century, South Africa's political life was dominated by white Afrikaners. (See the article on "Afrikaners" in this volume. Afrikaners are descendants of settlers mostly from the Netherlands.) English South Africans were prominent in commerce, industry, and the professions throughout much of this period. They remain influential as one of the best-educated and most affluent sectors of the population.

2 ● LOCATION

English South Africans have historic and language ties to England, but they see themselves as South African, not British. English are concentrated in and around South Africa's urban areas—the coastal cities of Cape Town, Port Elizabeth, East London and Durban, and the inland cities of Johannesburg, Pretoria, Bloemfontein, and Kimberley.

English presence in South Africa goes back to the end of the eighteenth century when Britain seized control of the Cape of Good Hope, the first white settlement area in Cape Town. The British government encouraged its citizens to emigrate to the Cape—mostly to establish a buffer between African tribesmen and farming colonists on

Cynthia Bassett

The successful white South African lives in a style similar to his or her counterpart in the United States—in single family houses on wide suburban streets or in apartments or semi-detached row houses.

the eastern frontier—and the first sizable group of 4,000 began to arrive in 1820.

Eventually the British government went to war with the native Zulus (see the article on Zulus in this volume), defeating them after a number of bloody battles. At the turn of the century, British forces fought the Anglo-Boer war and defeated the Afrikaners. South Africa was incorporated into the British Empire. In 1910 the Union of South Africa, a self-governing dominion within the British Empire, was created. Throughout this turbulent history, English South Africans settled all over the country.

3 ● LANGUAGE

English has been spoken in South Africa since the nineteenth century. It is the same as English spoken elsewhere in the world, but it has a distinctive South African accent and vocabulary. South African English pronunciation of the words yes, kettle, and axle are *yis, kittle,* and *eksel.*

South African English slang has borrowed some structures from Afrikaans, such as "I am going to the shop, will you come with?" It has also taken some words from African languages, such as *indaba* (gathering).

4 ● FOLKLORE

English South Africans share in holidays, legends, and myths with others in the English-speaking world. They celebrate Christmas with gifts, family gatherings, and dinner. They get together for parties and celebrations on New Year's Eve, and sing *Auld Lang Syne* at midnight.

5 ● RELIGION

Religious beliefs are an important part of the daily life of many South Africans. Most English South Africans belong to Protestant Christian denominations; a lesser number adhere to the Catholic church. Religion played a key role in opposition to the racial discrimination known as apartheid. Religious leaders such as Archbishop Desmond Tutu of the Anglican Church in South Africa became politically prominent in their campaigns for equality and democracy.

6 ● MAJOR HOLIDAYS

The English of South Africa observe national and religious holidays. These include Republic Day, May 31, honoring the date in 1961 that South Africa became a republic; Kruger Day, October 10, honoring the birth of Stephanus Johannus Paulus Kruger (1925–1904), an early Afrikaner political leader.

7 ● RITES OF PASSAGE

The rites of passage for English South Africans would be familiar to their counterparts in other parts of the world. After graduation from high school—known as matriculation in South Africa—it is common to go on to a technical college or to a university.

Few South African youths own cars before they get full-time jobs. The purchase of the first car is an important rite of passage, as is reaching the age of eighteen when it becomes legal to drive, to vote, and to drink alcohol. On the twenty-first birthday, it is usual to present the celebrant with a symbolic silver key to adulthood. Marriage usually occurs in the mid-twenties.

After university graduation—and sometimes before—it is common for young English South Africans to try to travel abroad. Typically, they travel to Britain and the European continent (fourteen hours away by air) but increasing numbers are traveling to the United States, Asia, Australia, and New Zealand. Because of the expense involved, many try to get work during their travels. It is not uncommon to find young English South Africans working in other countries as farm laborers, maids, nannies, and in other casual jobs.

In the past, military service was compulsory at age eighteen for white males only. Army duty brought English and Afrikaner South Africans together. As of the late 1990s, all races served in a volunteer defense force, further demolishing past racial barriers.

8 ● RELATIONSHIPS

In the past, English South Africans—like other ethnic and racial groups in the country—tended to keep to themselves with most social contacts confined to members of their own group. With the end of separation of the races (which began by stages in the 1980s and reached its peak with the beginning of democracy in 1994), whites and blacks have been brought together in schools, colleges, the workplace, and sports fields. As a result, people are being exposed to customs that may be different than their own. For instance, in some African cultures it is considered polite to sit down when a prominent person or someone elderly enters a room. English South Africans have been taught traditionally that younger people should stand up as a mark of respect. They are learning that their way is not necessarily practiced by everyone.

9 ● LIVING CONDITIONS

Under the apartheid system, whites (both English and Afrikaner) were afforded many advantages. For instance, they had better schools, better job opportunities, and better recreation and health facilities. English-speaking South Africans were part of that elite. As of the late 1990s, there are no longer legal barriers to race groups living anywhere. The typical English South African lives in a single family house on a wide suburban street or in an apartment or semi-detached row house with neighborhood playgrounds, shopping centers, and cinemas (movie theaters).

10 ● FAMILY LIFE

In English South African families, both parents typically work. Younger children are cared for after school by live-in domestic workers. With high interest rates and sharply rising property prices, it has become fairly common for young adults to continue to live at home for longer than they would have in the past. Sometimes families build separate structures on their property for their adult children or elderly parents.

English South African families celebrate birthdays, anniversaries, special achievements in school or in sports, and often take vacations together, renting cottages or apartments at the seaside. Many families keep one or two dogs or cats as pets.

11 ● CLOTHING

Everyday clothing is similar to that worn by middle-class people throughout the world. It is common to find men giving up traditional Western business suits at work for a more casual style of dress. This trend was set by President Nelson Mandela who wore colorful open-neck shirts even at formal meetings. Schoolchildren wear school uniforms. Sometimes these uniforms include the traditional blazer and tie for boys and girls, but this is hot and uncomfortable during the summer. Many schools have opted for open-neck clothes. Shorts and T-shirts are popular on weekends.

12 ● FOOD

English South Africans traditionally enjoyed roast beef or lamb with roasted potatoes and Yorkshire pudding, prepared on Sunday morning and eaten at a family lunch (followed by a nap). Lifestyles and dietary changes are changing this tradition. The traditional breakfast of bacon and eggs has also been given up on most mornings. English South Africans drink coffee or tea, and eat toast, breakfast cereal, or fruit. Lunch is often a sandwich or slice of pizza. Dinner might by grilled steak with fried or baked potatoes. Fried or baked fish is popular in coastal cities. In winter, *bredies* (stews) are popular. English South Africans like to garnish their food with chutney (pickled relish). Many enjoy a bread spread called Marmite, a dark-colored yeast extract with a salty taste. Fast foods are gaining in popularity.

13 ● EDUCATION

Almost all English South Africans are literate (can read and write). Education is compulsory to the age of sixteen. It generally takes twelve years to obtain a high school diploma or senior certificate which is required to continue studies at a technical college or university. University undergraduate degrees generally take three years to complete. (The academic year is longer than in the United States.) An additional year of study after a bachelor's degree can lead to an honors degree, followed by further work for master's degrees or doctorates.

It is becoming more difficult to get a good job without a bachelor's degree or a technical college diploma. Many families will sacrifice to ensure that their children are educated.

14 ● CULTURAL HERITAGE

English South African writers have achieved international renown for their depiction of dramatic events in South Africa. Probably the best-known such writer is Alan Paton (1903–88). His novel, *Cry the Beloved Country*, explores the impact of racism on whites as well as blacks. Another writer who has achieved international fame is Nadine Gordimer (1923–). Playwright Athol Fugard (1932–) has also achieved international fame with his dramatic portrayals of life through South Africa's race-tinged prism. Many English South Africans have developed a taste for African music, as performed by groups like Ladysmith Black Mambazo. American musician and entertainer Paul Simon has done much to bring this music to an international audience.

15 ● EMPLOYMENT

A typical work week ranges from forty to forty-six hours. There is no legally mandated minimum wage. Until 1979, special classes of labor were reserved for workers by race. The more highly paid jobs were reserved for, and are still largely held by, whites. After apartheid, this situation was changing. Some English South Africans express concern over affirmative action programs to correct the inequities created by apartheid. Some claim now that this has led to a new kind of apartheid in which whites are unable to get jobs and promotion because of their skin color.

16 ● SPORTS

Outdoor sports are very popular. Cricket and rugby are national obsessions. Other popular sports are soccer, field hockey (mostly female participants) played in winter, tennis, track and field athletics, competitive cycling, and swimming. Lawn bowls (bowling) is played mostly by older adults. Windsurfing, surfing, yachting, hiking, and mountaineering are all popular. Events that attract thousands of spectators and participants include annual road marathon races in Cape Town and Natal. Horse racing also has a large following, and two races in particular—the Cape Metropolitan handicap and the Durban July—are major media events. The fashions worn by the spectators get as much attention as the horses.

17 ● RECREATION

Popular recreation attractions in South Africa include Kruger National Park and several game reserves. Entertainment facilities include symphony halls, theaters, movies, nightclubs, and discos.

18 ● CRAFTS AND HOBBIES

English in South Africa enjoy the varied hobbies of citizens of any industrialized nation.

19 ● SOCIAL PROBLEMS

South Africa's transition to democracy in 1994 brought equal rights and new opportunities to the disadvantaged sectors of the population. It also sparked a dramatic increase in the rate of crime and violence—an result of poverty and high unemployment. Burglaries, muggings, carjackings, rapes, and murders all increased in the late 1990s. As a result, there is a growing interest in the possibility of emigration (moving out of the country), and growth of home security services and the development of gated communities.

South Africa's transition also made it a target for foreign narcotics traffickers who saw an opportunity to ship drugs through the newly opened borders. Illegal drugs are shipped through South Africa to North America and Europe in a complex network that makes themt difficult to trace.

20 ● BIBLIOGRAPHY

Crocker, Chester A. *High Noon in Southern Africa.* New York: Norton, 1992.

Mallaby, Sebastian. *After Apartheid.* New York: Random House, 1992.

Morris, Donald R. *The Washing of the Spears.* London, England: Jonathan Cape, 1972.

Paton, Alan. *Towards the Mountain, An Autobiography.* Cape Town: David Philip, 1980 (also published in the United States by Charles Scribner's Sons).

Reader's Digest Illustrated History of South Africa. Cape Town: Reader's Digest Association, 1994.

Suzman, Helen. *In No Uncertain Terms, A South African Memoir.* New York: Knopf, 1993.

WEBSITES

Embassy of South Africa, Washington, D.C. [Online] Available http://www.southafrica.net/, 1998.

Government of South Africa. [Online] http://www.polity.org.za/gnu.html, 1998.

Interknowledge Corp. South Africa. [Online] Available http://www.geographia.com/south-africa/, 1998.

Southern African Development Community. South Africa. [Online] Available http://www.sadc-usa.net/members/safrica/, 1998.

Xhosa

PRONUNCIATION: KOH-suh
LOCATION: South Africa (eastern, urban areas)
POPULATION: 6 million
LANGUAGE: Xhosa (Bantu)
RELIGION: Traditional beliefs (supreme being *uThixo* or *uQamata*); Christianity

1 ● INTRODUCTION

The word Xhosa refers to a people and a language of South Africa. The Xhosa-speaking people are divided into a number of subgroups with their own distinct but related heritages. One of these subgroups is called Xhosa as well. The other main subgroups are the Bhaca, Bomvana, Mfengu, Mpondo, Mpondomise, Xesibe, and Thembu. Unless otherwise stated, this article refers to all the Xhosa-speaking people.

XHOSA

Well before the arrival of Dutch in the 1650s, the Xhosa had settled the southeastern area of South Africa. They interacted with the foraging (food-gathering) and pastoral (nomadic herding) people who were in South Africa first, the Khoi and the San. Europeans who came to stay in South Africa first settled in and around Cape Town. As the years passed, they sought to expand their territory. This expansion was first at the expense of the Khoi and San, but later Xhosa land was taken as well. A series of wars between *trekboers* (Afrikaner colonists) and Xhosa began in the 1770s. Later, in the nineteenth century, the British became the new colonizing force (foreigners in control) in the Cape. They directed the armies that were to vanquish the Xhosa.

Christian missionaries established their first outposts among the Xhosa in the 1820s, but met with little success. Only after the Xhosa population had been traumatized by European invasion, drought, and disease did Xhosa convert to Christianity in substantial numbers. In addition to land lost to white annexation, legislation reduced Xhosa political autonomy. Over time, Xhosa people became increasingly impoverished. They had no option but to become migrant laborers. In the late 1990s, Xhosa make up a large percentage of the workers in South Africa's gold mines.

Under apartheid (a government policy requiring the separation of races), the South African government created separate regions that were described as *Bantustans* (homelands) for black people of African descent. Two regions—Transkei and Ciskei—were set aside for Xhosa people.

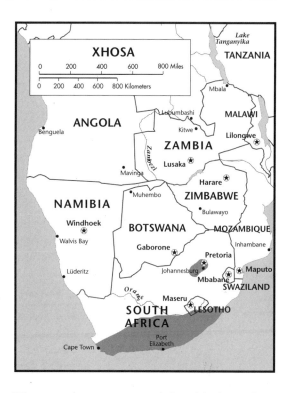

These regions were proclaimed independent countries by the apartheid government. Apartheid policy denied South African citizenship to many Xhosa. Thousands of people were forcibly relocated to remote areas in Transkei and Ciskei. The homelands were abolished with the change to democracy in 1994.

2 ● LOCATION

Before the arrival of the Europeans in the late 1600s, Xhosa-speaking people occupied much of eastern South Africa. The region extended from the Fish River to land inhabited by Zulu-speakers south of the modern city of Durban. This territory includes well-watered rolling hills near scenic coastal areas as well as harsh and dry regions further inland. Many Xhosa live in

111

Cape Town (iKapa), East London (iMonti), and Port Elizabeth (iBhayi). They can be found in lesser numbers in most of South Africa's major metropolitan areas. As of 1995, there were about 6 million Xhosa, making up approximately 17.5 percent of South Africa's population.

3 ● LANGUAGE

The Xhosa language is properly referred to as *isiXhosa*. It is a Bantu language closely related to Zulu, Swazi, and Ndebele. As with other South African languages, Xhosa is characterized by respectful forms of address for elders and in-laws. The language is also rich in idioms. To have *isandla esishushu* (a warm hand), for example, is to be generous.

Xhosa contains many words with click consonants that have been borrowed from Khoi or San words. The "X" in Xhosa represents a type of click made by the tongue on the side of the mouth. This consonant sounds something like the clicking sound English-speaking horseback riders make to encourage their horses. English speakers who have not mastered clicks often pronounce Xhosa as "Ko-Sa."

Names in Xhosa often express the values or opinions of the community. Common personal names include *Thamsanqa* (good fortune) and *Nomsa* (mother of kindness). Adults are often referred to by their *isiduko* (clan or lineage) names. In the case of women, clan names are preceded by a prefix meaning "mother of." A woman of the Thembu clan might be called *MamThembu*. Women are also named by reference to their children, real or intended; *NoLindiwe* is a polite name for Lindiwe's mother.

4 ● FOLKLORE

Stories and legends provide accounts of Xhosa ancestral heroes. According to one oral tradition, the first person on Earth was a great leader called Xhosa. Another tradition stresses the essential unity of the Xhosa-speaking people by proclaiming that all the Xhosa subgroups are descendants of one ancestor, Tshawe. Historians have suggested that Xhosa and Tshawe were probably the first Xhosa kings or paramount (supreme) chiefs.

Xhosa tradition is rich in creative verbal expression. *Intsomi* (folktales), proverbs, and *isibongo* (praise poems) are told in dramatic and creative ways. Folktales relate the adventures of both animal protagonists and human characters. Praise poems traditionally relate the heroic adventures of ancestors or political leaders.

5 ● RELIGION

The supreme being among the Xhosa is called *uThixo* or *uQamata*. As in the religions of many other Bantu peoples, God is only rarely involved in everyday life. God may be approached through ancestral intermediaries who are honored through ritual sacrifices. Ancestors commonly make their wishes known to the living in dreams.

Christianity in one form or another is accepted by most Xhosa-speaking people today. Cultural traditionalists are likely to belong to independent denominations that combine Christianity with traditional beliefs and practices. Xhosa religious practice is distinguished by elaborate and lengthy rituals, initiations, and feasts. Modern rituals typically pertain to matters of illness and psychological well-being.

6 ● MAJOR HOLIDAYS

Xhosa observe the same holidays as other groups of South Africa. These include the Christian holidays, Workers's Day (or May Day, May 1), the Day of Reconciliation (December 16), and Heritage Day (September 24). During the apartheid era, two unofficial holidays were observed to honor black people killed in the fight for equality and political representation. June 16 was a national day of remembrance for students killed by police in Soweto on that day in 1976. March 21 honored protestors killed by authorities during a demonstration in Sharpeville in 1960. Both of these anniversaries continue to be recognized with a day of rest, meetings, and prayer. Another important holiday is April 27, the date of the first national election in which black South Africans could vote.

7 ● RITES OF PASSAGE

After giving birth, a mother is expected to remain secluded in her house for at least ten days. In Xhosa tradition, the afterbirth and umbilical cord were buried or burned to protect the baby from sorcery. At the end of the period of seclusion, a goat was sacrificed. Those who no longer practice the traditional rituals may still invite friends and relatives to a special dinner to mark the end of the mother's seclusion.

Male initiation in the form of circumcision is practiced among most Xhosa groups. The *abakweta* (initiates-in-training) live in special huts isolated from villages or towns for several weeks. Like soldiers inducted into the army, they have their heads shaved. They wear a loincloth and a blanket for warmth. White clay is smeared on their bodies from head to toe. They are expected to observe numerous taboos (prohibitions) and to act deferentially to their adult male leaders. Different stages in the initiation process were marked by the sacrifice of a goat.

The ritual of female circumcision is considerably shorter. The *intonjane* (girl to be initiated) is secluded for about a week. During this period, there are dances, and ritual sacrifices of animals. The initiate must hide herself from view and observe food restrictions. There is no actual surgical operation.

8 ● RELATIONSHIPS

Xhosa have traditionally used greetings to show respect and good intentions to others. In interacting with others, it is crucial to show respect (*ukuhlonipha*). Youths are expected to keep quiet when elders are speaking, and to lower their eyes when being addressed. Hospitality is highly valued, and people are expected to share with visitors what they can. Socializing over tea and snacks is common.

In Xhosa tradition, one often found a girlfriend or boyfriend by attending dances. One popular type of dance, called *umtshotsho* or *intlombe*, could last all night. On some occasions, unmarried lovers were allowed to sleep together provided they observed certain restraints. A form of external intercourse called *ukumetsha* was permitted, but full intercourse was taboo. For Westernized Xhosa, romances often begin at school, church, or through mutual acquaintances. Dating activities include attending the cinema as well as going to school

Jason Lauré

Housing, standards of living, and creature comforts vary considerably among Xhosa. Xhosa people make up some of the poorest and some of the wealthiest of black South Africans.

dances, sporting events, concerts, and so forth.

9 ● LIVING CONDITIONS

During the early period of white rule in South Africa, Xhosa communities were severely neglected in terms of social services. In fact, rural areas were deliberately impoverished so as to encourage Xhosa to seek wage labor employment. In the later years of apartheid, some attempts were made to address major health concerns in these areas. However, most government money continued to be set aside for social services that benefited whites. As the Xhosa population in rural areas expanded through natural increase and forced removals, rural lands became increasingly overcrowded and eroded. In the twentieth-century, many men and women migrated to urban shantytowns (towns comprised of crudely built huts). Poverty and ill health are still widespread in both rural and urban communities. Since 1994, however, the post-apartheid government has expanded health and nutritional aid to the black population.

Housing, standards of living, and creature comforts vary considerably among Xhosa. Xhosa people make up some of the poorest and some of the wealthiest of black

South Africans. Poor people live in round thatched-roof huts, labor compounds, or single-room shacks without running water or electricity. Other Xhosa are among an elite who live in large comfortable houses in quiet suburban neighborhoods.

10 ● FAMILY LIFE

The traditional Xhosa family was patriarchal; men were considered the heads of their households. Women and children were expected to defer to men's authority. Polygynous marriages (multiple wives) were permitted where the husband had the means to pay the *lobolo* (bride wealth) for each, and to maintain them properly. Women were expected to leave their families to live with their husband's family.

The migrant labor system has put great strains on the traditional family. Some men have established two distinct families, one at the place of work and the other at the rural home. With the end of apartheid, some of the families previously separated by the labor laws are beginning new lives in urban areas. Some of these families live under crowded and difficult conditions in shantytowns and migrant labor compounds.

11 ● CLOTHING

Many Xhosa men and women dress similarly to people in Europe and the United States. Pants for women have only recently become acceptable. As a result of missionary influence, it has become customary for a woman to cover her hair with a scarf or hat. Many rural woman fold scarves or other clothes into elaborate turban shapes. They continue to apply white or ochre-colored mixtures to their bodies and faces. Other unique Xhosa dress includes intricately sewn designs on blankets that are worn by both men and women as shawls or capes.

12 ● FOOD

Xhosa people share many food traditions with the other peoples of South Africa. Staple foods are corn (maize) and bread. Beef, mutton (sheep meat), and goat meat are popular. Milk is often drunk in its sour form. Sorghum beer, also sour in taste, continues to be popular.

One particular food popularly identified with the Xhosa is *umngqusho*. This dish combines hominy corn with beans and spices. Xhosa also regularly eat the soft porridge made of corn meal flour that is widespread in Africa. Eggs were traditionally taboo for women, and a just-married wife was not allowed to eat certain types of meat. Men were not supposed to drink milk in any village where they might later take a wife.

The major mealtimes are breakfast and dinner. Children may go without lunch, although school lunch programs have been established by the government.

13 ● EDUCATION

The first Western-style schools for Xhosa-speakers were begun by missionaries. One of the most famous of the missionary institutions, the University of Fort Hare, boasts Nelson Mandela and a number of other famous African leaders as former students.

Under apartheid, African access to education was restricted and many of the best mission schools were shutdown. As a result, adult literacy rates (percentage able to read and write) dropped, in some areas to as low as 30 percent. Today, the goal is free education for all those aged seven to seventeen. Literacy and education are now seen as keys to success and are highly valued by most people.

14 ● CULTURAL HERITAGE

Xhosa traditional music places a strong emphasis on group singing and handclapping as accompaniment to dance. Drums, while used occasionally, were not as fundamental a part of musical expression as they were for many other African peoples. Other instruments used included rattles, whistles, flutes, mouth harps, and stringed-instruments constructed with a bow and resonator.

Missionaries introduced the Xhosa to Western choral singing. Among the most successful of the Xhosa hymns is the South African national anthem, *Nkosi Sikele' iAfrika* (God Bless Africa). It was written by a school teacher named Enoch Sontonga in 1897.

Xhosa written literature was established in the nineteenth century with the publication of the first Xhosa newspapers, novels, and plays. Early writers included Tiyo Soga, I. Bud-Mbelle, and John Tengo Jabavu.

15 ● EMPLOYMENT

Many rural Xhosa have left home to find employment in the city. Under white rule, Xhosa men were most frequently hired as miners and farm laborers. Women also worked as farm laborers, but work in domestic service was more valued. For those with high school and college educations, the greatest opportunities were in health care, education, and government administration. In the 1990s, Xhosa sought degrees in all fields. South Africa's migrant labor system has dramatically altered Xhosa social life and put strain on the family.

16 ● SPORTS

Xhosa children enjoy skipping rope, racing, swimming, and playing hopscotch. Boys enjoy wrestling and stick fighting.

The most popular sport in South Africa is soccer. There are many professional, school, and company teams. There are also organized competitions between schools in athletics (track and field).

17 ● ENTERTAINMENT

Popular entertainment includes attending movies, plays, and musical performances. Televisions and videocassette recorders are also popular. Most movies are imported from other countries, but a South African film industry is developing. Plays are often broadcast over TV and radio. Television broadcasts also include programs in Xhosa. Xhosa "soap operas" are a regular feature.

South Africa has a well-established music industry. The most popular musicians are typically those that perform dance tunes. Religious choirs are also popular.

18 ● CRAFTS AND HOBBIES

Folk craft traditions include beadwork, sewing, pottery making, house decoration, and weaving. Hand-woven materials were generally functional items such as sleeping mats, baskets, and strainers. Xhosa ceremonial clothing is often elaborately decorated with fine embroidery work and intricate geometric designs.

19 ● SOCIAL PROBLEMS

Most of the social problems found among Xhosa people today stem directly or indirectly from the apartheid past. These include high rates of poverty, fractured families, malnutrition, and crime. Competition for scarce resources has also led to conflict with other African ethnic groups. There are also divisions within the Xhosa community—between men and women, young and old, rural and urban, and highly educated and illiterate. These divisions may lead to tensions if not resolved in the post-apartheid era. One of the biggest challenges for South Africa as a whole is to meet rising expectations for education, employment, and improved standards of living.

20 ● BIBLIOGRAPHY

Ramphela, Mamphela. *A Bed Called Home: Life in the Migrant Labour Hostels of Cape Town.* Athens, Ohio: Ohio University Press, 1993.

Switzer, Les. *Power and Resistance in an African Society: The Ciskei Xhosa and the Making of South Africa.* Madison: University of Wisconsin Press, 1993.

Zenani, Nongenile. *The World and the Word: Tales and Observations from the Xhosa Oral Tradition.* Collected and edited by Harold Scheub. Wisconsin: University of Wisconsin Press, 1992.

WEBSITES

Embassy of South Africa, Washington, D.C. [Online] Available http://www.southafrica.net/, 1998.

Government of South Africa. [Online] http://www.polity.org.za/gnu.html, 1998.

Interknowledge Corp. South Africa. [Online] Available http://www.geographia.com/south-africa/, 1998.

Southern African Development Community. South Africa. [Online] Available http://www.sadc-usa.net/members/safrica/, 1998.

Zulu

PRONUNCIATION: ZOO-loo
LOCATION: KwaZulu-Natal Province of South Africa
POPULATION: 9.2 million
LANGUAGE: IsiZulu; Zulu; English
RELIGION: Mixture of traditional beliefs and Christianity

1 ● INTRODUCTION

For many people, the Zulu are the best-known African people. Their military exploits led to the rise of a great kingdom that was feared for a long time over much of the African continent. The Zulu are the descendants of Nguni-speaking people. Their written history can be traced back to the fourteenth century.

In the early nineteenth century a young Zulu prince, Shaka, came onto the scene and welded most of the Nguni tribes into the powerful Zulu Kingdom. Shaka ruled from 1816 to 1828, when he was assassinated by his brothers. During his reign, Shaka recruited young men from all over the kingdom and trained them in his own novel warrior tactics. After defeating competing armies and assimilating their people, Shaka established his Zulu nation. Within twelve years, he had forged one of the mightiest empires the African continent has ever known.

However, during the late 1800s, British troops invaded Zulu territory and divided the Zulu land into thirteen chiefdoms. The Zulu never regained their independence. Throughout the mid-1900s they were dominated by different white governments, first

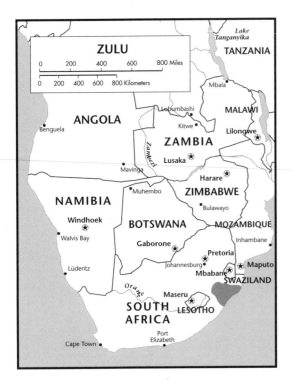

The subtropical climate brings lots of sunshine and brief, intense rain showers.

While many Zulu still live in traditionally structured rural communities, others have migrated to urban areas. However, links between urban and rural residents remain strong. A mixture of traditional and Western ways of life is clearly evident in the lives of almost all Zulu people.

3 ● LANGUAGE

The dominant language in South Africa is isiZulu. In KwaZulu-Natal, the most frequently spoken languages are Zulu and English. Zulu is idiomatic and proverbial and is characterized by many clicks. The Zulu language is characterized by *hlonipha* (respect) terms. Addressing those who are older than oneself, especially elderly and senior people, by their first names is viewed as lack of respect. Therefore terms like *baba* (father) and *mama* (mother) are used not only to address one's parents but also other senior males and females of the community.

4 ● FOLKLORE

Among the Zulu, the belief in ancestral spirits (*amadlozi* or *abaphansi*) has always been strong. These are the spirits of the dead. The Zulus recognize the existence of a supreme being. *UMvelinqangi* (One Who Came First) or *uNkulunkulu* (Very Big One) is God because he appeared first. This supreme being is far removed from the lives of the people and has never been seen by anyone. No ceremonies are, therefore, ever performed for uMvelinqangi. Zulu people believe that the spirits of the dead mediate

the British and later on, the Afrikaner. The Zulu have endeavored to regain a measure of political autonomy, both before South Africa's first democratic election in 1994 and in the subsequent period to the present. They have been unsuccessful, however, with both governments.

2 ● LOCATION

The 9 million Zulu-speaking people live mainly in KwaZulu-Natal Province of South Africa. Some are also scattered throughout the other provinces. KwaZulu-Natal borders on Mozambique in the north, Eastern Cape in the south, the Indian Ocean in the east, and Lesotho in the west. The capital city is Pietermaritzburg. KwaZulu-Natal is semi-fertile with a flat coastal plain, highlands to the west, and numerous rivers and streams.

between uMvelinqangi and the people on earth.

Zulus believe in a long life that continues after death. Getting old is seen as a blessing. This is based on the myth that long ago people did not die but rather lived for years. The Creator did not think that people should die. He, therefore, called a chameleon and said, "Chameleon, I am sending you to the people. Go and tell them that they are not to die." Although the chameleon was very slow, the Creator did not mind. He waited for the reply. However, after walking a long distance, the chameleon saw wild berries and decided to stop and eat them. It told itself that the Creator would not see it. Unfortunately, the Creator saw it and became very angry. He called a lizard, which came swiftly. The Creator told the lizard to go and tell the people that they are to die. The lizard sped off, passed the chameleon on the way, and delivered the message to the people. After a long time, the chameleon appeared, breathing heavily, and delivered its message. The people were very angry and said to it, "Why did you waste time? We have already received the lizard's message!" Thus, growing old among the Zulu is seen as a special privilege from the Creator. Elderly people are believed to be sacred, and are thus are always respected.

5 ● RELIGION

Ancestral spirits are important in Zulu religious life. Offerings and sacrifices are made to the ancestors for protection, good health, and happiness. Ancestral spirits come back to the world in the form of dreams, illnesses, and sometimes snakes. The Zulu also believe in the use of magic. Anything

beyond their understanding, such as bad luck and illness, is considered to be sent by an angry spirit. When this happens, the help of a diviner (soothsayer) or herbalist is sought. He or she will communicate with the ancestors or use natural herbs and prayers to get rid of the problem.

Many Zulu converted to Christianity under colonialism. Although there are many Christian converts, ancestral beliefs have far from disappeared. Instead, there has been a mixture of traditional beliefs and Christianity. This kind of religion is particularly common among urbanites. There are also fervent Christians who view ancestral belief as outdated and sinful.

6 ● MAJOR HOLIDAYS

The Zulu recognize the national holidays of the Republic of South Africa. In addition, they celebrate Shaka's Day every year in September. This holiday is marked by celebrations and slaughtering cattle to commemorate the founder of the Zulu Kingdom. On this important day, Zulu people wear their full traditional attire (clothing and weapons) and gather at Shaka's tombstone, kwaDukuza in Stanger. This is a very colorful day attended by both national and international dignitaries who represent their governments. *Izimbongi* (praise-poets) sing the praises of all the Zulu kings, from Shaka to the present king, Zwelithini.

7 ● RITES OF PASSAGE

Among the Zulu, birth, puberty, marriage, and death are all celebrated and marked by the slaughter of sacrificial animals to ancestors. Birth and puberty are particularly celebrated. To Zulu traditionalists, childlessness

Jason Lauré

Zulus celebrate Shaka's Day every year in September. This holiday is marked by celebrations and slaughtering cattle to commemorate the founder of the Zulu Kingdom. On this day, Zulu people wear their full traditional attire.

and giving birth to girls only are the greatest of all misfortunes. No marriage is permanent until a child, especially a boy, is born.

The puberty ceremony *(umemulo)* is a transition to full adulthood. Nowadays it is performed only for girls. It involves separation from other people for a period to mark the changing status from youth to adulthood. This is followed by "reincorporation," characterized by ritual killing of animals, dancing, and feasting. After the ceremony, the girl is declared ready for marriage. The courting days then begin. The girl may take the first step by sending a "love letter" to a young man who appeals to her. Zulu love letters are made of beads. Different colors

have different meanings, and certain combinations carry particular messages.

Dating occurs when a young man visits or writes a letter to a woman telling her how much he loves her. Once a woman decides that she loves this man, she can tell him so. It is only after they have both agreed that they love each other that they may be seen together in public. Parents should become aware of the relationship only when the man informs them that he wants to marry their daughter.

8 ● RELATIONSHIPS

In contrast to their known warriorism, the Zulu are very warm and amicable people at a personal level. *Ubuntu* (literally, "human-ness," "good moral nature," "good disposition") shapes the everyday life of the Zulu people. This comes from a notion that a human being is the highest of all species. There are hundreds of proverbs written about ubuntu. These proverbs relate to the treatment of people, good and bad behavior, pride, ingratitude, bad manners, moral degeneracy, conceit, cruelty, obstinacy, pretense, helping others, and so forth.

Sawubona is usually enough of a greeting for strangers, but a formal greeting is more appropriate for those who are familiar. The formal greeting includes a three-times handshake, while asking about the well-being of the person and his or her relations *(Ninjani?)*. Taking leave involves the standard *Sala /Nisale kahle* (Remain well), and the other person responds by saying, *Uhambe /Nihambe kahle* (Go well). It is customary for juniors and the young to initiate the greetings when they meet their seniors and their elders.

9 ● LIVING CONDITIONS

In South Africa, living conditions cannot be divorced from local politics. Conditions for the Zulu are similar to those of other black people. Zulu in most of the rural areas do not have adequate basic services such as electricity, clean water, formal housing, transport, hospitals, or clinics. Urban Zulu live in the so-called black townships and the areas fringing industrial cities. Their living conditions are, at least, better than those in rural areas. They constitute the Zulu middle class; their lifestyle is usually no different from that of other Western urbanites. Since the education available in rural black schools is inferior, the people in these areas are not equipped to migrate and seek a better life in the urban areas. If they migrate, most end up in the poor areas fringing cities.

In the rural areas of KwaZulu-Natal, a typical Zulu homestead will be circular and fenced, with a thatched-roof house.

10 ● FAMILY LIFE

The Zulu term for "family" *(umndeni)* includes all the people staying in a homestead who are related to each other, either by blood, marriage, or adoption. Most rural households comprise extended families, brothers with their wives, unmarried sisters, children, parents, and grandparents all staying together in the same homestead. As a sign of respect, parents and elders are not called by their first names; instead, kinship names (surnames) are used.

The Zulu family is patriarchal; a man is both the head of the family and the figure of authority. It is not unusual for young men to have as many girlfriends as they wish. If they can afford it, they can take more than one wife when they decide to get married. Traditionally, women were not supposed to go out and work, since they were a man's responsibility. Nowadays the status of Zulu women is slowly improving with more women receiving an education.

Marriage is exogamous; marriage to any person belonging to one's father's, mother's, father's mother's, and mother's mother's clan is prohibited. If it happens, the *ukudabula* (literally, "cutting of the blood relationship") ritual is performed.

© Corel Corporation

Zulu village women in Natal, South Africa. A typical Zulu homestead will be circular and fenced, with a thatched-roof house.

11 ● CLOTHING

Today, the everyday clothing of a Zulu is no different from that of any modern urbanite. Traditional clothing, however, is very colorful. Men, women, and children wear beads as accessories. Men wear *amabheshu*, made of goat or cattle skin, which looks like a waist apron, worn at the back. They decorate their heads with feathers and fur. Men also wear frilly goatskin bands on their arms and legs. Women wear *isidwaba*, a traditional Zulu black skirt made of goat or cattle skin. If a woman is not married, she may wear only strings of beads to cover the top part of the body. If she is married, she will wear a T-shirt. Zulu only wear their traditional clothes on special occasions, such as Shaka's Day and cultural gatherings.

12 ● FOOD

The rural Zulu economy is based on cattle and agriculture. Consequently, the main staple diet consists of cow and agricultural products. This includes barbecued and boiled meat; *amasi* (curdled milk), mixed with dry, ground corn or dry, cooked mealie-meal (corn flour); *amadumbe* (yams); vegetables; and fruits. The Zulu traditional beer is not only a staple food but a considerable source of nutrition. It is also socially and ritually important and is drunk on all significant occasions.

Drinking and eating from the same plate was and still is a sign of friendship. It is customary for children to eat from the same dish, usually a big basin. This derives from a "share what you have" belief which is part of *ubuntu* (humane) philosophy.

13 ● EDUCATION

Illiteracy (inability to read and write) is high among most black South Africans. However, education is slowly improving with the new government. Before, children went to school only if their parents could afford to send them. Schooling started at seven years of age and continued until about twenty-four years of age. Since education was not compulsory, pupils could take their time to finish matric (high school). Passing matriculation (graduating) was and still is regarded as a high achievement by the whole community. After matriculation, those parents who can afford it usually send their children to college.

Education and raising a child is like a cycle among the Zulu. Parents spend all they have to raise and educate their children. In turn, the children take care of their parents and their own children when they start working. A person who breaks this cycle is viewed as a community outcast, one who has forgotten about his or her roots.

14 ● CULTURAL HERITAGE

The Zulu are fond of singing as well as dancing. These activities promote unity at all the transitional ceremonies such as births, weddings, and funerals. All the dances are accompanied by drums. The men dress as warriors, wave their clubs, and thrust their cowhide shields forward.

Zulu folklore is transmitted through storytelling, praise-poems, and proverbs. These explain Zulu history and teach moral lessons. Praise-poems (poems recited about the kings and the high achievers in life) are becoming part of popular culture.

15 ● EMPLOYMENT

In the past, only able-bodied men were supposed to work. Before the 1970s, especially in rural areas, being able to send a written letter and get a reply meant that a young boy was ready to go and look for work. Now Zulus want to complete their high school education. In the mind of the Zulu, work should benefit either one's parents or children and siblings. The first salary (or the bigger portion), therefore, is usually given to parents in return for blessings.

16 ● SPORTS

Soccer is very popular for both young boys and men. Children learn the game by watching their older brothers play. Whenever boys are together and not engaged in some household or school activity, they play soccer. Young boys, especially those who live next to big rivers, also compete in swimming. Girls, if they are not at school, are expected to assist their mothers in the house. However, they can play games once they have finished their chores. One popular game played by girls, especially in rural KwaZulu, is *masishayana/maphakathi*. Two girls stand opposite each other, usually not more than 165 feet (50 meters) apart.

Another girl stands between them, facing the one who is holding a tennis ball. The idea of this game is to try to hit the girl standing in the middle while she tries to avoid being hit. If the ball hits her or touches her clothes, she is out. Being able to avoid being hit ten times earns the girl a point. Having the most points means winning a game and becoming the best player in your circle of friends. One sport which is participated in by both girls and boys is track and field, an organized school sport.

17 ● RECREATION

Ritual ceremonies also serve as part of the entertainment and recreation for the whole community. Zulu custom does not mandate formal invitations to gatherings where food will be served, such as weddings and birthday parties. The Zulu believe that food should be shared. Therefore, uninvited arrival at a celebration is an honor to the host. These celebrations include singing and dancing.

Television is very popular among urban Zulu households. Owning a television set is a luxury for rural Zulu since very few rural areas have electricity. Those who can afford to go to the movies do so. For urban teenagers, American youth culture, especially clothing and music, is very popular. Among adults, *stokvels* (voluntary or common-interest associations) provide financial assistance, friendship, and recreation.

18 ● CRAFTS AND HOBBIES

The Zulu, especially those from rural areas, are known for their weaving, craftmaking, pottery, and beadwork. Women and children weave everyday-use mats, beer sieves, and baskets for domestic purposes. They also make calabashes (decorated gourds used as utensils). Men and boys carve various household objects and ornaments from wood and bone. These include headrests, trays, scrapers, household utensils, and chairs. Beadmaking is mainly women's work because beads are believed to be a way of sending messages without being direct.

19 ● SOCIAL PROBLEMS

The Zulu terms *ubuntu* and *hlonipha* summarize everything about human rights. However, it is evident that some individuals in Zulu society, particularly women and children, enjoy fewer human rights than others.

20 ● BIBLIOGRAPHY

Haskins, J., et al. *From Afar to Zulu*. New York: Walker and Company, 1995.
Khuzwayo, W. "Kinship Substitutions." Paper presented at the PAAA Conference in Cameroon, West Africa, 1994.
Macnamara, M. *World Views*. Pretoria: J. L. van Schaik Pty, 1980.
West, M. *Abantu*. Cape Town: C. Struik Publishers, 1976.

WEBSITES
D.W.Web Design. Zulu Anthropology. [Online] Available http://www.africasafari.co.za/traditional.htm, 1998.
Embassy of South Africa, Washington, D.C. [Online] Available http://www.southafrica.net/, 1998.
Government of South Africa. [Online] http://www.polity.org.za/gnu.html, 1998.
Interknowledge Corp. South Africa. [Online] Available http://www.geographia.com/southafrica/, 1998.
Southern African Development Community. South Africa. [Online] Available http://www.sadc-usa.net/members/safrica/, 1998.

Spain

The Basques, Galicians, and Catalans consider themselves separate nations within Spain. They enjoy a fair amount of cultural, economic, and political independence. Estimates of the Gypsy population range from 50,000 to 450,000.

Spaniards

PRONUNCIATION: SPAN-yurds
LOCATION: Spain
POPULATION: 40 million
LANGUAGE: Castilian Spanish; Catalan; Galician; Basque
RELIGION: Roman Catholicism

1 ● INTRODUCTION

Spain is the second-largest nation in Europe, after France. It is a land of contrasts and extremes. Its terrain includes Mediterranean beaches, snow-capped Pyrenees Mountains, dry plains, coastal rice paddies, volcanic islands, and rolling hills. Its people have strong regional identities forged by this diverse geography and by the events of their history.

After colonization by the Greeks and Romans and invasion by Germanic tribes, Spain was conquered by the Muslim Moors in the eighth century AD. The Moors maintained control for nearly 800 years, and heavily influenced the culture. Finally, in the late fifteenth century, Isabel and Ferdinand, called the Catholic monarchs, conquered Granada, the last city in Spain held by the Muslims. The monarchs sponsored Christopher Columbus's voyage to America in 1492. Spain became the greatest world power during Europe's Age of Discovery. It reaped tremendous wealth from an empire that extended to virtually all areas of the globe.

After becoming a republic in 1931, the nation was torn apart by a civil war (1936–39). The end of the Spanish Civil War marked the beginning of General Francisco

Franco's repressive thirty six-year regime, which lasted until his death in 1975. Since then, Spain has been a parliamentary monarchy (having both a legislature and a ruler) under King Juan Carlos. Spain joined the European Community in 1986. In 1992 Spain hosted the Summer Olympic Games in Barcelona and the International Exposition in Seville.

2 ● LOCATION

Spain comprises approximately four-fifths of the Iberian peninsula (with Portugal accounting for the remainder). Spain also includes the Canary Islands in the Atlantic Ocean and the Balearic Islands in the Mediterranean Sea. Altogether, its total area is slightly less than the combined areas of the states of Utah and Nevada. Spain's average elevation is the second-highest in Europe after Switzerland. Three-fifths of the Spanish mainland is a broad plateau, called the *Meseta*, located in the center of the country.

Spain has a population of some 40 million people, with a much lower population density than most other European countries. Geographic barriers have helped preserve a keen sense of identity in all six of Spain's major ethnic groups. The Castilians, who live in the central Meseta, are the nation's dominant group, and Castilian Spanish is Spain's national language. The other groups are the Galicians, Basques, Catalans, Levante, and Andalusians.

3 ● LANGUAGE

According to the 1978 Constitution, Castilian Spanish is the national language. It is spoken by a majority of Spaniards and used in the schools and courts. Castilian is a Romance (Latin-based) language, as are most of the other regional languages, including Catalan and Galician. Basque is a pre-Roman language whose origin has not been clearly determined.

NUMBERS

English	Spanish
one	un, uno
two	dos
three	tres
four	cuatro
five	cinco
six	seis
seven	siete
eight	ocho
nine	nueve
ten	diez

DAYS OF THE WEEK

English	Spanish
Sunday	Domingo
Monday	Lunes
Tuesday	Martes
Wednesday	Miércoles
Thursday	Jueves
Friday	Viernes
Saturday	Sábado

4 ● FOLKLORE

Spanish folkloric tradition is very rich. Its origins include Celtic, Roman, Germanic, Jewish, and Moorish influences. Spain's ancient musical heritage includes bagpipe music in Galicia and Asturias, *sardanas (circle dances)* in Catalonia, flamenco dancing accompanied by the guitar in Andalusia, and the lively Aragonese dance called the *jota*. Bullfighting is the most widely known Spanish tradition. Some historians trace it to a cult of bull worship.

5 ● RELIGION

Historically, Spain has been one of Europe's most staunchly Catholic countries. Over 95 percent of the Spanish people (about 38 mil-

SPANIARDS

0   100   200   300 Miles

0   100   200   300 Kilometers

FRANCE

Paris

Nantes

Bordeaux

Bay
of
Biscay

Bilbao

Oporto

ANDORRA

PORTUGAL

Barcelona

Madrid

Lisbon

SPAIN

Sevilla

Málaga

Gibraltar (UK)

Balearic
Islands

Day of St. Peter and St. Paul (June 29), St. James's Day (July 25), and a National Day on October 12. Every city or town also celebrates the feast day of its patron saint with processions, dancing, and bullfights. Pamplona is known for its celebration of San Fermin, when bulls are turned loose in the streets. Barcelona's town fiesta, the Feast of La Merc, is marked by a week of celebrations. Madrid's Festival of San Isidro involves three weeks of parties, processions, and bullfights. The celebrations of Holy Week in many cities and towns of Spain include floats with scenes of the Passion and Death of Christ, and likenesses of the Madonna.

7 ● RITES OF PASSAGE

Baptism, first communion, marriage, and military service are considered rites of passage for Spaniards. The first three of these events are usually the occasion for big, expensive social gatherings in which the family shows its generosity and economic status. *Quintos* are the young men from the same town or village going into military service in the same year. They form a closely knit group that collects money from their neighbors to organize parties and serenade girls. In the mid-1990s, the government planned to replace required military service with an all-volunteer army.

8 ● RELATIONSHIPS

Spaniards are considered to be friendly and outgoing. It is customary to shake hands, and in a social setting women usually kiss their friends on both cheeks. Groups of young people go together to discos, organize parties and excursions, and date among themselves. The average citizen spends a

lion) are Roman Catholic. Many Spaniards observe baptism and other important Catholic rites but do not attend church regularly. A 1967 law guarantees freedom of religion. As of 1993, Spain had 300,000 Muslims, 250,000 Protestants, and 15,000 Jews. Spaniards, like the Catholics in other countries, believe strongly in divine help from the saints and especially from the Virgin Mary. *Cofradías*, Catholic lay societies devoted to particular saints, play an important role in religious life in many areas of the country.

6 ● MAJOR HOLIDAYS

Spaniards celebrate New Year's Day (January 1) and the major holidays of the Christian calendar. Other national holidays include St. Joseph's Day (March 19), the

A market vendor in Barcelona, Spain.

great deal of time outside of the house. There is an active street life; many people live downtown, frequent bars and restaurants, and go to bed late. Workers typically finish their day with a walk *(paseo)* with friends or family and/or visits to neighborhood bars for drinks, appetizers *(tapas),* and conversation. Dinner is often eaten as late as 10:30 PM.

Spaniards move from place to place less than Americans do. When Spaniards do move, it is typically for a job and many hope to return to their birthplace and settle there. Regional loyalties are usually strong.

9 ● LIVING CONDITIONS

Spain today is a consumer society that relies on credit cards. Spaniards love to go shopping and are interested in cars, gadgets, and entertainment. Cars are commonplace and have become a problem in big cities (due to limited parking, pollution, congested traffic, and car theft). The public transportation system in Spain is excellent. Consequently, many people who work in cities have moved to towns on the outskirts that are now part of suburbia. In the 1970s and 1980s there was a building boom, so there is no housing shortage. Rent and the price of apartments are high.

10 ● FAMILY LIFE

Today's Spanish families, much smaller than in the past, usually have two children. The mother has most of the responsibility for child-rearing. The father's relationship with his children can be formal and remote. When children reach adolescence, their relationship with their families changes based on gender. A teenage male, while continuing to honor his mother, begins spending much of his time with other young men. Teenage girls and their mothers tend to grow closer than ever. Even after a daughter is grown and married, her mother generally continues to play an important role in her life. Spanish people usually marry within their own social class. Only church marriages were recognized in Spain until 1968, when civil ceremonies were first allowed by law. Divorce has been legal since the 1980s. Women have an ever-increasing role in Spanish society.

11 ● CLOTHING

Both in town and in the country, Spaniards conform to the average European fashion standards. Boutiques and ready-to-wear shops can be found all over the country. Many young people wear sports clothes and blue jeans. However, the average Spaniard pays more attention to personal appearance than his or her American counterpart. Children who attend private schools wear school uniforms.

12 ● FOOD

Spain has a wide variety of regional dishes. As in other Mediterranean countries, Spaniards use lots of olive oil, fresh vegetables, and garlic. Galicia is known for its seafood and stews. Catalonia is known for its fish casseroles and for cured and smoked meats. The regional dish *paella* originated in Valencia and has become a national delicacy. It consists of a rice-and-saffron base and can include mostly seafood *(a la marinera)* or several kinds of meats *(mixta)*. Spaniards love cured ham *(jamón serrano)*, several kinds of sausage (including *chorizo* and *salchichón),* and cheese (especially a variety called *queso manchego)*. A wide variety of seafood is also popular. Spanish wine, champagne *(cava),* sherry, brandy, and beer are all excellent.

13 ● EDUCATION

School is free and required between the ages of six and fourteen. Secondary education or vocational training is available for students aged fourteen to sixteen. Private schools, mostly run by the Roman Catholic Church and subsidized by the government, educate nearly one-third of Spain's children. The adult literacy rate (ability to read and write) is estimated at 98 percent. Spain has thirty-one state-run universities and an increasing number of private ones. Students receive a diploma after three years of general study and a *Licenciatura* (degree) upon completing a program of specialized study lasting two or more years.

14 ● CULTURAL HERITAGE

Spain enjoyed a Golden Age of literature in the sixteenth and seventeenth centuries. *Don Quixote* by Miguel de Cervantes is widely regarded as the first great novel. It eventually became the most widely translated work other than the Bible. In modern times, poet and dramatist Federico García Lorca won international acclaim. Several

© Stephanie Maze/Woodfin Camp & Assoc.

Two men deep in discussion in a public square.

1828) were among Spain's great artists. In the twentieth century, great painters include Pablo Picasso (1881-1973), perhaps the single most powerful influence on twentieth-century art, as well as Joan Miró (1893-1983), Salvador Dali (1904-89), and others.

15 ● EMPLOYMENT

In the past, agriculture, livestock, and mining were the mainstays of the Spanish economy. Under the regime of General Francisco Franco, (1939-75) industrial expansion was emphasized and the bulk of Spanish employment shifted to industry. Jobs in the service sector (directly serving the public) were the most common, as of 1991 statistics, followed by industry. Agriculture and fishing together came in third. Typical crops grown in the north are potatoes, beans, corn, and vegetables. In the central areas, crops include wheat, soybeans, sunflowers, lentils, chickpeas, and grapes and other fruits. In the Mediterranean area, vegetables, rice, and fruits, especially citrus, are grown. Spain's fishing fleet is the largest in the world.

16 ● SPORTS

The most popular sport is soccer (called *fútbol*). League matches are played on Saturday and Sunday afternoons from September through May, with tournaments in the summer. Madrid has two teams in the top division, and Barcelona's team, known as Barsa, is world-famous. It forms the basis of a sporting club with more than 100,000 members, one of the oldest such clubs in Europe. Basketball and tennis are also gaining popularity as spectator sports. Spanish world-class champions today are cyclist Miguel Induráin, golfer Seve Ballesteros

Spanish authors, including playwright José Echegaray, poet Vicente Aleixandre, and novelist Camilo José Cela, have been recipients of the Nobel Prize. Musically, Spain gave the world the guitar. Great Spanish composers have included Isaac Albéniz, Enrique Granados, Manuel de Falla, and Joaquín Rodrigo. Spain has also produced virtuoso performers such as Pablo Casals and Andrés Segovia.

Spain is particularly known for its contribution to painting. In earlier centuries, El Greco (c.1541–c.1614), Diego Velázquez (1599–1660), and Francisco Goya (1746–

© Kim Newton/Woodfin Camp & Assoc.

The fiesta brava *(bullfight) is a popular form of entertainment throughout Spain. This ritualized fiesta involves grace, courage, and spectacle.*

and tennis players Arantxa Sánchez Vicario and Conchita Martínez. Participant sports include hunting and fishing, sailing, soccer, cycling, golf, horseback riding, and skiing.

17 ● RECREATION

The most characteristically Spanish form of entertainment is the bullfight *(fiesta brava)*. Popular throughout the country, this ritualized fiesta involves grace, courage, and spectacle. In an afternoon of bullfighting, six bulls are usually killed by three different matadors.

Young people enjoy going to the beach in the summer, and to the countryside and the mountains for hikes and picnics. In the evenings, they go dancing or have a drink with friends. The mild Spanish climate has encouraged an active night life, much of it outdoors in the streets, plazas, and sidewalk taverns and restaurants.

Spaniards go to concerts, to the theater, and to movies. People of all ages are fond of television, perhaps the main source of entertainment today.

18 ● CRAFTS AND HOBBIES

Spanish handicrafts include lace and leather goods, gloves, basketry, tapestries, carpets, wrought iron, ceramics, and products of gold and silver. Each region has specialties, including leather in Córdoba; lace and carpets in Granada; pearls in the Balearic Islands; and jewelry, swords, and knives in Toledo. The Spanish government has taken steps to assure that traditional crafts, or *artesanía,* survive against competition from mechanized industry. Spain is also known for its handmade musical instruments, especially guitars.

19 ● SOCIAL PROBLEMS

Terrorism by separatist groups, particularly Basque rebels, has plagued Spain in recent years. The nation has also faced major economic adjustments following its 1986 entry into the European Community (EC). Spain suffers from a high rate of unemployment, with a notably large percentage of unemployed university graduates. Finally, like the rest of the developed countries, Spain shares a drug problem, crime in big cities, and illegal immigration from Africa, Latin America, and Eastern Europe.

20 ● BIBLIOGRAPHY

Eames, Andrew. *Barcelona.* Insight Guides. Boston: Houghton Mifflin, 1995.
Fodor's Spain. Fodor's Travel Publications, 1996.
Hooper, John. *The New Spaniards.* Suffolk, England: Penguin, 1995.
Leahy, Philippa. *Discovering Spain.* New York: Crestwood House, 1993.
Steinberg, Rolf, ed. *Continental Europe.* Insight Guides. Singapore: APA Publications, 1989.

WEBSITES

Spanish Foreign Ministry. [Online] Available http://www.docuweb.ca/SiSpain/, 1998.
Tourist Office of Spain. [Online] Available http://www.okspain.org/, 1998.
World Travel Guide. Spain. [Online] Available http://www.wtgonline.com/country/es/gen.html, 1998.

Andalusians

PRONUNCIATION: an-duh-LOO-zhuns
LOCATION: Southern Spain
POPULATION: About 6.6 million
LANGUAGE: Castilian Spanish (Andalusian dialect)
RELIGION: Roman Catholicism

1 ● INTRODUCTION

Andalusia is located in southern Spain. It has a distinctive culture influenced by its hot Mediterranean climate, its historical tolerance of diverse ethnic groups (including Jews and Gypsies), and, most important, its long period of rule by the Moors. (Moors are Muslims who invaded from North Africa and seized control of the region in the eighth century AD.)

The word "Andalusia" is derived from the Moorish name for Spain—*Al-Andalus.* The Moors ruled all of Spain for three centuries, and Andalusia until nearly 1500. This period was a time of both cultural and economic wealth for the region. Andalusia reaped the benefits of Islamic advances in philosophy, medicine, the arts, and other fields, as well as the religious tolerance practiced under Moorish rule. In addition, the Moors brought to the region sophisticated irrigation and cultivation techniques that made the land bloom.

When Christian forces based in Castile finally drove the Moors out of Granada (a province in Andalusia) in 1492, their religion (as well as that of the Jews) was suppressed. Consequently, the rich cultural life that had flourished in Andalusia was largely destroyed. Much of the region's wealth was confiscated, and a long period of economic decline began. The conquering Castilians—warriors rather than farmers—let the extensive irrigation systems of the Moors deteriorate, turning the fertile farms into pastureland. Large portions of land were placed under the control of absentee landlords, and the *latifundio*, or large landed estates, became a way of life. This situation has continued to the present day, leaving Andalusia one of Spain's poorest regions. In addition, Andalusia never built a strong industrial base and continued to rely on outmoded farming methods well into the twentieth century. However, since the end of the repressive Franco regime (1975) and Spain's entry into the European Community (EC) in 1986, Andalusia has seen some economic progress. The Spanish government designated it as an autonomous region in 1985.

2 ● LOCATION

Andalusia is located in the southernmost part of the Iberian peninsula, between the Sierra Morena Mountains and the Mediterranean Sea. It is bound by Portugal to the west; the Spanish provinces of Extremadura, Castile-La-Mancha, and Murcia to the north; the Mediterranean to the southeast; and the Gulf of Cádiz to the southwest. Andalusia is the largest region in Spain, and also the least densely populated. It is a land of contrasts, containing Spain's highest mountains (the Sierra Nevada chain), its hottest lowlands (the Andalusian Plains), the white beaches of the Costa del Sol, and the Las Marismas marshes—home of the Coto Dona, a national park.

3 ● LANGUAGE

According to the 1978 constitution, Castilian Spanish, the language of the central and southern parts of the country, is the national language of Spain. It is spoken by a majority of Spaniards and used in the schools and courts.

NUMBERS

English	Spanish
one	un, uno
two	dos
three	tres
four	cuatro
five	cinco
six	seis
seven	siete
eight	ocho
nine	nueve
ten	diez

DAYS OF THE WEEK

English	Spanish
Sunday	Domingo
Monday	Lunes
Tuesday	Martes
Wednesday	Miércoles
Thursday	Jueves
Friday	Viernes
Saturday	Sábado

Andalusia also has its own regional dialect—Andalusian—that contains words derived from Arabic, reflecting the region's period of Moorish rule.

4 ● FOLKLORE

The development of bullfighting in Andalusia was preceded by bull rituals and cults. Bulls are found in stone carvings as well as in the prehistoric cave paintings of the region. The Catholicism of Andalusia has a strong element of belief in the miraculous. Some scholars believe it is possible to trace the region's devotion to the Virgin Mary to

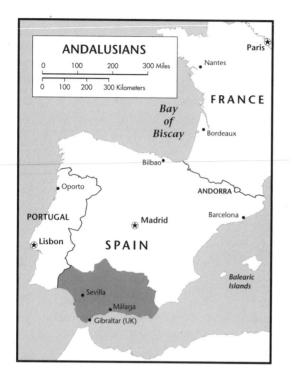

ANDALUSIANS

0   100   200   300 Miles
0   100   200   300 Kilometers

Paris

Nantes

FRANCE

Bay
of
Biscay

Bordeaux

Bilbao

Oporto

ANDORRA

PORTUGAL

Madrid

Barcelona

Lisbon

SPAIN

Balearic
Islands

Sevilla

Málaga

Gibraltar (UK)

Paul (June 29), St. James's Day (July 25), and a National Day on October 12. Additional festivals and celebrations of many kinds take place in the region throughout the year. The most famous is Seville's *Semana Santa,* or Holy Week, celebration, which begins on Palm Sunday and ends on Easter Saturday. On each day, up to eleven processions of floats pass through town, organized by members of religious brotherhoods called *cofradías.* The nighttime processions by candlelight are especially beautiful.

Seville is also noted for its *feria,* a type of fair. Seville's feria takes place shortly after Easter and lasts an entire week. During this time the town is on holiday and almost all normal business shuts down. The Monday following the festival, which is also a public holiday, is popularly called Hangover Monday *(Lunes de la Resaca).*

the mother goddesses of pre-Christian religions.

5 ● RELIGION

Like people in the other regions of Spain, Andalusians are overwhelmingly Catholic. They are particularly known for the colorful Holy Week *(Semana Santa)* celebrations held in their cities and towns. The Catholicism of Andalusians is distinguished by an especially strong belief in the power of intercession by saints and the Virgin Mary.

6 ● MAJOR HOLIDAYS

Andalusians celebrate the major holidays of the Christian calendar, as well as Spain's other national holidays. These include New Year's Day (January 1), St. Joseph's Day (March 19), the Day of St. Peter and St.

7 ● RITES OF PASSAGE

Baptism, first communion, marriage, and military service are considered rites of passage for Andalusians, as they are for most Roman Catholic Spaniards. The first three of these events are the occasion, in most cases, for big and expensive social gatherings in which the family shows its generosity and economic status. *Quintos* are the young men from the same town or village going into military service in the same year. They form a closely knit group that collects money from neighbors to organize parties and serenade girls. In the mid-1990s, the government planned to replace required military service with a voluntary army.

A village scene in Andalusia.

8 ● RELATIONSHIPS

In the cities, office hours begin at 9:00 AM and traditionally include an extended afternoon lunch break beginning at 2:00 PM. Workers then return to their offices from 4:00 to 7:00 PM. The day typically ends with a walk with friends or family or visits to neighborhood bars for drinks, *tapas* (appetizers), and conversation. Dinner is often eaten as late as 10:30 PM.

In greetings, it is customary to shake hands, and in social settings women usually kiss their friends on both cheeks. Young groups formed by co-workers, fellow students, or people from the same town go together to discos, organize parties and excursions, and date among themselves. It is not unusual to have lifelong friends known since kindergarten.

9 ● LIVING CONDITIONS

Reflecting the Andalusians' Moorish heritage, houses in the region have traditionally been designed with the goal of protecting residents from the heat of the sun. Often built of stucco with thick walls and few windows, Andalusia's older houses may also be built of stone. Windows overlook patios filled with potted plants. The house is often built around a shady central courtyard—sometimes including a fountain—in which the family can relax and cool off. Houses in Seville often have intricately carved wrought-iron gates over their doors and windows.

10 ● FAMILY LIFE

Most Andalusian households consist of nuclear families (parents and children only). Sometimes one or more grandparents are included. Women have almost exclusive responsibility for child-rearing. Male participation in domestic life is sharply limited, and fathers generally maintain a more distant and formal role. As elsewhere in Spain, there is a strict standard of modesty and chastity for women before marriage. In the 1980s, high unemployment in Spain forced many young adults to continue living with their parents. This led to a rebirth of the traditional formalized courtship, or *noviazgo*.

Married women in Andalusia maintain close ties to their mothers. Common-law marriages among laborers are not unusual. Only church marriages were formally recognized in Spain until 1968, when civil ceremonies were first allowed by law. Divorce has been legal since the 1980s. The tradition of *machismo*—the public assertion of masculinity—continues to define much of men's behavior. Andalusian women have a high degree of economic independence, and compete favorably with men for the region's scarce jobs.

11 ● CLOTHING

For everyday activities, both casual and formal, Andalusians wear modern Western-style clothing. However, traditional costumes can be seen at the region's many festivals and in flamenco dance performances.

Women's attire consists of solid-colored or polka-dot dresses with tightly fitted bodices and flounced skirts and sleeves. These are worn with *mantillas* (lacy scarves worn over the hair and shoulders), long earrings, and hair ornaments such as combs or flowers. Male flamenco dancers wear white shirts with black suits and broad-brimmed black hats.

During the Holy Week (*Semana Santa*) festivals, members of religious fraternities called *cofradías* wear all-white costumes consisting of long robes, masks, and high-pointed hats. These are similar to those worn during the Spanish Inquisition of the fifteenth century and later adopted by the Ku Klux Klan in the United States.

12 ● FOOD

Andalusians have a preference for extremely late meals. Lunch may be eaten as late as 5:00 in the afternoon, and dinner as late as midnight. Sometimes meals are skipped altogether in favor of *tapas*. These are snacks or appetizers eaten—with regional variations—throughout Spain. Tapas are, in fact, said to have originated in Andalusia. Popular tapas in all of Spain include shrimp-fried squid, cured ham, chorizo (spicy Spanish sausage), and potato omelettes (called *tortillas*).

The most famous Andalusian dish is *gazpacho*, a cold soup made with tomatoes, peppers, cucumbers, and olive oil. The other dish for which Andalusia is known is fish fried in batter, available at special shops called *freidurías*. A salad of lettuce and tomatoes is served with most dishes, but these are usually the only vegetables that accompany a meal. Andalusia's most popular drink is lager beer, served ice-cold.

13 ● EDUCATION

Andalusian children, like other Spanish children, receive free, required schooling between the ages of six and fourteen. Following this, many students begin the three-year *bachillerato* (baccalaureate) course of study. They may then opt for either one year of college preparatory study or vocational training. The University of Seville is highly regarded throughout Spain.

14 ● CULTURAL HERITAGE

The most important element of Andalusian culture is flamenco dancing. Flamenco dances, accompanied by a singer and guitarist, feature expressive hand and chest movements, clapping *(tapoteo)*, and foot tapping *(zapoteo)*. The greatest performances are said to be distinguished by a type of inspiration called *duende*. All performers strive for this quality. The authentic flamenco song, sung a cappella (without musical accompaniment), is the *cante jondo*, an anguished lament expressing love, sadness, and loss. The cante jondo has almost exclusively Arabic roots. When these songs are of a religious nature, they are called *saetas*. Another type of Andalusian folk song, and one which is very popular today, is the *sevillana*.

15 ● EMPLOYMENT

Andalusia is primarily an agricultural region. Important crops include various grains, sunflowers, and olives. Most of the region's farm laborers work on large estates *(latifundios)*. Here they perform largely unskilled, repetitive tasks such as sowing

© Kim Newton/Woodfin Camp & Assoc.

Girls in traditional dress at a flamenco festival in in the city of Seville.

and harvesting. Unemployment has always been high. In the mid-1980s, some 40 percent of the work force under the age of twenty-five was unemployed. Many people move to the cities to work in factories or they move to the coast to obtain jobs in the tourist industry. Such emigration is more common among men than among women.

16 ● SPORTS

The Andalusians share the rest of Spain's passion for soccer (called *fútbol*). The Spanish national sport of bullfighting originated in Andalusia, where Spain's oldest bullrings are located (in Seville and Ronda). At the beginning of the bullfight, or *corrida,* the *torero* (bullfighter) sizes up the bull while performing certain ritualized motions with his cape. Next the *picadores,* mounted on horseback, gore the bull with lances to weaken him, and the *banderilleros* stick colored banners into his neck. Finally, the torero confronts the bull alone in the ring. Exceptionally good performances are rewarded by giving the torero one or both of the bull's ears. Andalusia's other sports include tennis, swimming, hunting, and horseback riding.

17 ● RECREATION

In a region with extremely hot weather much of the year, Andalusian life moves at a leisurely and casual pace. Much social life centers around the neighborhood bars where one can relax with a cold drink and a plate of *tapas.* People also enjoy staying home and watching television, which is found even in the smallest village.

18 ● CRAFTS AND HOBBIES

In addition to their leather crafts, Andalusians are known for their ceramics, which are distinguished by the geometric designs that originated with the Moors. (Islamic culture prohibits the representation of living things in art.) The art of Andalusian builders and stone carvers has survived in such famous buildings as the Alhambra Palace in Granada, the Giralda Tower in Seville, and the mosque in the city of Córdoba.

19 ● SOCIAL PROBLEMS

Andalusia is a poor region with high rates of unemployment and emigration. Much of the land is concentrated in large holdings *(latifundios)* by wealthy (and often absentee) landowners. The wages of Andalusia's landless laborers, or *braceros,* are the lowest in Spain. They are subject to long, seasonal periods of unemployment, often adding up to half the year.

20 ● BIBLIOGRAPHY

Cross, Esther, and Wilbur Cross. *Spain.* Chicago: Children's Press, 1994.

Jacobs, Michael. *A Guide to Andalusia.* London, England: Viking, 1990.

Schubert, Adrian. *The Land and People of Spain.* New York: HarperCollins, 1992.

WEBSITES

Tourist Office of Spain. [Online] Available http://www.okspain.org/, 1998.

World Travel Guide. Spain. [Online] Available http://www.wtgonline.com/country/es/gen.html, 1998.

Basques

PRONUNCIATION: BASKS
LOCATION: Northwest Spain and southwest France
POPULATION: 3 million(2.5 million in Spain)
LANGUAGE: Euskera (Basque language); Spanish; French
RELIGION: Roman Catholicism

1 ● INTRODUCTION

The Basques are a single people who live in two countries—northwest Spain and southwest France. The Basques may be the oldest ethnic group in Europe. They are thought to have inhabited the southwestern corner of the continent since before Indo-European peoples came to the area approximately 5,000 years ago. Surviving invasions by the Romans, Visigoths, Arabs, French, and

Spanish, they resisted domination by outsiders until the Middle Ages (AD 476–1450). At that time, much of their territory was seized by Spaniards, Gascons, and Catalans. In 1516, the Basques on the Spanish side of the Pyrenees Mountains agreed to Castilian rule but won the right to keep a degree of self-government. By 1876, all Basque lands were divided between France and Spain.

During the regime of General Francisco Franco (1939–75) the Basque language and culture in the Spanish provinces were ruthlessly suppressed (prohibited). By the 1950s, resistance groups had formed, most notably the *Euskadi Ta Askatasuna* (ETA)— Basque Homeland and Liberty. The ETA committed terrorist acts throughout the 1970s and 1980s, even after Spanish rule over the Basques was liberalized following Franco's death in 1975.

Three of the four Spanish Basque provinces—Vizcaya, Guipúzcoa, and Navarra— were unified in 1980 as the Basque Autonomous Community. Its inhabitants were granted limited autonomy, recognition of their language and culture, and control over their schools and police force. However, the ETA—although representative of only a small minority—has continued to fight for full Basque independence. There has been little or no comparable activity among the French Basques, who have not been subjected to the same type of repression as those in Spain. However, separatist sympathizers on the French side have provided the ETA with material assistance and safe havens.

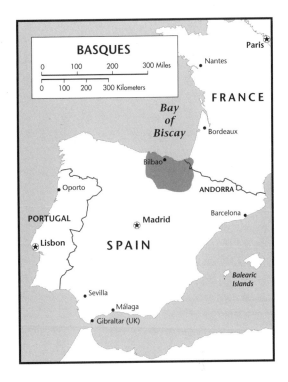

2 ● LOCATION

Basque country consists of four regions on the Spanish side of the Pyrenees (Vizcaya, Guipúzcoa, Navarra, and Alava) and three on the French side (Labourd, Basse-Navarre, and Soule). Basques call these territories collectively, *Euskal-Herria* (Land of the Basques) or *Euskadi*. It has been nearly a thousand years since these regions were unified politically. The area is geographically varied, containing the ridges and foothills of the Pyrenees and a short coastal plain along the Bay of Biscay (an inlet along the Atlantic Ocean), as well as steep, narrow valleys and mountain streams.

With some 3 million inhabitants (2.5 million in Spain and half 0.5 million in France), the land of the Basques is a densely populated area. Blood types and other genetic information suggest that they are an ancient people who inhabited the region long before the arrival of other European groups. According to a Basque saying, "Before God was God and boulders were boulders, the Basques were already Basques."

3 ● LANGUAGE

The Basque language, also known as Euskera, is Europe's oldest living language. It is unrelated to Spanish, French, or any other Romance language and belongs to no other known language family. It was the universal language of rural Basques until the end of the nineteenth century. At that time it had no written literary tradition. During Franco's regime in the mid-twentieth century, all Spanish regionalism (devotion to the uniqueness of one's own region) was suppressed. This caused the number of Basque speakers in Spain to decline sharply (as opposed to France, where the figures are higher). In recent years, Basques in both Spain and France have promoted—with some success—the use of their traditional language. Every province and town in Spain's Basque country has two official names—a Spanish one and a Basque one. Both appear on all road signs.

The Basque language is extremely difficult and complex. (Regional folklore has it that the Devil tried to learn Basque for seven years and gave up.) In addition, there are a number of different dialects. Basque is also rather exotic when contrasted with other Western tongues. For example, intensity may be expressed by repeating a word twice ("very hot" is *bero-bero*). This language feature is unknown among European languages but common among Polynesian ones. The language also lacks generic terms for "tree" and "animal": there are names for specific trees (oak, maple, etc.), but not for trees in general.

SAMPLE WORDS AND PHRASES

English	Basque
welcome	ongi-etorri
beach	hondartza
yes	bai
no	ez
see you later	gero arte
hello, how are you?	kaixo, zer moduz?

A common Basque proverb is "Happiness is the only thing we can give without having" (*Izan gabe eman dezakegun gauza bakarra da zoriona*).

4 ● FOLKLORE

Through centuries of storytelling, the Basques have evolved a rich and colorful mythology. In ancient times their land was supposed to have been peopled by a race of giants called *jentillak*. These giants lived side by side with human inhabitants until the coming of Christ. At that time they disappeared, leaving behind only one of their number named *Olentzero*. Today, Olentzero is a sort of folk icon or mascot who appears in the form of dolls and straw figures in processions, homes, and sometimes even churches. The *laminak* were female sprites, similar to leprechauns, who could wield either a helpful or harmful influence.

Basque folklore also encompasses various rituals and dances. The *Katcha-Ranka* is a dance performed in fishing villages. A person representing St. Peter is carried in a coffin through the village and to the waterfront. Dancers then symbolically beat him as a threat to ensure a good catch when they go out fishing.

5 ● RELIGION

Almost all Basques are Roman Catholic. Traditionally, an unusually high percentage chose to become priests or nuns. However, this number has fallen since the Second Vatican Council (1962), as has church attendance in general. Two of the Church's most renowned theologians, St. Francis Xavier and St. Ignatius Loyola (founder of the Jesuit order) were of Basque origin. Basque Catholicism, like that in many other areas of Spain, is characterized by a strong devotion to the Virgin Mary.

6 ● MAJOR HOLIDAYS

As elsewhere in Spain, most Basque holidays are those found in the Christian calendar. Special religious observances include St. Joseph the Workman's Day in May, and St. John of Compostela Day in August. In addition, villages celebrate their own festivals with performances by folk musicians, dancers, and *bertsolariak,* traditional singer/storytellers who can improvise and sing rhymes on any topic.

The famous running of the bulls in celebration of San Fermín takes place every year in the Basque town of Pamplona. Every day for a week, six bulls are let loose in the streets to run to the bullfighting stadium. Crowds of white-clad young men dare fate by running ahead of the bulls and swatting them with rolled-up newspapers.

7 ● RITES OF PASSAGE

Besides baptism, First Communion, and marriage, military service could be considered a rite of passage for Basques as it is for most Spaniards. The first three of these events are the occasion, in most cases, for big and expensive social gatherings in which the family shows its generosity and economic status. *Quintos,* the young men from the same town or village going into the military in the same year, form a closely knit group that collects money from their neighbors to organize parties and serenade girls. In the mid-1990s, the period of required military service had been greatly reduced, and the government planned to replace required military service with a voluntary Army.

8 ● RELATIONSHIPS

A special relationship developed in rural communities where families often lived on individual farms in relative isolation. This was especially true with the nearest neighbor, called the *lehen auzo,* or "first neighbor." The role played by first neighbors sometimes even goes beyond that of blood relatives. The best man and chief bridesmaid at weddings are chosen from the household of the lehen auzo. In addition, its members are informed of a serious illness or impending death before the family's closest relatives are told. In an emergency, the lehen auzo temporarily takes over the running of the neighbor's farm. When there is a death in the family, custom traditionally requires that the lehen auzo be informed before the village bell tolls. The wider neighborhood, or *auzoa,* is also an important source of social support.

9 ● LIVING CONDITIONS

People in the rural regions of Basque country live in large, stone farm houses called baserriak (the plural of baserria). They are often as high as three stories. Animals are kept on the ground floor, the family lives on the second floor, and hay and other crops are stored on the third. Baserriak may either be built at a distance from one another or located in clusters of about ten or twelve. In cities and towns, the Basques, like other Spanish urban dwellers, generally live in apartment buildings.

10 ● FAMILY LIFE

In rural areas, Basque households generally include either the maternal or paternal grandparents, as well as unmarried aunts or uncles. It is not uncommon for cousins, even first cousins, to marry. The most important concern for rural dwellers is the continuation of the family farm, or basseria. In every family, one son or daughter is designated from childhood as heir to the farm. When he or she gets married, ownership of the farm is transferred to the new couple as part of the wedding arrangements. All adults in the household participate in child-rearing. The whole family helps with the farm work, including children and grandparents, who assist with easier tasks.

In urban areas, the nuclear family (parents and children) is the norm, sometimes joined by an elderly grandparent or unmarried aunt. Families who can afford it may have a live-in nanny or servant.

11 ● CLOTHING

Basques wear modern Western-style clothing for both casual and formal occasions. The single most distinctive item of traditional Basque clothing—still worn throughout the country—is the flat, wide, black beret worn by Basque men. It is customary to dress in white and red during the Festival of San Fermín, which is the occasion for the traditional running of the bulls in Pamplona.

12 ● FOOD

The Basques are known for their excellent cuisine, much of which involves seafood. The Basque version of bouillabaisse, or fish stew, is called ttoro and includes mussels, crayfish, congers (eels), the head of a cod-fish, and three other kinds of fish. Other specialties include fresh tuna with tomatoes, garlic, and spices; txangurro (spider crab); and kokotchas, made with hake (merluza—a type of fish), garlic, and parsley. Gazpacho, a cold soup made with tomatoes, peppers, cucumbers, and olive oil, is common fare in all of Spain. Red peppers are a dietary staple and find their way into seafood sauces, chicken recipes, and omelettes. They are even strung across the walls of Basque houses as a decoration. Gateau Basque (Basque cake) is made from eggs, flour, sugar, and rum. A favorite national beverage is txakoli (also called txakolina), a fruity, white wine produced in coastal areas, often in small family cellars.

13 ● EDUCATION

School for the Basques, as for other Spanish children, is free and required between the ages of six and fourteen. Many students then begin the three-year bachillerato (baccalaureate) course of study. They may then opt for either one year of college preparatory study or vocational training. About one-third of Spain's children are educated at private schools, many of them run by the Catholic Church.

14 ● CULTURAL HERITAGE

Traditional Basque plays known as *pastorales,* which possibly related to medieval mystery plays, are still performed at festivals. In the fine arts, well-known Basques include writer and philosopher Miguel de Unamuno y Jugo, composer Maurice Ravel, and sculptor Eduardo Chillida.

15 ● EMPLOYMENT

About 20 percent of the Basque population is engaged in agriculture. The traditional farm holding, or *basseria,* is a family enterprise in which each household raises its own crops (corn, wheat, and vegetables) and livestock (chickens, pigs, cows, and sheep). However, certain resources, including pasture lands and fuel wood, are held in common by each village. Basque herders still follow the seasonal patterns of their ancestors. They move herds of sheep, cows, and goats up to mountain pasture lands from June to October while their wives take charge of the family farm. Fishing, a significant Basque industry, is undergoing modernization. However, one can still see women on the docks of fishing villages repairing nets with needles and thread.

The Basque country has long been known as a center of Spanish industry, especially the city of Bilbao. The region's history as the nation's iron and steel capital has led to the development of automobile and machine tool manufacturing. Shipbuilding is another profitable industry.

16 ● SPORTS

The Basque national game is *pelote,* a game like handball or squash played at very high speeds. The game has been played for centuries in an outdoor court called a *frontón,* which often shares a wall with the village church. Today, it is also played in indoor courts as well. The fastest form of pelote, called *cesta punta,* is played on an outdoor court with a second wall called a *jai-alai* (a term that has come to designate the game itself in countries throughout the world as its popularity has grown).

Another competitive sport popular among the Basques is rowing. Every fishing village has a thirteen-member team, and thousands attend the annual rowing championship at San Sebastián.

One of the most prized attributes among the Basques has historically been physical strength. This is displayed in the traditional Basque sports of stone-lifting (*harrijasotzaileak*) and log-chopping (*aizkolariak*).

17 ● RECREATION

Like other people throughout Spain, the Basques spend many leisure hours socializing with friends at *tapas* bars, which serve light food and drinks. They also enjoy each other's company at the more than 1,500 gourmet societies, or *txokos,* in their region. These are private dining clubs that were formerly male-only but now welcome women (although men still tend to do the cooking). Television is a popular form of relaxation. Spain has a private television station (TV Vasca) that broadcasts in the Basque language. *El mus* is a popular Basque card game.

18 ● CRAFTS AND HOBBIES

The traditional Basque decorative arts consist primarily of woodcarving and engraving on stone. Both are practiced mainly on door lintels (upper frames) and tombstones. The Basques have a well-developed tradition of oral storytelling, which was one of their main forms of entertainment before urbanization (and television). Basques would often invite their neighbors over for an evening of tale-spinning. Basque folk music is sung and played on traditional instruments including the *txistu,* a three-holed flute, and the bagpipe-like *dultzaina.* Dozens of folk dances have been preserved, and many villages have folk-dance groups that perform regularly. Two especially spirited dances are the *Bolant Dantza* (flying dance) and *La Espata Dantza* (sword dance).

19 ● SOCIAL PROBLEMS

The iron, steel, chemical, and paper industries of the Basque region have created a serious pollution problem in its cities. Motor vehicle emissions have made the situation even worse. There is considerable river pollution as well. Bilbao's metals industries must deal with outmoded facilities and increased competition from the European Community (EC). In 1994, the city's unemployment rate climbed to 27 percent. Clashes between ETA separatists and Spanish forces have left more than 600 dead in the past three decades.

20 ● BIBLIOGRAPHY

Collins, Roger. *Basques.* London, England: Basil Blackwell, 1990.

Facaros, Dana, and Michael Pauls. *Northern Spain.* London, England: Cadogan Books, 1996.

Westwood, Webster. *Basque Legends.* New York: AMS Press, 1977.

WEBSITES

Tourist Office of Spain. [Online] Available http://www.okspain.org/, 1998.

Castilians

PRONUNCIATION: cass-TIL-ee-uhns
LOCATION: central Spain
POPULATION: about 30 million
LANGUAGE: Castilian Spanish
RELIGION: Roman Catholicism

1 ● INTRODUCTION

The Castilians, who inhabit Spain's central plateau, have dominated Spain politically since the sixteenth century AD. The area traditionally referred to as Castile comprises two present-day regions: Castile-and-León and Castile-La Mancha. Its original inhabitants were Iberians and Celts who were later conquered by the Romans and the Moors. The *Reconquista*—the centuries-long crusade to drive the Moors from Spain—was centered in Castile. The region was known for its religious devotion and fierce warriors. The hero El Cid, who became the subject of an epic poem, modeled these qualities.

The Moors, who had occupied Granada (a province in Andalusia) since the eighth century AD, were finally expelled from the region in 1492. The marriage of Isabella of Castile to Ferdinand of Aragon in 1469 made Castile a center of political and military power. Castile also became the site of an engine of authority that eventually got out of control—the Spanish Inquisition, which began in 1478. The Spanish Inquisition was begun by Ferdinand and Isabella to investigate heresy (dissent from established church doctrine).

In the following centuries, the fortunes of Castile rose and fell with those of the country. Castile was caught up in the nineteenth- and twentieth-century struggles between supporters of the monarchy and those who desired the formation of a republic. In the twentieth century, Spain remained officially neutral in both world wars. Coming to power at the end of the Spanish Civil War (1936–39), the regime of Francisco Franco aided the Axis powers (Nazi Germany and its allies) in World War II (1939–45). As a result, Spain was left out of the Marshall Plan that aided in the postwar reconstruction of Europe. Predominantly rural areas like Castile experienced large-scale emigration. Since Franco's death in 1975 and the installation of a democratic regime (a parliamentary monarchy) in 1978, Castile has had greater opportunities for economic development. Spain joined the European Community (EC) in 1986.

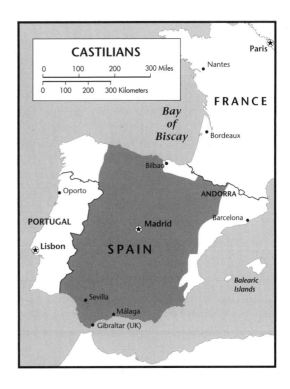

2 ● LOCATION

Castile is located within Spain's central plateau, or *meseta,* which accounts for approximately 60 percent of the country's total area. It is a region of hot, dry, windswept plains broken in places by chains of low mountains. There are few trees, and much of the terrain is covered by either *encinas,* which are similar to dwarf oaks, or scrub. The main bodies of water are the Duero and Tagus rivers.

Castile is thought to account for about three-fourths of Spain's population of approximately forty million people. Most Castilians are concentrated in major urban areas such as Madrid, Toledo, and Valladolid. The rural areas are much less densely populated, and their population continues to

fall as residents relocate to the cities or emigrate abroad.

3 ● LANGUAGE

Several distinct languages are spoken throughout Spain. However, Castilian (*castellano*) is the country's national language. It gained this status due to Castile's political dominance since the sixteenth century. Used in government, education, and the media, it is the language people in other countries identify as Spanish. Two of the main regional languages—Catalan and Gallego— are Romance languages that bear some degree of similarity to Castilian. Euskera, spoken in the Basque country, is very different both from Spanish and from all other European languages. Spain's linguistic differences have been a major source of political tension.

NUMBERS

English	Spanish
one	un, uno
two	dos
three	tres
four	quatro
five	cinco
six	seis
seven	siete
eight	ocho
nine	nueve
ten	diez

DAYS OF THE WEEK

English	Spanish
Sunday	Domingo
Monday	Lunes
Tuesday	Martes
Wednesday	Miércoles
Thursday	Jueves
Friday	Viernes
Saturday	Sábado

4 ● FOLKLORE

The Castilians' great hero was El Cid Campeador. An actual historical figure (Rodrigo Díaz de Vivar) of the eleventh century AD, his life passed into legend with the composition of the Spanish national epic, *The Poem of the Cid*. El Cid was a warrior of the *Reconquista* (the Christian reconquest of Spain from the Moors). He was celebrated for qualities that are still important to Castilians: a strong sense of honor, devout Catholicism, common sense, devotion to family, and honesty.

The Castilians traditionally describe their climate in the following proverb: *Nueve meses de invierno y tres mese de infierno* (Nine months of winter and three months of hell).

5 ● RELIGION

The Castilians, like the Spanish population in general, are overwhelmingly Roman Catholic. They are known for their adherence to Church doctrine and their high degree of religious observance. Many attend church every Sunday, and a number of women go to services every day. However, the traditionally strong influence of village priests over many areas of their parishioners' lives has declined in recent years.

6 ● MAJOR HOLIDAYS

Besides New Year's Day and the major holidays of the Christian calendar, Castilians celebrate Spain's other national holidays. These include St. Joseph's Day (March 19), the Day of St. Peter and St. Paul (June 29), St. James's Day (July 25), and a National Day on October 12. The most important religious holidays in Castile are Easter (March or April) and Christmas (December 25). In addition, every village observes the feast day of its patron saint. These gala celebrations include many distinctly secular (nonreligious) events, such as bullfights, soccer matches, and fireworks. Residents parade through the streets carrying huge papier-maché figures called *gigantes* (giants) and *cabezudos* (big heads or fat heads). The gigantes are effigies of King Ferdinand and Queen Isabella. The cabezudos portray a variety of figures from history, legend, and fantasy. Madrid's Festival of San Isidro involves three weeks of parties, processions, and bullfights.

7 ● RITES OF PASSAGE

Baptism, first communion, marriage, and military service are rites of passage for

Castilians, as they are for most Spaniards. The first three of these events are the occasion, in most cases, for big and expensive social gatherings in which the family shows its generosity and economic status. *Quintos* are the young men from the same town or village going into the military in the same year. They form a closely knit group that collects money from their neighbors to organize parties and serenade girls. In mid-1990s, the government planned to replace required military service with a voluntary army.

8 ● RELATIONSHIPS

Tempered by the harsh, barren landscape of their homeland, Castilians are known for toughness, frugality (not being wasteful), and endurance. Rural inhabitants are isolated by Castile's vast expanses of arid land and rely closely on their immediate neighbors. They live in small clusters of houses and tend to be suspicious of outsiders and of new ideas.

9 ● LIVING CONDITIONS

Although Castile contains large cities such as Madrid and Toledo, it is still primarily a rural region. Much of its population is dependent on agriculture. In rural villages, the traditional house combined the family's living quarters with a stable and barn that had a separate entrance. The kitchen was arranged around an open-hearthed fireplace *(chimenea)*. The most common building material is stucco, although stone houses are common among wealthier inhabitants.

10 ● FAMILY LIFE

Castilians tend to delay marriage until about the age of twenty-five. By this time, the

© Robert Frerck/Woodfin Camp & Assoc.
Plaza Mayor in Castile, Spain, features a unique architectural style.

couple has likely achieved a degree of financial independence. Courtships are carefully supervised, since any scandal reflects not only on the couple themselves but also on the reputations of their respective families. During the marriage ceremony, members of the wedding party hold a white veil over the bride and groom to symbolize the future submissiveness of the wife to her husband. Newlyweds are expected to set up their own household. However, it is common for the bride's parents to help them buy or build a house. Only church marriages were recognized in Spain until 1968, when civil ceremonies were first allowed by law. Divorce has been legal since the 1980s. A man is much more likely to divorce his wife than vice versa.

11 ● CLOTHING

For everyday activities, both casual and formal, Castilians wear modern Western-style clothing similar to that worn elsewhere in Western Europe and in the United States. Traditionally, black clothing was worn to church. The elderly in rural villages still observe this custom.

12 ● FOOD

Pork and other pig products—ham, bacon, and sausages—are staples of the Castilian diet. The region's most famous dish is *cochinillo asado,* roast suckling pig. Another popular dish is *botillo,* composed of minced pork and sausages. Beans of all kinds are a regional staple. *Tapas,* the popular snacks eaten throughout Spain, are also popular in Castile. Like people in other parts of Spain, Castilians take an extended lunch break at midday and eat dinner late—any time between 9:00 PM and midnight.

13 ● EDUCATION

Castilians, like other Spanish children, receive free, required schooling between the ages of six and fourteen. Many students then begin the three-year *bachillerato* (baccalaureate) course of study. Upon completion they may opt for either one year of college preparatory study or vocational training. Castile is home to Spain's oldest university—the Pontifical University of Salamanca, founded in 1254, as well as the one with the highest enrollment—the University of Madrid.

14 ● CULTURAL HERITAGE

Castile's literary tradition dates back to the twelfth-century epic poem *Cantar del Mio Cid* (Poem of the Cid), celebrating the life and exploits of Rodrigo Díaz de Vivar. He was a Castilian warrior who gained fame in the *Reconquista,* the campaign to drive the Moors from Spain. The fictional Cid, embodying the ideal Castilian, captured the popular imagination of generations. He eventually served as the subject of a play by the French playwright Corneille, and a Hollywood movie starring Charlton Heston. The most famous Castilian author is Miguel de Cervantes. He wrote the seventeenth-century classic *Don Quixote,* a masterpiece of world literature and a milestone in the development of the modern novel. At the turn of the twentieth century, the poet Antonio Machado wrote of Castile's decline from its one-time position of power in the following terms:

> *Castilla miserable, ayer cominadora, envuelta en sus andrajos, desprecia cuanto ignora.*

This translates as "Miserable Castile, yesterday lording it over everybody, now wrapped in her rags, scorns all she does not know."

15 ● EMPLOYMENT

Castilian agriculture consists mostly of small family farms that raise barley, wheat, grapes, sugar beets, and other crops. Many farms also raise poultry and livestock, and almost all farm families have at least one or two pigs. Income from the family farm is usually supplemented by a small business or by salaried jobs—often in government—held by one or more family members. Tourism is a major employer in the city of Burgos, and Valladolid is an industrial center and grain market. Food processing employs many workers in Salamanca.

16 ● SPORTS

The most popular sports in Castile are soccer (called *futból*) and bullfighting. Other favorite sports include cycling, fishing, hunting, golf, tennis, and horseback riding. Horse racing takes place in Madrid at Zarzuela Hippodrome.

17 ● RECREATION

Castile's warm climate has fostered an active nightlife in its cities. Much of the nightlife takes place outdoors in the streets, plazas, and sidewalk taverns and restaurants. After work, Castilians often go for a stroll *(paseo),* stopping to chat with neighbors along the way or meeting friends at a local cafe. A dinner date in Madrid may take place as late as 10:00 PM or 11:00 PM and be followed by a trip to a local club. Sunday afternoon is another traditional time for a stroll. Castilians, like people throughout Spain, also enjoy relaxing at home with their favorite television programs.

18 ● CRAFTS AND HOBBIES

Castilian pottery is typically decorated with brightly colored pictures of birds and other animals. Fine swords have been made of Toledo steel—famous for its strength and flexibility—since the Middle Ages (AD 476–c.1450). Craftspeople continue this tradition to the present day. Steel is inlaid with gold and silver, and intricate designs are crafted on swords, as well as on jewelry and other objects. The Spanish government has taken steps to ensure that traditional crafts, or *artenia*, survive against competition from mechanized industry.

19 ● SOCIAL PROBLEMS

As in Spain's other predominantly rural areas, Castile has suffered from a high rate of emigration in the years since World War II (1939–45). Between 1960 and 1975, the population of Castile-León declined from 2.9 million to 2.6 million people; that of Castile-La Mancha dropped from 1.4 million to 1 million. The Castilian provinces of Avila, Palencia, Segovia, Soria, and Zamora had smaller populations in 1975 than in 1900.

20 ● BIBLIOGRAPHY

Cross, Esther and Wilbur Cross. *Spain.* Enchantment of the World Series. Chicago: Children's Press, 1994.

Facaros, Dana, and Michael Pauls. *Northern Spain.* London, England: Cadogan Books, 1996.

Lye, Keith. *Passport to Spain.* New York: Franklin Watts, 1994.

Schubert, Adrian. *The Land and People of Spain.* New York: HarperCollins, 1992.

WEBSITES

Spanish Foreign Ministry. [Online] Available http://www.docuweb.ca/SiSpain/, 1998.

Tourist Office of Spain. [Online] Available http://www.okspain.org/, 1998.

World Travel Guide. Spain. [Online] Available http://www.wtgonline.com/country/es/gen.html, 1998.

Catalans

PRONUNCIATION: CAT-uh-lanz
LOCATION: Northeast Spain
POPULATION: About 6 million
LANGUAGE: Catalan
RELIGION: Roman Catholicism

1 ● INTRODUCTION

The Catalan people live in an area of northeast Spain called Catalonia. Historically, Catalonia also included Valencia, Andorra, the Balearic Islands, and the French department (or province) called Pyrenees Orientales. Speakers of the Catalan language can still be found in these areas. Following centuries of foreign rule, Catalonia became an independent political entity in AD 988 and united with the Kingdom of Aragon in 1137. Together, the two regions established an empire that eventually extended to Sardinia, Naples, Sicily, and Greece. After the marriage of King Ferdinand and Queen Isabella in the fifteenth century, the kingdoms of Aragon and Catalonia were united with Castile and León. After this union, the Catalans struggled for centuries to preserve their political and cultural identity.

By the nineteenth century, Catalonia had become a major economic power in Spain due to trade and industrialization. It has remained one of Spain's wealthiest and most developed regions. It has attracted large numbers of immigrants from the south throughout the twentieth century. During the years of Francisco Franco's dictatorship (1939–75), Catalan regionalism was suppressed and the local language outlawed. In 1979, Catalonia became an autonomous region with its capital at Barcelona. In 1992, it gained the international spotlight as host to the Summer Olympic Games.

2 ● LOCATION

Catalonia is located in Spain's northeastern corner. It is roughly the size of the state of Maryland. It is bound to the north by the Pyrenees mountains, to the east and south by the Mediterranean Sea, to the southwest by Valencia, and to the west by Aragon. The region is dominated by the Pyrenees. Catalonia is divided into four administrative provinces: Lleida, Girona, Barcelona, and Tarragona. A fifth region within Catalonia is Andorra, a small country jointly governed by France and Spain.

Catalonia has a population of approximately 6 million people, roughly 15 percent of Spain's total population. Much of the region's population growth—up from barely 2 million in 1900—is due to immigration. Over 25 percent of Catalonia's inhabitants live in Barcelona.

3 ● LANGUAGE

Catalan is the official language of Catalonia. It is also spoken in Valencia, Andorra, the Balearic Islands, and the French department (or province) of Pyrenees Orientales. Catalan is a Romance language like French, Italian, and Castilian Spanish. It is similar to the Provençal language spoken in the south of France. From the late 1930s to the mid-1970s, Catalan, like other regional languages in Spain, was suppressed by the Franco regime. Now the language can be heard on television and radio and is taught in the schools. Road signs in Catalonia are printed in both Catalan and the national language, Castilian. The most common Catalan names are Jordi (the equivalent of George) for men, and Montserrat and Núria for women. Catalan was the official host language for the 1992 Summer Olympics in Barcelona.

EXAMPLES

English	Catalan
beach	platja
good day	bon dia
please	si us plau
welcome	benvinguts
common sense	seny

4 ● FOLKLORE

Catalan folklore has been strongly influenced by Roman Catholicism. Saints and visions of the Virgin Mary play a prominent role in legends, tales, and customs.

5 ● RELIGION

The majority of Catalans, like most other people in Spain, are Roman Catholic. However, the role of religion has decreased in the lives of many people in the region. This is due to the industrialization and modernization of Catalonia, as well as to outside cultural influences. Most Catalans mark major events such as baptism and marriage with the appropriate religious ritual. However, many are not regular churchgoers. Religious minorities include Protestants, evangelical Christians, and Jews.

6 ● MAJOR HOLIDAYS

Catalans celebrate the standard holidays of the Christian calendar. Other religious dates include Epiphany *(Reis)* on January 6; Easter Monday, in March or April; the Feast of St. George *(Sant Jordi),* Catalonia's patron saint, on April 23; Pentecost *(Pasqua Granada),* in May; and several summer festivals marked by fires and fireworks, including the feasts of St. Anthony on June 13 (in Balears); St. John on June 24; and Sts. Peter and Paul on June 29. The Catalan national holiday is *La Diada* on September 11. The Day of the Dead *(Dia Dels Difunts)* is celebrated on November 2. Boxing Day (December 26) is also observed.

Towns and villages celebrate their patron saints' days every year in a "main festival," or *fiesta major.* This climaxes in an all-night dance. All Catalan festivals are marked by the dancing of the *sardana,* the Catalan national dance. Another typical feature is the presence of ritual figures called giants *(gegants)* and bigheads *(capgrosses),* enormous papier-mache forms that are carriend in processions. The grotesque bigheads are objects of jokes and mockery.

7 ● RITES OF PASSAGE

Besides baptism, first communion, and marriage, military service can be considered a rite of passage for Catalans, as it is for most Spaniards. The first three of these events are the occasion, in most cases, for big and expensive social gatherings in which the family shows its generosity and economic status. *Quintos* are the young men from the same town or village going into the military in the same year. They form a closely knit group that collects money from their neighbors to organize parties and serenade girls. In the mid-1990s, the period of required military service has been greatly reduced. The government planned to replace required military service with a voluntary army.

8 ● RELATIONSHIPS

The Catalans generally have a reputation for being hard-working, ambitious, and conservative. In contrast to the passionate flamenco of the Andalusians, their national dance is the stately *sardana*. They tend to regard themselves as European rather than Spanish. They spend little time in other parts of Spain, preferring to vacation either in their own region or abroad in France, Italy, or England.

9 ● LIVING CONDITIONS

Homes in northern Catalonia often house an extended family above a first floor that is used as a barn and/or storage area. Traditionally, Catalan homes and workplaces were often combined into a single building. This type of arrangement has become less common with urbanization and the spread of multistory apartment buildings.

10 ● FAMILY LIFE

Economic interests have traditionally played an important role in rural, and even some urban, marriages. According to custom, one son inherited all the family property. This resulted in the creation of many wealthy estates but also in a high rate of emigration. In cities, the nuclear family (parents and children) make up the household. In the country, a family may include grandparents as well as aunts and uncles. Men have a limited role in child-rearing, which is primarily the responsibility of the mother and female relatives or nannies. The last three decades have seen a weakening of family ties among many Catalans.

11 ● CLOTHING

Catalans wear modern Western-style clothing. Their tastes tend to be more conservative than those of their neighbors in other regions. Traditional male Catalan garb includes the distinctive *barretina,* a sock-shaped, red woolen hat that can be seen at festivals. It is often worn with a white shirt and black slacks and vest. Women's festive costumes include elaborate lacework in both black and white.

12 ● FOOD

Catalonia has a rich culinary tradition. The earliest Spanish cookbook in existence was written in the Catalan language in the fourteenth century. Typically Mediterranean fla-

© Stephanie Maze/Woodfin Camp & Assoc.
Dancers in Barcelona, Spain.

tomáquet, bread smeared with tomato and sprinkled with oil and salt.

13 ● EDUCATION

Catalan children, like other Spanish children, receive free, required schooling between the ages of six and fourteen. Many students then begin the three-year *bachillerato* (baccalaureate) course of study. Following this, they may opt for either one year of college preparatory study or vocational training. Schooling in Catalonia was dominated by the Catholic Church until the 1970s. An expansion of educational services followed the Franco regime. Study of the Catalan language is required in the region's schools.

14 ● CULTURAL HERITAGE

In art and architecture, Catalonia is especially prominent in connection with two widely separated periods: Romanesque, and modernist. The region contains some 2,000 buildings erected during the Romanesque period, which flourished from around AD 1000 to 1250. At the turn of the twentieth century, the modernist style was championed by architects including Antoni Gaudí, Josep Puig I Cadafalch, and Lluís Domènech. Great painters include Pablo Picasso, Joan Miró, and Salvador Dalí. Each has a museum in Barcelona devoted to his work. Well-known contemporary Catalan writers include Salvador Espriu and Llorenç. Prominent twentieth-century musicians from Catalonia include cellist Pablo Casals and opera singers Montserrat Caballé and José Carreras.

vors predominate in Catalan cuisine. These include olive oil, garlic, onions, tomatoes, nuts, and dried fruits. A favorite Catalan dish is *escudella I carn d'olla,* a boiled meal-in-a-pot comparable to the French *pot-au-feu.* Meats and sausages are simmered with vegetables; the broth is then served with pasta as a first course, with the rest served as the main course. Catalonians are fond of mushrooms. About six dozen edible varieties grow in their homeland. Mushrooms often appear sautéed as an appetizer *(tapas)* or as an ingredient in soups, sauces, and stews. A Catalan staple, eaten as a snack or a meal accompaniment, is *pa amb*

15 ● EMPLOYMENT

About 10 percent of Catalans in the labor force are engaged in agriculture, 45 percent in industry, and 45 percent in the service sector (jobs that serve the public directly). Catalan has a thriving tourism business. Much agricultural work is performed on small, family-owned plots. Fruits and vegetables are grown, and animals, including cattle, pigs, and sheep, are raised. Catalonia is one of the top five industrialized regions of Europe. Catalan industrialization began with textile production in the nineteenth century. Other important industries include chemicals, leather, construction materials, automobiles, and appliances. The region also has the greatest number of small, high-tech companies in Spain.

16 ● SPORTS

Soccer (called *fútbol*) is Catalonia's most popular participant sport. Fishing, sailing, and hiking or climbing in the Pyrenees are other favorite outdoor activities. Winter sports include Nordic and cross-country skiing, ice skating, and ice hockey. Squash, tennis, and golf are also widely played. The 1992 Summer Olympics were held in Barcelona.

17 ● RECREATION

Like other people in Spain, the Catalans enjoy watching television. The fine arts have played an important role in the Catalonian heritage. Catalans enjoy going to opera houses, theaters, and museums in Barcelona and other cities. Catalans generally vacation in their own region, usually going to the same place every year. They also enjoy traveling abroad to other European countries.

18 ● CRAFTS AND HOBBIES

The Catalan national dance is the *sardana.* It is performed at festivals and other special occasions throughout the country. Dancers form a circle, holding their clasped hands high in the air. Short, quiet steps alternate with longer, bouncy ones. The bands that play music for the sardana are called *coblas.* They consist of the *flabiol,* a three-holed flute that is played with one hand while the player beats a small, elbow drum called a *tabal;* woodwind instruments called *tenoras* and *tibles;* the brass *trompeta, fiscorn,* and *trombó;* and the *contrabaix,* or double bass. A regular sardana session, or *audació,* consists of half a dozen dances, each lasting about ten minutes. Marathon sessions called *aplecs,* however, include twenty-four dances played by three or four different coblas and last all day. Group singing is very popular among Catalans, and many belong to traditional Catalan choirs.

19 ● SOCIAL PROBLEMS

As Spain's most prosperous region, Catalonia has been spared many social problems. Catalan efforts to maintain cultural identity and independence have remained peaceful—unlike those of the Basques. The traditional Catalan family structure has been weakened in the postwar decades. Immigration to the region has resulted in social and cultural discrimination.

20 ● BIBLIOGRAPHY

Lye, Keith. *Passport to Spain.* New York: Franklin Watts, 1994.

Schubert, Adrian. *The Land and People of Spain.* New York: HarperCollins, 1992.

Williams, Roger. *Catalonia.* Insight Guides. Singapore: APA Publications, 1991.

WEBSITES

Spanish Foreign Ministry. [Online] Available http:/ /www.docuweb.ca/SiSpain/, 1998.

Tourist Office of Spain. [Online] Available http:// www.okspain.org/, 1998.

World Travel Guide. Spain. [Online] Available http://www.wtgonline.com/country/es/gen.html, 1998.

Galicians

PRONUNCIATION: guh-LISH-uhns
ALTERNATE NAME: Gallegos
LOCATION: Northern Spain
POPULATION: 2.7 million
LANGUAGE: Gallego; Castilian Spanish
RELIGION: Roman Catholicism

1 ● INTRODUCTION

Galicia is one of three autonomous regions in Spain that have their own official languages in addition to Castilian Spanish, the national language. The language of the Galicians is called Gallego, and the Galicians themselves are often referred to as Gallegos. The Galicians are descended from Spain's second wave of Celtic invaders (from the British Isles and western Europe) who came across the Pyrenees mountains in about 400 BC. The Romans, arriving in the second century BC, gave the Galicians their name, derived from the Latin *gallaeci*.

Galicia was first unified as a kingdom by the Germanic Suevi tribe in the fifth century AD. The shrine of St. James (Santiago) was established at Compostela in 813. Christians throughout Europe began flocking to the site, which has remained one of the world's major pilgrim shrines. After the unification of the Spanish provinces under King Ferdinand and Queen Isabella in the fifteenth century, Galicia existed as a poor region geographically isolated from the political center in Castile to the south. Their poverty was worsened by frequent famines. With the discovery of the New World in 1492, large numbers emigrated from the region. Today, there are more Galicians in Argentina than in Galicia itself.

Although Francisco Franco was a Galician himself, his dictatorial regime (1939-75) suppressed the region's moves toward political and cultural autonomy. Since his death, and the installation of a democratic regime (parliamentary monarchy) in Spain, however, a revival of Galician language and culture has taken place. A growing tourism industry has improved the region's economic outlook.

2 ● LOCATION

Galicia is located in the northwest corner of the Iberian peninsula. The region is bounded by the Bay of Biscay to the north, the Atlantic Ocean to the west, the River Mió to the south (marking the border with Portugal), and León and Asturias to the east. Galicia's coastline contains a number of scenic estuaries *(rías)*, which are drawing increasing numbers of tourists to the region. The area's mild, rainy, maritime climate is in sharp contrast to the dry, sunny lands of southern Spain. About one-third of Galicia's population live in urban areas.

3 ● LANGUAGE

Most Galicians speak both Castilian Spanish, the national language of Spain, and Gallego, their own official language. Gallego has come into much wider use since Galicia attained the status of an autonomous

GALICIANS

0	100	200	300 Miles
0	100	200	300 Kilometers

romance; clairvoyants, called *barajeras*; and the evil *brujas,* or witches. A popular saying goes: *Eu non creo nas bruxas, pero habel-as hainas!* (I don't believe in witches, but they exist!).

5 ● RELIGION

Like their neighbors in other parts of Spain, the vast majority of Galicians are Roman Catholic. Women tend to be more religious than the men are. Galicia contains numerous churches, shrines, monasteries, and other sites of religious significance. The most notable is the famous cathedral at Santiago de Compostela in La Coruña province. Santiago has been one of the world's great pilgrimage shrines since the Middle Ages (AD 476–c.1450). It is surpassed only by Rome and Jerusalem as spiritual centers of the Catholic Church. According to local legend, a shepherd discovered the remains of St. James here in the year AD 813. The central role that Catholicism plays in Galician culture is also evident in the tall stone crosses called *cruceiros* found throughout the region.

region after the end of Franco's dictatorial rule. Like Catalan and Castilian, Gallego is a Romance language (one with Latin roots). Gallego and Portuguese were a single language until the fourteenth century, when they began to diverge. Today, they are still similar to each other.

4 ● FOLKLORE

Galician folklore includes many charms and rituals related to the different stages and events of the life cycle. Popular superstitions sometimes merge with Catholicism. For example, amulets (charms) and ritual objects thought to ward off the evil eye are often available near the site of a religious rite. Supernatural powers are attributed to a variety of beings. These include *meigas,* providers of potions for health and

6 ● MAJOR HOLIDAYS

Galicians celebrate the major holidays of the Christian calendar. In addition, they celebrate the festivals of a variety of saints. Nighttime festivities called *verbenas* are held on the eve of religious holidays. Many Galicians also participate in pilgrimages, called *romer'as*. Secular (nonreligious) holidays include the "Disembarking of the Vikings" at Catoira. This holiday commemorates and reenacts an attack by a Viking fleet in the tenth century.

7 ● RITES OF PASSAGE

Besides baptism, first communion, and marriage, military service can be considered a rite of passage for Galicians, as it is for most Spaniards. The first three of these events are the occasion, in most cases, for big and expensive social gatherings in which the family shows its generosity and economic status. *Quintos* are the young men from the same town or village going into the military in the same year. They form a closely knit group that collects money from their neighbors to organize parties and serenade girls. In the mid-1990s, the period of required military service had been greatly reduced. The government planned to replace required military service with an all-voluntary army.

8 ● RELATIONSHIPS

Galicia is a mountainous land of ever-present rain and mists and lush greenery. The mood associated with the area is one of Celtic dreaminess, melancholy, and belief in the supernatural. There is a special term—*morriña*—associated with the nostalgia that the many Galician emigrants have felt for their distant homeland. Galicians are fond of describing the four main towns of their region with the following saying: *Coruña se divierte, Pontevedra duerme, Vigo trabaja, Santiago reza* (Coruña has fun, Pontevedra sleeps, Vigo works, and Santiago prays).

9 ● LIVING CONDITIONS

City dwellers typically live either in old granite houses or newer brick or concrete multistory apartment buildings. Outside of the largest cities, most Galicians own their own homes. They live in some 31,000 tiny settlements called *aldeas*. Each aldea numbers between 80 and 200 people. The aldeas are usually made up of single-family homes of granite. Animals are kept either on the ground floor or in a separate structure nearby. Hemmed in by Portugal, Galicia was historically unable to expand its territory. Consequently, its inhabitants were forced to continually divide up their land into ever smaller holdings as the population grew. Village farmhouses are distinguished by the presence of granite granaries, called *hórreos*. Turnips, peppers, corn, potatoes, and other crops are grown. Crosses on roofs call for spiritual as well as physical protection for the harvest.

10 ● FAMILY LIFE

The nuclear family (parents and children) is the basic domestic unit in Galicia. Elderly grandparents generally live independently as long as both are alive. Widows tend to remain on their own as long as they can, although widowers tend to move in with their children's families. However, this is less often the case since Galicians often relocate from their native villages or leave the region altogether. Married women retain their own last names throughout their lives. Children take their father's family name but attach their mother's after it. Galician women have a relatively high degree of independence and responsibility. They often perform the same kinds of work as men in either agriculture or trade. Over three-fourths of Galician women have paid jobs. Women also shoulder the bulk of responsibility for household chores and child-rearing, although men do help in these areas.

© Robert Frerck/Woodfin Camp & Assoc.

A scene near the river Camarinas in the Galicia region of Spain.

11 ● CLOTHING

Like people elsewhere in Spain, Galicians wear modern Western-style clothing. Their mild, rainy, maritime climate requires somewhat heavier dress than that worn by their neighbors to the south, especially in the wintertime. Wooden shoes are an item of traditional dress among rural dwellers in the interior of the region.

12 ● FOOD

Galician cuisine is highly regarded throughout Spain. Its most striking ingredient is seafood, including scallops, lobster, mussels, large and small shrimp, oysters, clams, squid, many types of crab, and goose barna-

cles (a visually unappealing Galician delicacy known as *percebes).* Octopus is also a favorite, seasoned with salt, paprika, and olive oil. *Empanadas,* a popular specialty, are large, flaky pies with meat, fish, or vegetable fillings. Favorite empanada fillings include eels, lamprey (a type of fish), sardines, pork, and veal. *Caldo gallego,* a broth made with turnips, cabbage or greens, and white beans, is eaten throughout the region. *Tapas* (appetizer) bars are popular in Galicia as they are elsewhere in Spain. Galicia is famous for its *tetilla* cheese. Popular desserts include almond tarts *(tarta de Santiago),* a regional specialty.

13 ● EDUCATION

Schooling in Galicia, as in other parts of Spain, is free and required between the ages of six and fourteen. At that time, many students begin the three-year *bachillerato* (baccalaureate) course of study. They may then opt for either one year of college preparatory study or vocational training. The Galician language, Gallego, is taught at all levels, from grade school through university. About a third of Spain's children are educated at private schools, many of them run by the Catholic Church.

14 ● CULTURAL HERITAGE

The Galician literary and musical heritage stretches back to the Middle Ages (AD 476–c.1450). The Gallegan songs of a thirteenth-century minstrel named Martin Codax are among the oldest Spanish songs that have been preserved. In the same period, Alphonso X, king of Castile and León, wrote the *Cántigas de Santa María* in Gallego. This work consists of 427 poems to the Virgin Mary, each set to its own music. It is a masterpiece of European medieval music that has been preserved in performances and recordings up to the present day. Galician lyric and courtly poetry flourished until the middle of the fourteenth century.

More recently, Galicia's best-known literary figure has been the nineteenth-century poet Rosal'a de Castro. Her poetry has been compared to that of the American poet Emily Dickinson, who lived and wrote at approximately the same time. Twentieth-century Galician writers who have achieved fame include poets Manuel Curros Enríquez and Ramón María del Valle-Inclán.

15 ● EMPLOYMENT

The Galician economy is dominated by agriculture and fishing. The region's small farms, called *minifundios,* produce corn, turnips, cabbages, small green peppers called *pimientas de Padrón*, potatoes said to be the best in Spain, and fruits including apples, pears, and grapes. While tractors are common, ox-drawn plows and heavy carts with wooden wheels can still be seen in the region. Much of the harvesting is still done by hand. Traditionally, Galicians have often emigrated in search of work, many saving for their eventual return. Those who do return often go into business, especially as market or restaurant owners. Galicia also supports tungsten, tin, zinc, and antimony mining, as well as textile, petrochemical, and automobile production. There is also a growing tourism industry, especially along the picturesque Atlantic coast.

16 ● SPORTS

As in other parts of Spain, the most popular sport is soccer *(fútbol)*. Basketball and tennis are also gaining popularity as spectator sports. Participant sports include hunting and fishing, sailing, cycling, golf, horseback riding, and skiing.

17 ● RECREATION

Like people in other parts of Spain, Galicians enjoy socializing at the region's many *tapas* (appetizer) bars, where they can buy a light meal and a drink. The mountains, estuaries, and beaches of their beautiful countryside provide abundant resources for outdoor recreation.

18 ● CRAFTS AND HOBBIES

Galician craftspeople work in ceramics, fine porcelain, jet (*azabache*—a hard, black form of coal that can be polished and used in jewelry), lace, wood, stone, silver, and gold. The region's folk music is enjoyed in vocal and instrumental performances. Folk dancing is popular as well. Accompaniment is provided by the bagpipe-like Galician national instrument, the *gaita*, which reflects the Celtic origins of the Galician people.

19 ● SOCIAL PROBLEMS

Galicia is one of the poorest regions in Spain. Historically, many of its inhabitants have emigrated in search of a better life. In the years between 1911 and 1915 alone, an estimated 230,000 Galicians moved to Latin America. Galicians have found new homes in all of Spain's major cities, as well as in France, Germany, and Switzerland. So many emigrated to Buenos Aires, Argentina, in the twentieth century that the Argentines call all immigrants from Spain *gallegos* (Galicians). In recent years, a period of relative prosperity has caused emigration to decline to less than 10,000 people per year.

20 ● BIBLIOGRAPHY

Facaros, Dana, and Michael Pauls. *Northern Spain*. London, England: Cadogan Books, 1996.

Lye, Keith. *Passport to Spain*. New York: Franklin Watts, 1994.

Schubert, Adrian. *The Land and People of Spain*. New York: HarperCollins, 1992.

Valentine, Eugene, and Kristin B. Valentine. "Galicians." *Encyclopedia of World Cultures (Europe)*. Boston: G. K. Hall, 1992.

WEBSITES

Spanish Foreign Ministry. [Online] Available http://www.docuweb.ca/SiSpain/, 1998.

Tourist Office of Spain. [Online] Available http://www.okspain.org/, 1998.

World Travel Guide. Spain. [Online] Available http://www.wtgonline.com/country/es/gen.html, 1998.

Sri Lanka

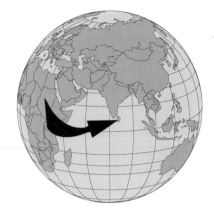

The people of Sri Lanka are called Sri Lankans. Ethnic groups include the Sinhalese making up about 74 percent of the total population; Tamils, making up 18 percent of the total. Other groups together make up almost 8 percent. A small group of Veddas, an aboriginal (native) tribe represent less than 1 percent.

Sinhalese

PRONUNCIATION: sin-huh-LEEZ
LOCATION: Sri Lanka
POPULATION: 15 million
LANGUAGE: Sinhala
RELIGION: Buddhist (Theravada); small numbers of Christians and Muslims

1 ● INTRODUCTION

The Sinhalese are the major ethnic group of Sri Lanka, an island located off the southern tip of India. It is believed that the Sinhalese are descendants of peoples that came from northern India and settled the island around the fifth century BC. The name *Sinhalese* reflects the popular myth that the people are descended from a mythical Indian princess and a lion (*sinha* means "lion" and *le* means "blood").

The ruler of Sri Lanka converted to Buddhism during the third century BC. Since that time, the Sinhalese have been mainly Buddhist in religion and culture. Ancient Buddhist texts provide stories of the early history of the Sinhalese people. By the first century BC, a thriving Sinhalese Buddhist civilization existed in the northern part of Sri Lanka. For some reason, this civilization collapsed in the thirteenth century.

Like many other peoples of south Asia, the Sinhalese later came under the influence of European nations. The Portuguese landed on Ceylon (the English name for Sri Lanka) in 1505 and soon gained control of much of the island. The Dutch replaced the Portuguese in the mid-seventeenth century, who were in turn driven out by the British in 1798. The island and its people formed part of Britain's Indian Empire until 1948, when Ceylon was granted independence. The country adopted the name Sri Lanka in 1972. Its capital is Colombo.

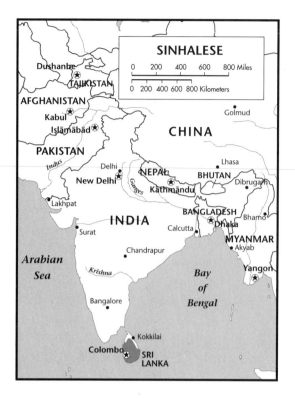

southwestern flanks of these mountains and the nearby lowlands are known as the island's "wet zone." These areas receive as much as 196 inches (500 centimeters) of rain per year from the southwest monsoon. The northern and eastern lowlands lie in the shadow of the mountains and form Sri Lanka's dry zone. In this area, rainfall averages less than 79 inches (200 centimeters) and drops below 39 inches (100 centimeters) in places. The island has an equatorial climate, with little variation in temperature throughout the year. Average monthly temperatures at Colombo range only between 71.6°F (22°C) in the winter months and 78.8°F (26°C) in the summer months.

3 ● LANGUAGE

The Sinhalese speak Sinhala, an Indo-Aryan language brought to Sri Lanka by the north Indian peoples that settled the island in the fifth century. Because it was geographically separated from other Indo-Aryan tongues, Sinhala developed in its own way. It has been influenced by Pali, the sacred language of southern Buddhism. To a lesser extent, it has also been influenced by Sanskrit. It also has borrowed words from Dravidian languages of southern India, mostly Tamil. Sinhalese is written in its own alphabet.

4 ● FOLKLORE

The Sinhalese have many legends about heroes and kings. When Prince Vijaya first came to the island of Lanka from northern India, so the tale goes, his men were imprisoned by the evil Kuveni, the queen of a Yaksha clan. (The Yakshas were a group of often demonic mythological creatures who possessed magical powers.) When Vijaya went to search for his men, he found Kuveni

2 ● LOCATION

According to 1995 estimates, the Sinhalese population is about 15 million people. This is about 80 percent of Sri Lanka's population. The Sinhalese are distributed over most of the island, except for the far northern districts near Jaffna and the eastern coastal areas where the Hindu Tamils live.

The island of Sri Lanka is 25,332 square miles (65,610 square kilometers) in area. It is separated from the Indian mainland by a strait only 22 miles (35 kilometers) wide. The main feature of the landscape is the Central Highlands, averaging more than 5,000 feet (1,500 meters) in altitude and reaching a maximum altitude of 8,281 feet (2,524 meters) at Pidurutala Peak. The

A Sinhalese newspaper.

and threatened to kill her. Kuveni, who had taken on the form of a beautiful maiden, begged for her life. She promised to release the men, give Vijaya a kingdom, and become his wife. Using her magic powers, Kuveni helped Vijaya destroy the Yakshas. Vijaya ruled as king in Lanka, the couple lived together for many years, and Kuveni gave birth to a son and a daughter. However, when a marriage was arranged for Vijaya with an Indian princess from the mainland, Vijaya banished Kuveni from his life. As she was leaving, Kuveni cursed the king for this, and as a result he and the ruler who followed had no children. A magical dance was needed to remove the curse.

5 ● RELIGION

Most Sinhalese people follow Buddhism. They accept the religion's basic concepts of *dharma, samsara, karma,* and *ahimsa.* Dharma refers to the Law (the teachings of Buddha); samsara, to the life cycle of birth-death-rebirth; karma relates to the effects of good or bad deeds on a person's rebirths; and ahimsa is the doctrine of nonviolence toward living things. Buddhists believe that these Four Noble Truths point the way to achieving *nirvana* (the Buddhist equivalent of salvation). However, the Sinhalese follow the southern or *Theravada* (also called *Hinayana*) form of Buddhism. This form remains true to the original teachings of Buddha, holding that there is no God, that Buddha was an ordinary mortal who should be respected but not worshiped, and that everyone is responsible for working out his or her own salvation. Buddhism is reflected in every aspect of daily Sinhalese life. Buddhist monks *(bhikkus)* play an important role in the Sinhalese community and often have a fair amount of political power. Monks serve the religious needs of the people, but Sinhalese people also worship at the temples *(devale)* of Hindu gods. The Sinhalese also believe in demons, ghosts, and evil spirits. They have a number of folk magicians to deal with such beings. Small numbers of Sinhalese are Christians (mostly Roman Catholic) or Muslims (followers of Islam).

6 ● MAJOR HOLIDAYS

Major festivals for the Sinhalese include the Sinhalese New Year in April and the *Vesak* festival in May, which commemorates the birth, enlightenment, and death of the Buddha. During the *Esala Perahera,* a two-week festival held in the city of Kandy, the Tooth Relic of the Buddha is paraded through the streets on the back of an elephant. Thousands gather to see the relic and its accompanying procession of decorated elephants, temple officials, schoolchildren, dancers, and acrobats. A fire-walking festival held at Katagarama attracts pilgrims from all over

Cynthia Bassett

Most Sinhalese people follow Buddhism. They accept the religion's basic concepts of dharma, samsara, karma, *and* ahimsa.

the island, as do other sacred centers of Buddhism.

7 ● RITES OF PASSAGE

Sinhalese rites of passage involve a mixture of Buddhist customs and folk traditions. In rural areas, difficulties in pregnancy are often blamed on evil spirits or black magic. A magician *(kattadiya)* may be called in to deal with the situation with charms and *mantras* (sacred words). The birth of a child is eagerly awaited, and male babies are preferred. The newborn baby is given a few drops of human milk with a touch of gold to endow the child with strength and beauty.

Offerings are made both at the temple and to Buddhist monks. There are few formal ceremonies. But the time when a child is taught to read letters (at about three years of age) is an important one.

No special rites mark a boy's reaching adolescence, but a girl's first menstruation is marked by a ceremony.

Death rites are fairly simple. The Sinhalese do not believe in the existence of a soul, but instead that a human being is a combination of five elements. At the time of death, these elements are dispersed (separated) and the most important one, consciousness, will be reborn in a new existence, according to the laws of karma.

If possible, *bhikkus* (Buddhist monks) are called to the bedside of a dying man to chant from the Buddhist scriptures. After death, the dead person's face is covered with a handkerchief and the big toes are tied together. Oil lamps are lit, flowers are spread on the bed, and religious books are read during the night. The body is prepared, then either cremated or buried. Bhikkus preside at the funeral ceremony, and a white cloth is offered to the leader of the bhikkus, who delivers a brief sermon. All those who attend the funeral take a bath to rid themselves of the pollution of death, and relatives gather for a simple meal. Close relatives wear white clothes, a sign of mourning in southern Asia.

8 ● RELATIONSHIPS

Ayubowan (greeting) is the word used by the Sinhalese when they meet or part. They usually also clasp their hands in front of them and bow slightly. The European style of shaking hands, however, is replacing traditional forms of greeting. Women often kiss friends and relatives on both cheeks.

The Sinhalese are well known for their hospitality in entertaining guests. Typically, the Sinhalese do not say "Thank you," but instead say something that translates roughly as, "May you receive merit."

9 ● LIVING CONDITIONS

Although many of the Sinhalese live in cities and towns, where their living conditions differ little from those of other city populations in southern Asia, the Sinhalese are by and large a rural people. They live in villages, hamlets, and isolated farmsteads scattered across the island.

A typical agricultural village is made up of a cluster of houses on slightly higher land surrounded by rice paddies. Nearby, especially in the dry zone, may be one of the many tanks constructed over the centuries to store water for irrigation. The village itself usually has a well, a temple, and perhaps a school and an informal clinic. Traditional building materials of mud (for walls) and thatch (for roofs) are being replaced by cement and tiles. Each house stands in a garden in the midst of coconut, mango, papaya, and other trees. In front of the house is a porch, where men sit during the day and sleep at night. A single door opens into the house, where women and children sleep. There are typically two rooms and a kitchen, but sometimes the fireplace is in a lean-to attached to the back of the house. Most villagers sleep on mats. Only the wealthier people have beds and simple wooden tables and chairs. Some households have their own well. Many houses have pit-latrines (toilets) dug in the garden.

10 ● FAMILY LIFE

The Sinhalese have *castes* (inherited social and economic status levels) based historically on occupation. But the system is much less rigid than the caste system in India. There are no Brahmans (priests), caste rankings are less significant, and in the cities caste observance is rapidly disappearing. Caste is, however, important in marriage. About half of the Sinhalese population belongs to the highest caste, the agricultural *Goyigama*. Other castes include washermen *(Hinna)*, metalworkers *(Navandanna)*, and drummers *(Berawa)*. The *Rodiya* (formerly traveling beggars) are considered to be among the lowest castes.

The Sinhalese marry within their caste, but they also have further limitations. Each caste is subdivided into *microcastes (pavula)*, and women must marry men of equal or higher status within the caste. Marriages are usually arranged, and cross-cousin marriages are preferred (that is, with a man's father's sister's daughter or mother's brother's daughter). Preparations include the casting of horoscopes and negotiation of the dowry (if any is to be paid). The actual ceremony is relatively simple. In some cases, there may be no formal ceremony.

The wife usually moves in with the husband's family, but couples who can afford it prefer to set up their own household. A woman takes on the responsibility of running the household. She may also work to contribute to the family income. Her main role, however, is to bear and raise children, preferably sons. In general, women are treated with respect in Sinhalese society.

11 ● CLOTHING

The traditional clothing of the Sinhalese is the *sarama*, a type of sarong (a wrapped garment). Men may wear a shirt with the sarama; when they go bare-chested, they throw a scarf around their shoulders. Women wear a tight-fitting, short-sleeved jacket with the sarama. In the cities, Sinhalese have adopted Western-style clothes. Women wear skirts and blouses, but they prefer the Indian *sari* for formal and ceremonial occasions.

12 ● FOOD

Rice, eaten with a serving of *curry* (a spicy dish), is the staple food of the Sinhalese. A family usually has three meals a day, although "morning tea" may be nothing more than that—tea, perhaps with rice cakes, fruit, or leftovers from the previous evening meal. Lunch consists of rice served with vegetable and meat curries and sauces such as *sambol*, a spicy mixture of grated coconut and chili, peppers, pickles, and chutneys. The evening meal is rice eaten with as many curry dishes as a family can afford.

Although orthodox Buddhists are strict vegetarians, many Sinhalese eat meat, poultry, fish, and eggs. Many Sinhalese dishes are cooked in coconut milk. A meal is usually followed by fresh fruits or sweets. Tea and coconut milk are the usual drinks. *Pan*, or betel nut (seed of the betel palm) eaten with lime, is taken after meals and often throughout the day.

13 ● EDUCATION

The Sinhalese literacy rate (the proportion of people able to read and write) is around 90 percent, among the highest of any community in southern Asia. Education is required up to the age of fourteen, and parents are responsible for making sure their children attend school. Education is free from kindergarten to the university level, but there is a shortage of places for qualified university applicants. The number of Sinhalese girls who remain in school to complete their educations is higher than average in southern Asia.

Cynthia Bassett

Sri Lankans are unique among south Asians in terms of literacy and educational levels. The overall literacy rate among the population over ten years of age is the highest of any developing country.

14 ● CULTURAL HERITAGE

The heritage of the Sinhalese is basically that of Buddhist civilization in Sri Lanka. This includes early literary works (the *Dipavamsa* from AD 350 and the *Mahavamsa from* AD 550) chronicling the history of Buddhism on the island. It also includes architecture, temple and cave paintings, and massive sculptures such as the 46-foot-long (14-meter-long) reclining Buddha at Polonnaruwa. The Sinhalese developed their own form of classical dance, usually performed by men, with rapid footwork and acrobatic movements. The "devil dancing" of the southern coastal lowlands developed from folk ceremonies to exorcise (drive away) demons. *Kolam* is a form of dance-drama involving masked dancers who retell stories from myth and legend.

15 ● EMPLOYMENT

About 80 percent of the Sinhalese people are rural and engaged primarily in subsistence farming (growing only enough to survive on). Sri Lanka's commercial plantations—producing tea, coconut products, rubber, cinnamon, cardamom (another spice), and pepper—provide some jobs for the population. Manufacturing industries in Sri Lanka are poorly developed and show only slow growth. However, the recently established clothing industry in a free-trade zone near Colombo now accounts for nearly half the value of Sri Lanka's exports. Sinhalese people in the cities and towns are engaged in government work, the professions, business, trade, and the service industries. Still, unemployment is a severe problem in Sri Lanka.

16 ● SPORTS

Sinhalese children play in the same ways as other young people in southern Asia—tag, hide-and-seek, dolls, marbles, and so forth. Indoor activities include board games and various string games such as cat's cradle.

Gambling is popular among adults, but many traditional sports such as cockfighting have been banned. Buffalo fights and elephant fights are still staged as part of Sinhalese New Year celebrations. Sports such as cricket, soccer, field hockey, and track-and-field were introduced by the British and are still played in schools and colleges. Cricket is by far the most popular spectator sport.

17 ● RECREATION

The Sinhalese have radio and television programming and can also see English and Sinhala movies. In rural areas, however, there is often little extra income to spend on such activities, so villagers relax in more traditional ways. They spend time sharing news with their neighbors and visiting local fairs. They go on pilgrimages and watch religious processions, folk dances, folk theater, and puppet shows.

18 ● CRAFTS AND HOBBIES

Sinhalese crafts include wood and ivory carving, stonework, and metalwork in brass, gold, and silver. Pottery and basketry are traditional cottage industries. Sri Lanka has been known for centuries for its gemstones; jewelry making and the cutting of sapphires, rubies, and semiprecious stones continue to this day

19 ● SOCIAL PROBLEMS

In terms of some social characteristics (health and education, for example), the Sinhalese are not typical of southern Asia. But they do face many problems of the region. Sri Lanka is basically an agricultural country, but growing enough food is a problem, and landlessness in rural areas is increasing. Unemployment and underemployment are serious problems, and slow industrial growth limits economic expansion and job creation.

None of this is helped by the continuing ethnic conflict between the Sinhalese and the Tamils on the island. Tamil separatists in northern areas around Jaffna are engaged in armed rebellion against the government, which is controlled by the Sinhalese. This has included random terrorism, the assassination of a prime minister, much loss of life, and constant charges of human rights violations. This rebellion creates a serious economic burden; in addition, millions of valuable tourist dollars have been lost. Until this conflict is resolved, it is unlikely that Sri Lanka can deal with its social and economic problems.

20 ● BIBLIOGRAPHY

Johnson, B. L. C., and M. Le M. Scrivenor. *Sri*

Lanka: Land, People, and Economy. London, England: Heinemann, 1981.

Wijisekera, Nandadeva. *The Sinhalese.* Colombo, Sri Lanka: Gunasena, 1990.

Yalman, Nur. *Under the Bo Tree: Studies in Caste, Kinship, and Marriage in the Interior of Ceylon.* Berkeley: University of California Press, 1967.

WEBSITES

Embassy of Sri Lanka, Washington, D.D. [Online] Available http://piano.symgrp.com/srilanka/, 1998.

World Travel Guide. Sri Lanka. [Online] Available http://www.wtgonline.com/country/lk/gen.html, 1998.

Tamils

PRONUNCIATION: TAHM-uhls

ALTERNATE NAME: Telugu

LOCATION: Sri Lanka (northeast area); India (Tamil Nadu region)

POPULATION: 67 million in India; 3 million in Sri Lanka

LANGUAGE: Tamil

RELIGION: Hindu majority; Muslim; Christian

1 ● INTRODUCTION

The Tamil name comes from "Damila." This is the name of a non-Aryan people mentioned in early Buddhist and Jain records. The Tamil have roots in western India, Pakistan, and areas farther to the west. The peoples of the Indus civilization spoke a Dravidian language around 2500 BC. Dravidian speech and associated cultural traits spread into southern India and northern Sri Lanka, especially in the centuries after 1000 BC. By the early centuries BC, a distinctive culture had developed.

Many Tamils settled in northern Sri Lanka in ancient times. Several south Indian kingdoms challenged Sinhalese rule of the island, including such dynasties as the Pandyas, Cheras, and Pallavas. An impressive Tamil civilization emerged under the Cholas, who ruled from the tenth to the thirteenth centuries. Chola sea power allowed them to bring Sri Lanka and even parts of Southeast Asia under their control. The fourteenth century saw virtually the entire region incorporated into the Vijayanagar empire.

After the British took control of India and Sri Lanka (then known as Ceylon), they established a plantation economy. Coffee, coconut oil, tea, and cinnamon were produced on the island. The British moved many Tamils to Ceylon to work on these plantations.

After Ceylon become independent in 1948, a Sinhalese government took control. It changed the name of Ceylon to Sri Lanka in 1972.

2 ● LOCATION

Most Tamils, about 67 million, live in India. Tamils, however, are a significant minority group in Sri Lanka (about 3 million) and live in other parts of Asia, as well as Fiji, Africa, the West Indies, Europe, and the United States.

Ancient literature describes the land of Tamils as stretching from Tirupati, a sacred hill northwest of Madras, to India's southern tip at Cape Comorin. Many Tamils in Sri Lanka identify with this homeland, which runs along the shores of the Bay of Bengal in India. The Western Ghats in India

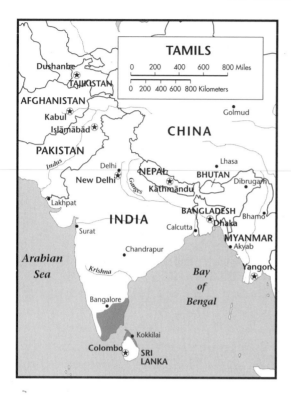

TAMILS

0   200   400   600   800 Miles

0   200 400 600 800 Kilometers

3 ● LANGUAGE

Tamil belongs to the Dravidian language family. Several dialects are spoken, including Pandya, Chola, and Kangu. The Tamil spoken by the Indian or estate Tamils also is considered a dialect. There is a difference between spoken and written Tamil. Tamil has two written forms—Vattelluttu (round script) which is used for everyday, and Grantha, a traditional script.

4 ● FOLKLORE

A highly venerated figure in south India is the sage *(rishi)* Agastya. According to legend, all the sages once gathered in the Himalayas. Their wisdom had so much weight that the earth started to sink. The sages asked Agastya, who was heavier than the rest, to go south so that the earth could rise to its original position. Agastya left, taking water from the sacred Ganges River with him. One day, a crow knocked over the pot holding that water. The water began to flow, forming the Kaveri, a river that Tamils consider holy.

5 ● RELIGION

Tamils are mostly Hindu, although some are Muslim or Christian. Tamil Hindus generally perform daily prayers *(puja)*. Shiva is the most important deity, although Vishnu and other gods are worshiped. Vinayaka, a form of the god Ganesha, is particularly popular. Tamils also give special importance to the Mother Goddess, a tradition that may date to the Indus Valley civilization. The Mother Goddess is worshiped as Durga, but also assumes the form of local *ammans,* or goddesses, such as Mariamman, who protects against disease. Many Tamils also

form the western boundary. The climate is tropical with moderately hot summers and gentle winters. Tamil Nadu, the modern state in India, receives about 31 to 47 inches (80 to 120 centimeters) of rain a year. This makes it a lush area.

Many Sri Lankans divide Tamils into two categories. One group is the Ceylon or indigenous Tamils whose ancestors settled on the island in ancient times. The other group, the Indian or estate Tamils, represents the descendants of the plantation workers whom the British brought from India in the nineteenth and early twentieth centuries. Tamils today make up approximately 18 percent of Sri Lanka's population.

worship village deities, and believe in such popular superstitions as spirits and the evil eye.

6 ● MAJOR HOLIDAYS

Although Tamils celebrate major Hindu festivals, the most important regional festival is Pongal. This mid-January celebration marks the end of the rice harvest. Newly harvested rice is boiled in milk and offered to Surya, the sun god. On the third day of the festival, cattle are decorated and worshiped, and bullfights and bull races take place. The Tamil New Year, in mid-April, is celebrated widely. Several shrines in the Indian state of Tamil Nadu are centers of pilgrimage. The island of Rameswaram, between India and Sri Lanka, is considered sacred.

7 ● RITES OF PASSAGE

Tamil superstitions shape life for pregnant women. They are not supposed to cross a river or climb a hill during pregnancy. During the fifth or seventh month of their pregnancy, women receive bangles or bracelets from their husband's families. After the baby is born, naming and hair-shaving ceremonies are performed.

Customs marking the coming of age of children vary. When a girl reaches puberty, Tamils celebrate with a feast.

Tamil tradition requires people to avoid saying that a person is dead. Instead, the person is said to have reached the world of Lord Shiva, to have attained a position in heaven, or to have reached the world of the dead. Tamil cremate or bury the dead, with burial being more common among lower castes. The body is prepared for the funeral

Cynthia Bassett

A Tamil dancer in traditional dress.

by being washed, perfumed, and dressed in new clothes. Families observe the anniversary of a death by gathering together, giving gifts to priests, and feeding the poor.

8 ● RELATIONSHIPS

Tamils use the typical Hindu *namaskar*, the joining of the palms of the hands in front of the body, to say hello as well as good-bye. Guests are entertained with coffee and snacks. When a visitor leaves, he or she generally says "I'll go and come back." The host responds, "Go and return."

9 ● LIVING CONDITIONS

Tamil villages are built near or around a temple. Priests (usually Brahmans) live in areas known as *agraharam*. Villages usually have a school, shops, shrines to local deities, and a cremation and burial ground. Wells provide water and a nearby "tank" or reservoir, catches and stores rainwater for irrigation. Individual houses vary from the one-room, thatched mud huts to two-story brick and tile structures.

10 ● FAMILY LIFE

A Dravidian emphasis on matrilineal ties (links with the wife's relatives) strongly influences Tamil family relations. Marriage between cousins is common, and the preferred match is with a man's mother's brother's daughter. In some castes, the marriage of a man to his sister's daughter is customary. Tamils marry within their caste. Marriages are arranged, and the bride's family usually pays for the wedding and a dowry. The actual ceremony usually takes place on a marriage platform with a canopy of thatched coconut leaves. Rituals include walking around a sacred fire, blowing conch shells, and throwing rice and colored water. The newlywed couple moves to the husband's village. Parents, children, and their elderly or unmarried relatives generally live together.

11 ● CLOTHING

Tamils traditionally wear the *dhoti* or loincloth. The dhoti is made by wrapping a long piece of white cotton around the waist and then drawing it between the legs and tucking it into the waist. Women wear the *sari* (a length of cotton or silk wrapped around the waist, with one end draped over the shoulder) and a blouse. Women wear their hair long, keeping it oiled and plaited, often with jasmine blossoms braided into it. They also wear gold jewelry. College-educated or career women may adopt Western styles, and many young men now wear shirts and pants.

Dress is an important indicator of caste, and many groups wear their clothes in a special style. For example, Tamil Brahman men wear the *dhoti* with the ends tucked in at five places *(panchakachcham)*. Tamil Brahman women wear a sari that is eighteen cubits long (a cubit is an ancient measure equal to about half a meter, or roughly eighteen inches), with the *kachcham* (the ends tucked in various ways). Non-Brahman women wear a shorter sari, without the tuck. Tribal women wear a smaller garment that reaches just below the knees, and they often leave the upper body bare.

12 ● FOOD

Most people eat three meals a day. Breakfast consists of coffee and items such as *idlis* (steamed rice cakes), *dosas* (pancakes made of rice and lentils), and *vadas* (fried doughnuts made from lentils). Lunch is boiled rice, curried fish or mutton, vegetables, *sambar* (a sauce made with lentils, vegetables, and tamarind), and *rasam* (a thin, peppery soup). The last dish served is usually curds, which is mixed with rice. The evening meal is a repeat of lunch, but with fewer dishes. People drink both coffee and tea, but coffee is more popular. Milk also is important. Non-vegetarians eat poultry, eggs, fish (including prawns), and mutton.

Some low castes eat pork, but this is taboo for Muslims.

13 ● EDUCATION

Tamil centers of learning date back to Buddhist times. The British colonial government and Christian missionaries emphasized an English approach to education during the nineteenth century. Education is seen as a step to a better job, and literacy among Tamils is quite high.

14 ● CULTURAL HERITAGE

Tamil literary traditions date to the first and fifth centuries when three literary academies, called *sangam,* flourished. Writings include epics and secular poetry, but the glory of Tamil literature lies in the religious works of medieval saints and poets. These involve two distinct traditions, one devoted to the worship of Shiva and the other consisting of the Vaishnavite hymns written by poets known as the Alvars. Tamil literature also flourished from the tenth to thirteenth centuries.

Bharata-natyam, one of the four great Hindu classical dance styles, evolved in Tamil region and so did Carnatic classical music. Tamil temples, with their towering *gopurams* (gateways), are well known in southern India. These temples are covered with large, carved statues of gods and figures from Hindu mythology.

Tamil folk culture includes oral literature, ballads, and songs performed or recited by bards and minstrels. Songs and dances are accompanied by music played on instruments such as the *tharai,* an S-shaped horn, and the *thambattam,* a type of drum. Folk dances include *Kolattam,* performed by young girls with sticks in both hands who rhythmically strike the sticks of the neighbors as they dance. *Kavadi* is a dance form as well as a religious act, in which pilgrims carry a symbolic structure (the kavadi) on their shoulders as they dance their way to the shrine of Subrahmanya, Shiva's son. In one dance, the dummy-horse show, the actors don the costume of an elaborately decorated horse and look as if they are actually riding on horseback. Various forms of folk drama and street theater are also performed for the amusement of the people.

15 ● EMPLOYMENT

Tamils work in agriculture, particularly in Sri Lanka. Rice and millet are the main food crop. Oilseeds and cotton are important cash crops. Tea is also grown in Sri Lanka. The Vellala are an important group of farming castes. In addition to cultivators, Tamils have a full range of trading, service, and artisan castes that pursue their traditional caste occupations. Fishing is important in coastal areas.

16 ● SPORTS

Tamil children play tag, leapfrog, and hide-and-seek. One particular game requires a player to stand on one leg and try to catch the members of the opposing team within a square playing area marked out on the ground. Another game is something like Simon Says. An adult says *Kombari, Kombari* (They have horns), and the children repeat this statement. The leader then goes on to list animals with horns. Occasionally a statement such as "elephant has horns" is made, and the children who repeat the incorrect statement are out.

Adult games include stick fighting *(Silambam),* wrestling, and *Thayam,* which is like chess. Tamils also enjoy Western sports.

17 ● RECREATION

Movies, and, more recently, television are the leading forms of entertainment. Even in rural areas, people tend to prefer them to the more traditional folk dances or street-corner theaters. The Tamil movie industry is centered in Madras, India.

18 ● CRAFTS AND HOBBIES

Every young Tamil girl learns a folk art known as *kolam.* This involves using the thumb and the forefinger to draw designs and floral motifs with a white powder. Kolam is drawn on the ground in front of houses, particularly on festive occasions. In India, Tamils are known for their handmade silk saris, pottery figures of various gods, bronze work, and brass and copper inlaid with silver. Painted wooden toys and cloth dolls are popular. Tamil artisans skillfully carve materials such as shell and horn. Woodworkers have made the massive, elaborately carved doors of temples, and they produce furniture such as tables with legs in the shape of elephant heads.

19 ● SOCIAL PROBLEMS

Tamils suffer discrimination and economic hardship in Sri Lanka. The government, which is led by Sinhalese, has established policies that prevent the teaching of Tamil in schools, keep Tamils from owning land, and deny the right of citizenship to the Indian or estate Tamils. Many have tried to leave the country and settle in Tamil Nadu in southern India.

Discrimination has led to a separatist movement in the northern areas around Jaffna. In this movement, Tamils are engaged in armed rebellion against the government. The ongoing conflict has produced a great deal of terrorism, the assassination of a prime minister (Rajiv Gandhi in 1991), and much loss of life. The Sinhalese government, however, continues to enforce anti-Tamil policies.

20 ● BIBLIOGRAPHY

Dolcini, Donatella. *India in the Islamic Era and Southeast Asia (8th to 19th century).* Austin, Tex.: Raintree Steck-Vaughn, 1997.

Kalman, Bobbie. *India: The Culture.* Toronto, Canada: Crabtree Publishing Co., 1990.

Pandian, Jacob. *The Making of India and Indian Traditions.* Englewood Cliffs, N.J.: Prentice Hall, 1995.

WEBSITES

Consulate General of India in New York. [Online] Available http://www.indiaserver.com/cginyc/, 1998.

Embassy of India, Washington, D.C. [Online] Available http://www.indianembassy.org/, 1998.

Interknowledge Corporation. [Online] Available http://www.interknowledge.com/india/, 1998.

World Travel Guide. India. [Online] Available http://www.wtgonline.com/country/in/gen.html, 1998.

Sudan

Native Sudanese include Arabs (an estimated 39 percent of the population); Nilotic or Negroid peoples, of whom the Dinka form the largest portion and constitute about 10 percent of the national population. In all, there are nearly 600 ethnic groups.

Sudanese

PRONUNCIATION: soo-duh-NEEZ
LOCATION: Sudan
POPULATION: 25 million
LANGUAGE: Arabic; English; 100 distinct indigenous languages
RELIGION: Islam; Christianity; indigenous beliefs

1 ● INTRODUCTION

The history of the Sudan, "Land of the Blacks," has been predominantly one of invasion and conquest. The earliest known events date back to 750 BC.

Between the years of 1898 and 1956 the Sudan was ruled primarily by Great Britain. The present boundaries of the People's Republic of the Sudan were finalized during this period by agreements between the British and other European nations trying to establish interests in the region. They largely disregarded local tribal, cultural, and linguistic boundaries. This disregard has been responsible for much of the contemporary political upheavals and distress in the Sudan. The country has been sharply divided between north and south, and people from the south have struggled unsuccessfully to either secede or gain a voice in the government.

In the forty years since independence (1956), three periods of parliamentary rule have alternated with three of army rule. The longest period of stability and prosperity was during the administration of Jaafar Nimeri (1969–85). In the first ten years of his presidency, Sudan's economy boomed. By the early 1980s, however, Sudan faced recession, drought, and political instability caused partly by large numbers of refugees from neighboring countries. Opposition to Nimeri quickly mounted when he introduced a severe form of the *Shari'a* (Islamic law). He was ousted in a peaceful coup (overthrow) in 1985. However, after a brief period (1986–89) of democratic rule the

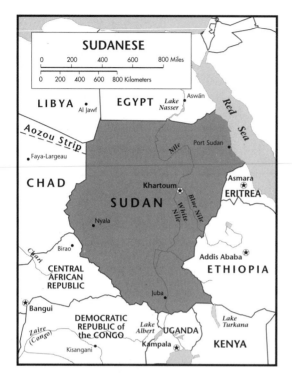

SUDANESE

| 0 | 200 | 400 | 600 | 800 Miles |

| 0 | 200 | 400 | 600 | 800 Kilometers |

LIBYA   •Al Jawf   EGYPT   Lake Nasser   •Aswān

Red Sea

Aozou Strip

•Faya-Largeau   Nile   Port Sudan

CHAD   Khartoum★   Asmara★   ERITREA

SUDAN   White Nile   Blue Nile

•Nyala

•Birao   Addis Ababa★

Chari   CENTRAL AFRICAN REPUBLIC   ETHIOPIA

Juba•

★•Bangui

Zaire (Congo)   DEMOCRATIC REPUBLIC of the CONGO   Lake Albert   UGANDA   Lake Turkana

Kisangani•   Kampala•★   KENYA

land. Its most important physical feature is the Nile River, which traverses the entire length of the country.

The Sudan has a population of approximately 25 million, with almost 600 distinct ethnic or tribal groups. The country remains predominantly rural, but towns have expanded rapidly since the Sudan gained its independence from Britain in 1956.

3 ● LANGUAGE

Arabic is the official language of the Sudan. Many other languages continue to be used in the home. At Independence, it was estimated that one hundred distinct languages were spoken in the country. Today, all educated people speak the local or colloquial form of Arabic—the language of government, schools, and of most northern Sudanese. In the south and west, English is spoken alongside the variety of indigenous languages, of which Dinka is the most widespread.

4 ● FOLKLORE

The Sudanese have a rich and varied folklore that embodies much of their indigenous wisdom. It continues to be passed on orally, at least in the countryside. Stories center on human rather than animal or supernatural themes. A favorite character in Muslim Sudan is Fatima the Beautiful. She outwits a variety of male relatives and rivals in a series of amazing feats. She usually ends up marrying the man of her choice, and often vindicates her whole family as well. Umm Ba'ula, the mother of bogeys, is a supernatural figure in warning stories told to small children. She bears a large basket for carrying away disobedient children.

army once again seized power. The country has since become increasingly isolated, both politically and economically. The civil war shows no sign of abating (as of 1998). Innocent bystanders from both north and south have lost their liberty and even their lives for attempting to disagree with the government's harsh interpretation of Islamic rule.

2 ● LOCATION

The People's Republic of the Sudan is the largest country in Africa. It is located in the northeastern part of the continent along the Red Sea and borders Egypt, Libya, Chad, the Central African Republic, the Democratic Republic of the Congo (former Zaire), Uganda, Kenya, Ethiopia, and Eritrea. Its landscapes include rocky desert, savanna (grasslands), and mountainous rain-

5 ● RELIGION

Sudan is now an Islamist state, and the majority of its population is Muslim. Islam was introduced to the northern Sudan by Arab traders in the seventh century AD. Islam coexisted for many centuries with an earlier branch of Christianity, though Islam ultimately absorbed it. Many peoples, particularly in southern and western Sudan, are not Muslim. Some are Christian, and others continue to practice indigenous beliefs.

6 ● MAJOR HOLIDAYS

The major holidays in the Sudan are religious holidays. In Muslim areas, the celebrations at the end of the fasting month of Ramadan and to mark God's sparing of Ishmael (the *Eid* of Sacrifice) are most important. They are marked with special foods, new clothes, and family visits. The birthday of the Prophet (the *Moulid*) is also celebrated. In Christian areas, the major holidays are also religious events. The day independence was gained from Britain is officially recognized on January 1.

7 ● RITES OF PASSAGE

The major rite of passage for most children in northern Sudan is circumcision. It is routinely performed on both girls and boys between the ages of four and eight. (Female circumcision is often referred to by outsiders as "female genital mutilation" and is becoming an international human rights issue.) After circumcision, gender segregation becomes marked. Young girls help their mothers and aunts with domestic chores and childcare. Young boys spend more time with male peers and enjoy a greater freedom.

© Betty Press/Woodfin Camp & Assoc.
Two women in Khartoum, Sudan.

Marriage is celebrated with great ritual even in poor neighborhoods. It is at least partly arranged, seen as an alliance between families rather than simply between two individuals. Payment of bride-price by the groom's family to the bride's family is an essential part of the marriage process.

8 ● RELATIONSHIPS

The Sudanese are intensely social people. Greetings are warm and often effusive. Accompanied by handshaking, the Arabic greeting *Izeyik* is exchanged, followed by

© Michael Yamashita/Woodfin Camp & Assoc.

A man builds a dwelling with the help of his friends and children.

inquiries about each other's health, *Qway-seen?* (Are you well?), to which the standard reply is to thank God—*Al-humdulilah.*

When greeting a man outside her own family, a woman is expected to keep her eyes down. In public, a woman generally assumes a more modest manner than within her home. The Western concept of dating is virtually unknown in Muslim parts of Sudan.

9 ● LIVING CONDITIONS

Although Sudan is regarded as one of the poorest countries in the world, its people have long found ways to accommodate their harsh environment. In the rural areas of the north, the mud-baked flat-roofed houses remain cool even in the hottest temperatures. In the south, conical grass huts provide warmth and safety from heavy rains and more variable climates. In towns and cities, housing ranges from European-style villas to make-shift huts and lean-tos (*rakuba*).

10 ● FAMILY LIFE

The family is at the heart of Sudanese life. Large families are universally desired. Women's roles are primarily those of homemaker and mother. An emphasis on male offspring and the male line is found throughout the country. Families are overwhelmingly patrilineal (tracing descent through the paternal line) and patriarchal (ruled by men). While nuclear families (husband, wife, and children) are becoming common, extended families are still found and are often polygynous (with more than one wife).

With the imposition of the *Shari'a* (Islamic law), patrilineal, patriarchal families and increasingly limited women's roles are the trend of the 1990s.

11 ● CLOTHING

Western-style clothing (long trousers, with a shirt) is commonly worn by Sudanese men in professional workplaces. Elsewhere they prefer traditional dress: long pastel-colored robes *(jalabiya),* a skullcap *(tagia)* and a length of cloth *('imma)* covering their head. Laborers wear baggy pants *(sirwal)* covered by a thigh-length tunic *(ragi).* Women in public today are bound to wear Islamic dress. For much of the twentieth century, this was simply a 30-foot (9-meter) length of material *(tob)* wound around their body. Today it also includes an Islamic shawl *(hijab)* pulled over the head, and may include a sort of heavy overcoat *(chadur)* common for women in Iran. In the privacy of their own homes, women simply wear light dresses.

12 ● FOOD

For most Sudanese, the staple food is *durra* (sorghum), used to make breads and porridges. These are eaten with various types of stew, beans, lentils, and salads. Sheep is the favorite meat. Meals are eaten communally and by hand from a round tray on which various bowls of food are surrounded by breads used for dipping. Meals are segregated by gender.

13 ● EDUCATION

Quranic schooling, based on memorizing the Quran (or Koran, the Islamic holy book), has a long history in the Sudan. Secular (nonreligious) formal education goes back only to the early twentieth century and is still not universal. Adult literacy (ability to read and write) is only 30 percent.

14 ● CULTURAL HERITAGE

The cultural heritage of contemporary Sudanese is particularly evident in their music. Singing, drumming, and dancing are indispensible to any major celebration. Western, Arab, and Indian, as well as African, performers have become popular through film, television, and radio.

Sudan's greatest novelist is Tayeb Salih. His novel *Season of Migration to the North,* which draws on his country's colonial experience, has been translated into many languages.

15 ● EMPLOYMENT

Despite massive migration to urban areas since independence, many Sudanese continue to work in agriculture. This includes both subsistence cultivation—growing sorghum, vegetables, peanuts, and beans for family consumption—and commercialized agriculture.

Agricultural work in Muslim areas is subject to gender segregation. In poorer families, females usually carry out tedious tasks such as picking cotton while males perform the heavier work of clearing the land, digging irrigation ditches, and planting. In families more comfortably situated, women are expected to work only inside the home.

16 ● SPORTS

Like many African countries, Sudan has a love affair with soccer. Most small boys learn to play, even if they have to use a wooden ball. Among the educated, tennis and (to a lesser extent) volleyball are played. Sudanese regularly compete against other African countries in most major sports but have yet to develop the resources for Olympic competition.

17 ● RECREATION

Television has become very popular throughout the country. Even in rural areas, the men's club usually owns a TV that village children are able to watch. Among the most popular programs are nightly soap operas (musalsal) and Islamic programs.

Open-air cinemas, found in all the towns and larger villages, are attended by mainly male audiences. Women spend their spare time visiting with friends and family, attending celebrations, or simply chatting quietly.

18 ● CRAFTS AND HOBBIES

Before marriage, a girl learns how to use specific homemade cosmetics including incense, oils, smoke-baths, henna decoration, and perfumes. These are believed to enhance sensuality. Throughout the country, people employ charms or amulets to stimulate fertility, as well as to decorate themselves. The most elaborate folk craft is basketry.

19 ● SOCIAL PROBLEMS

Since independence, the Sudan has undergone a series of upheavals that have intensified in recent years. The major problems stem from divisions between the Arab Muslims of the north and the Negroid, non-Muslims of the south; and the political and cultural domination of the whole country by the government. A civil war that broke out in 1983 shows no sign of abating as of mid-1998.

Desertification (increasing barrenness of the land) and widespread hunger are other problems. As crops wither on the stalk, whole villages have been abandoned and large numbers of animals have been left to die. Food shortages are common. In addition, there have been massive relocations of people to larger villages, to towns, and even outside the country.

20 ● BIBLIOGRAPHY

Deng, F. M. *Tradition and Modernization: A Challenge for Law among the Dinka of the Sudan.* New Haven, Conn.: Yale University Press, 1987.

Evans Pritchard, E. E. *Kinship and Marriage among the Nuer.* Oxford, England: Clarendon Press, 1951.

Gruenbaum, E. "The Islamist State and Sudanese Women." *Middle East Report* (Nov. 1992).

Holt, P., and M. Daly. *The History of the Sudan.* 3rd ed. London, England: Weidenfeld and Nicolson, 1979.

Karrar, Ali S. *The Sufi Brotherhoods in the Sudan:* Chicago: Northwestern University Press, 1992.

Kenyon, Susan, ed. *The Sudanese Woman.* London, England: Ithaca Press. 1987.

Kenyon, Susan, ed. *Five Women of Sennar. Culture and Change in Central Sudan.* Oxford,

England: Clarendon Press, 1991.

Mohamed-Salih, Mohamed A., and Margaret A. Mohamed-Salih, eds. *Family Life in Sudan.* London, England: Ithaca Press, 1986.

Pons, V., ed. *Urbanization and Urban Life in the Sudan.* Khartoum: Development Studies and Research Centre, University of Khartoum, 1980.

al-Shahi, A. and F. C. T. Moore. *Wisdom from the Nile.* Oxford: Clarendon Press, 1978.

Spencer, W. *The Middle East.* 4th ed. Guilford, Conn.: Dushkin Publishing Group, 1992.

WEBSITES

ArabNet. [Online] Available http://www.arab.net/sudan/sudan_contents.html, 1998.

World Travel Guide. Sudan. [Online] Available http://www.wtgonline.com/country/sd/gen.html, 1998.

Dinka

PRONUNCIATION: DEEN-kuh
LOCATION: Republic of Sudan
POPULATION: Over 1 million
LANGUAGE: Dinka
RELIGION: Monotheistic worship

1 ● INTRODUCTION

The Dinka are one of the largest ethnic groups in the Republic of Sudan. They belong to a group of cultures known as the Nilotic peoples, all of whom live in the southern Sudan.

In 1983, a civil war erupted in the Sudan, pitting the largely Arab and Muslim northern Sudan against the black African peoples of the south. Lasting into the 1990s, the war has had dire consequences for the Dinka and other Nilotic peoples. Tens of thousands of Dinka have died; countless others have become refugees. Rebel groups and international human rights organizations have accused the Sudanese government of attempting genocide against (extermination of) the Dinka.

2 ● LOCATION

The Dinka inhabit a vast region in the south of the Sudan that forms a seasonal swampland when the Nile River floods. Due to civil war, large numbers of Dinka have migrated from the southern Sudan to the northern Sudanese capital of Khartoum, as well as to Kenya, Uganda, Europe, and the United States.

3 ● LANGUAGE

Linguists classify Dinka as a major language family in the Nilotic category of African languages. The Dinka have a diverse vocabulary with which to describe their world. It is estimated that they have more than 400 to refer to cattle alone—their movements, their diseases, and their variety in color and form.

English	Dinka
cow	weng
beer	mou
husband	moc
wife	tieng
child	mieth

4 ● FOLKLORE

The Dinka tradition of oral literature is extensive and a considerable amount has been recorded. Two figures stand out prominently, Col Muong and Awiel Longar. Col Muong has an enormous appetite for all things in life. When he is hungry, he is said to eat an entire herd of cattle or an entire field of grain. Stories about him suggest that

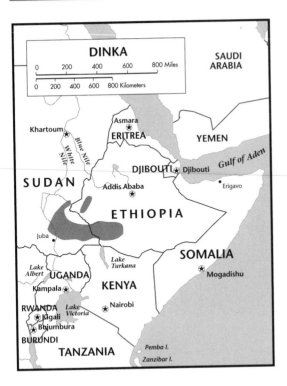

DINKA

SAUDI ARABIA

YEMEN

Khartoum

ERITREA

Asmara

DJIBOUTI   Djibouti   Gulf of Aden

SUDAN

Addis Ababa

Erigavo

ETHIOPIA

Juba

SOMALIA

Lake Albert   UGANDA   Lake Turkana

Kampala   KENYA   Mogadishu

RWANDA   Lake Victoria   Nairobi

Kigali

Bujumbura

BURUNDI

TANZANIA   Pemba I.

Zanzibar I.

people should do the best they can with what they have. Awiel Longar figures as the common ancestor of all Dinka peoples.

5 ● RELIGION

Dinka religion may be regarded as monotheistic (believing in one deity). *Nhialic* (creator) is thought to be the source of all life and death. Lesser manifestations of the creator's power are honored by the Dinka through ritual sacrifices. Rituals are performed at births, deaths, to cure disease, and in times of crisis.

6 ● MAJOR HOLIDAYS

Celebrations take place in the autumn when the whole tribe is together. To honor their traditional spiritual and political leaders, the Dinka enacted day-long ceremonies marked

by large public gatherings and the sacrifice of many cattle.

7 ● RITES OF PASSAGE

Birth, marriage, and death are all marked by standardized customs involving public ceremonies. These are typically accompanied by animal sacrifice. In the passage to adult status, young men, rather more than young women, are publicly recognized. Adult males decorate initiates' heads with a series of deep gashes that form permanent scars.

8 ● RELATIONSHIPS

When men become adults, they no longer refer to themselves by their birth names. Instead they adopt "ox-names"—derived from characteristics of their favorite cattle. Thus, a man may be known as *Acinbaai* (a man who never leaves his herd of cattle). Children's names often reflect the circumstances of their birth.

9 ● LIVING CONDITIONS

Traditionally, the Dinka dwelled in round clay huts with conical thatched roofs. Homesteads were typically surrounded by a garden and separated from each other by an open expanse of grassland forest. Garden soil would typically maintain its fertility for ten to twelve years. Following this, the area would be set afire and a new homestead erected nearby.

10 ● FAMILY LIFE

Polygamy (multiple spouses) is common among the Dinka. Men of high social standing may have as many as fifty to one hundred wives. In polygamous marriages, wives cooperate in performing household duties, although each rears her own children. Much of Dinka public life is dominated by men. However, women play a significant and even powerful role in local life.

11 ● CLOTHING

The Dinka wear very little clothing and no shoes. Men go naked, and the women may wear goatskin skirts. Both men and women wear strings of beads around their necks. Women also wear bangles on their arms and legs, and they may also wear elaborate jewelry in their ears.

12 ● FOOD

Dinka have traditionally produced all the material resources needed to sustain their livelihood via a combination of horticulture (gardening) with pastoralism (nomadic herding), fishing and occasional hunting. Millet is the mainstay of the Dinka diet. Depending on the season, it is supplemented with cow milk, fish, meat, beans, tomatoes, or rice.

13 ● EDUCATION

The Dinka lacked any formal system of education until literacy (reading and writing) was introduced via mission schools in the late 1930s. Even today, most Dinka lack the ability to read and write. The educational system has disappeared due to war.

14 ● CULTURAL HERITAGE

Song and dance play an important role in Dinka culture. A set of drums is found in every Dinka settlement. Artistic expression is associated with cattle, which they often imitate in songs and dances. There are also

battle songs, songs of initiation, and songs celebrating the tribe's ancestors.

Following is a typical Dinka song:

O Creator

Creator who created me in my mother's womb

Do not confront me with a bad thing

Show me the place of cattle,

So that I may grow my crops

And keep my herd.

15 ● EMPLOYMENT

Tending herds of cattle and growing millet form the basis of the livelihood and economy of the Dinka. Labor is clearly divided along gender lines, with men in their twenties and thirties devoting their time to cattle-herding. Women are responsible for growing crops, although men clear new fields for planting. Women also cook and draw water.

16 ● SPORTS

Dinka men engage in mock sparring, using spears or sticks and shields, in order to develop their fighting skills.

17 ● RECREATION

There is little time for recreation during the dry season, when much of the Dinka population disperses to follow the herds. Song and dance accompany social events such as marriages, which take place during the rainy season.

18 ● CRAFTS AND HOBBIES

Dinka men make spears and fishing hooks. Women make clay cooking pots using a coiling technique. Besides making pots, which are essential for carrying water, Dinka women also weave baskets and sleeping mats.

19 ● SOCIAL PROBLEMS

Since the civil war that began in the 1980s, numerous Dinka villages have been destroyed by burning or bombing. Thousands of Dinka women have been raped and their husbands castrated in their presence. Many Dinka have been abducted and sold as slaves in the northern Sudan. Violence against the Dinka is now on a level that has no precedent in their remembered past.

20 ● BIBLIOGRAPHY

Burton, John W. "Dinka." *Encyclopedia of World Cultures.* Boston: G. K. Hall, 1992.

Deng, Francis Mading. *Dinka Cosmology.* London, England: Ithaca Press, 1980.

Deng, Francis Mading. *Dinka Folktales: African Stories from Sudan.* New York: Africana Publishing, 1974.

Deng, Francis Mading. *The Dinka and Their Songs.* London, England: Oxford University Press, 1973.

Lienhardt, R. G. *Divinity and Experience: The Religion of the Dinks.* Oxford, England: Clarendon Press, 1961.

Ryle, John. *Warriors of the White Nile.* Amsterdam, The Netherlands: Time-Life Books, 1982.

WEBSITES

ArabNet. [Online] Available http://www.arab.net/sudan/sudan_contents.html, 1998.

World Travel Guide. Sudan. [Online] Available http://www.wtgonline.com/country/sd/gen.html, 1998.

Suriname

Suriname has one of the most diverse populations in the world. The two largest ethnic groups are the Creoles, mixed-race descendents of black plantation slaves (about 35 percent of the population), and the Hindustanis (about 33 percent), descendants of indentured laborers from India. The Bushmen (10 percent) are descended from Africans who escaped from the plantations into the forests of the interior. Other groups include the Javanese (about 16 percent), Chinese, and Europeans. The Amerindians (3 percent), Suriname's original inhabitants, include the Arawak, Carib, and Warrau.

Surinamese

PRONUNCIATION: sir-ih-nahm-EEZ
LOCATION: Suriname
POPULATION: 410,000 in Suriname; 200,000 in The Netherlands
LANGUAGE: Dutch (official); English; Spanish; Sranan; Hindi; Sranan Tongo (Taki-Taki)
RELIGION: Christianity; Hinduism; Islam

1 ● INTRODUCTION

Suriname became a British colony in 1650 and a Dutch colony in 1667. The Dutch made what has been called the worst land-swap deal in history. They took Suriname in exchange for Nieuw Amsterdam—or New York, as the British called it.

The Dutch imported west African slaves to Suriname to work on sugarcane and coffee plantations. Later indentured workers (contract laborers) were brought from Java, China, and India to work in the fields. It is

in this rich ethnic mixture that the modern Surinamese have their roots.

Suriname's journey from independence in 1975 has been marred by military coups, political repression, and guerrilla warfare.

2 ● LOCATION

Formerly called Dutch Guiana, Suriname is the smallest country in South America. It also has the smallest population, estimated at 410,000 in 1990. Located on the north-central coast of South America, it has an area of 63,251 square miles (163,820 square kilometers). Suriname has a narrow coastal plain. Much of it is swampy and requires drainage systems and dikes. Low, forested mountain ranges cover 80 percent of the country.

3 ● LANGUAGE

The official language of Suriname is Dutch, but many people speak English. Sranan (a

SURINAMESE

0   250   500   750 Miles

0   250   500   750 Kilometers

ATLANTIC
OCEAN

TRINIDAD AND
TOBAGO

Caracas

Orinoco   Ciudad Guayana

VENEZUELA   Georgetown
GUYANA   Paramaribo

Cayenne

SURINAME   French Guiana
(FRANCE)

Macapá

Negro   Amazon   Belém

Manaus   Santarém

Amazon   Tocantins

BRAZIL

Pôrto Velho

Rio Branco

lai tori riddles are overwhelmingly of African origin.

5 ● RELIGION

The main religion in Suriname is Christianity, followed by Hinduism and Islam. Some Christian groups also follow traditional African practices such as Obeah and Winti. Winti is a largely secret religion from West Africa. It recognizes a multitude of gods and ghosts, each having its own myths, rites, offerings, taboos (forbidden acts), and magical forces.

6 ● MAJOR HOLIDAYS

The Muslim holiday *Eid al-Fitr* celebrates the end of fasting during Ramadan. The Hindu festival of *Holi Phagwa* is a lively event. Water, paint, and colored powder are thrown into the streets at people passing by. Independence Day, a major national holiday, is on November 25.

7 ● RITES OF PASSAGE

Naming ceremonies at birth are important among Surinamese of all religions. Wedding ceremonies are elaborate and colorful, with generous feasting. Circumcision of males is practiced by Muslims.

Hindus practice a birth ceremony called *jatakarma*. Traditionally it takes place before the umbilical cord is cut. The naming ceremony occurs ten days after the child is born. The different Christian sects baptize children according to their own religious traditions.

8 ● RELATIONSHIPS

Hindus in Suriname do not observe the caste system of the villages of India. How-

Creole language), Hindi, and other Asian Indian, African, and Amerindian languages are also spoken. Altogether, twenty-two languages are spoken. The most common language is Sranan Tongo, also called Taki-Taki. It combines elements of English, Dutch, and several African languages.

4 ● FOLKLORE

Many Surinamese folk tales are based on African traditions. They emphasize the African belief in the unity between all forms of life. They also stress the continuing link between the living and the dead. Many of the stories take place in Africa. One particular type of folktale involves a cunning spider who outwits humans and animals. Riddles play an important part in Creole folklore. Despite European influence, the

ever, Brahmins (people of the highest-ranking Brahmic caste) retain their special religious role, interpreting sacred rituals and Sanscrit texts.

Anyone visiting a friend or acquaintance is expected to call on everyone they know in the same neighborhood. Not to do so is considered extremely rude.

9 ● LIVING CONDITIONS

Life expectancy is sixty-eight years for men and seventy-three for women, among the highest in South America.

The country's economy suffered during the 1980s because of political instability. Health is generally good. Sanitary conditions and nutrition are generally adequate.

10 ● FAMILY LIFE

Many of the Maroons (who are descended from escaped black African slaves) have more than one wife. Care of their children is entrusted to one parent at a time. Children spend their first four to six years with their mother. Many are then given to the father or another relative. There may be further shifts at later ages based on the child's developing needs or the parents' situation.

11 ● CLOTHING

Many of the Javanese women in Suriname still wear sarongs as they would in Indonesia. The Creole women continue to wear the *kotomissie*, a traditional costume. It includes a handkerchief called an *angisa*.

12 ● FOOD

The food of Suriname reflects the country's ethnic diversity. *Warungs*—Javanese food

Anne Kalosh

Diners at a lodge on Kumalu Island, Suriname. Surinamese cuisine reflects the ethnic diversity of the population, which includes Javanese and Creole influences.

stalls—serve *bami goreng* (fried noodles) and *nasi goreng* (fried rice). Creole food uses tubers, such as cassava and sweet potatoes. Plantains, similar to bananas, are eaten with chicken and seafood, including shrimp.

Rice is the staple diet for most people. *Pom* is puréed taro root, spiced and served with *kip* (chicken). *Moksie alesie* is a rice dish with meat, chicken, white beans, tomatoes, peppers, and spices.

13 ● EDUCATION

Education is free and compulsory from the age of six years to twelve years. Most students leaving primary education continue into secondary school. Higher education is provided by the government at the Anton de Kom University. Literacy rates (percent of the population who can read and write) are about 95 percent for both men and women.

14 ● CULTURAL HERITAGE

Drums are used to accompany the intense dancing during competitions known as "dance feasts." The drums of the Maroons must never be touched by a female.

At night the mellow sounds of metallic music are heard in the capital city, Paramaribo. This is the famous traditional Javanese "gamelan" music.

15 ● EMPLOYMENT

The Asian Indians are mostly small farmers. Creoles in urban areas work mostly in retail, politics, and the professions. The Javanese work mainly on Dutch-owned plantations. Many families depend on relatives in the Netherlands who send home money. Some Surinamese add to their incomes by working illegally in neighboring Guyana and French Guiana. There are no unemployment benefits or other social welfare benefits.

16 ● SPORTS

Soccer is played in towns and villages everywhere. A great hero of the game is Ruud Gullit, of Suriname descent. He became the captain of the Dutch national team. Another popular sport is swimming.

17 ● RECREATION

Birdsong competitions are held in parks and public plazas on Sundays and holidays. People carrying their songbirds (usually small black tua-tuas) in cages are a frequent sight on the streets of Paramaribo. They may be on the way to a training session or simply taking the bird for a stroll.

Young people enjoy outings, sporting events, and movies, as well as dancing.

18 ● CRAFTS AND HOBBIES

Many of the Maroons' huts display the fine woodcarvings for which they are famous and that adorn furniture, tools, and boots. The Afro-centered Maroon culture is also known for its sculpture.

19 ● SOCIAL PROBLEMS

Certain parts of the interior are controlled by groups of armed rebels. Warfare has driven many refugees from Maroon villages across the border into camps in French Guiana.

The country is also undergoing a continuing economic crisis. Inflation was around 54 percent by mid-1993 and was heading toward 100 percent.

20 ● BIBLIOGRAPHY

Beatty, Noelle B. *Suriname,* Major World Nations. New York: Chelsea House Pub., 1997.

Chin, Henk E. *Surinam: Politics, Economics, and Society.* New York: F. Pinter, 1987.

Hoefte, Rosemarijn. *Suriname.* Santa Barbara, Calif.: Clio Press, 1990.

Lieberg, C. *Suriname.* Chicago: Children's Press, 1995.

Sedoc-Dahlberg, Betty. *The Dutch Caribbean: Prospects for Democracy.* New York: Gordon and Breach, 1990.

WEBSITES

World Travel Guide. Suriname. [Online] Available http://www.wtgonline.com/country/sr/gen.html, 1998.

Swaziland

The people of Swaziland are called Swazis. There are more than seventy clans, of which the Nkosi Dlamini—the royal clan—is dominant. There are small groups of Europeans, Asians, and people of mixed race.

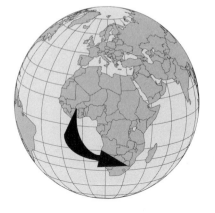

Swazis

PRONUNCIATION: SWAH-zeez
LOCATION: Swaziland
POPULATION: About 1 million
LANGUAGE: SiSwati
RELIGION: Christianity (various sects); traditional religious beliefs

1 ● INTRODUCTION

In the late sixteenth century, the first Swazi king, Ngwane II, settled southeast of modern-day Swaziland. His grandson, Sobhuza I, unified the resident Nguni and Sotho people within a central government. Swaziland became a British protectorate following the Anglo-Boer War of 1899–1902. It became an independent nation in 1968.

2 ● LOCATION

The Swazi reside primarily in Swaziland. It is a small landlocked country of 6,704 square miles (17,363 square kilometers) in southern Africa. There are four distinctive levels of terrain: the highveld, middleveld, lowveld, and the Lubombo mountain range. (A veld is a grassland.)

The total number of Swazis is about 1 million people. The two major cities are Mbabane and Manzini.

3 ● LANGUAGE

The Swazi language is referred to as "siSwati." It is a tonal Bantu language of the Nguni group, closely related to Zulu. It is spoken in Swaziland and in the Eastern Transvaal province of the Republic of South Africa. Little writing has been published in siSwati.

4 ● FOLKLORE

The Swazis suffered relatively little political disruption from colonial rule. Thus their oral tradition may be the richest still existing in southern Africa. Elder Swazis recount the histories of their forebears dating back several centuries. The first king, Ngwane II, is commemorated in one of many royal

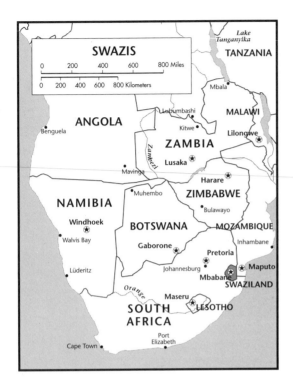

praise-songs, "Nkosi Dlamini"—"You thwarted the Lebombo in your flight."

One folktale tells the story of two daughters of a great Swazi king. The king had two wives, and with each wife, had one daughter. The half-sister princesses, Mulembe and Kitjila, loved each other, but Mulembe was the daughter of the king's favorite wife, and Mulembe was the older of the king's two daughters. Mulembe and her mother had the finest clothes of the finest fabrics, and the two could do no wrong in the king's eyes. The king insisted that the two sleep only on the skins of the rare golden otter. Kitila and her mother wore only common cowhide clothing. As the two half-sisters grew, Kitila developed as a more lovely and sweet person, but she was always pushed aside so that

Mulembe would always be considered the fairest in the land.

5 ● RELIGION

Followers of the traditional Swazi religion believe in a supreme being known as Mkhulumnqande. He created the Earth but is not worshiped and demands no sacrifices. Ancestral spirits *(emadloti)* play an important role in traditional religion. Spirits are believed to take many forms. They can possess people and influence their health.

Swazis also belong to many Christian sects. These range from Catholic and Afrikaner Calvinist to nationalistic "Zionist" churches.

6 ● MAJOR HOLIDAYS

National holidays in Swaziland include New Year's Day (January 1), Commonwealth Day (the second Monday in March), National Flag Day (April 25), Birthday of King Sobhuza II (July 22), Somhlolo (Independence) Day (September 6), United Nations Day (October 24), Christmas Day (December 25), and Boxing Day (December 26). Other Christian holidays are celebrated, including Good Friday and Easter Monday (in late March or early April).

Traditional religious holidays are also celebrated. The most important is the iNcwala (First Fruit) Ceremony, the annual ritual of kingship. Celebrated during a three-week period in December or January every year, it includes sacred songs and dances. Special branches from a type of acacia shrub are collected by young men. These are used to build a sacred enclosure where the first fruits of the season will be consumed by the king or leader. Once the leader has tasted the first fruits and has reappeared to the people present at the ceremony, everyone can enjoy the new growing season.

Another traditional religious holiday is Umhlanga (Reed Dance) Day, the last Monday in August. The Reed Dance honors iNdlovukazi, the Queen Mother. The dancers are women who gather reeds from a special area the week before the celebration. The dancers wear anklets, bracelets, necklaces, and colorful sashes with streamers. The colors of the streamers denote whether the woman is single, engaged to marry, or married.

7 ● RITES OF PASSAGE

A newborn baby is welcomed into the world with white "luck" beads placed around its waist, wrists, and/or ankles.

At puberty, a boy joins his *libutfo* (age regiment). Here he learns about manhood and service to the king. A girl, upon having her first menstruation, is isolated in a hut for several days. She is instructed by her mother about observances and taboos.

Following puberty, a girl's and boy's families begin marriage negotiations. The groom and his family transfer bride-wealth *(lobola)* to the bride's family. This includes valuables such as cattle (and in modern times, possibly cash). Besides gift exchanges, the marriage ceremony also includes singing, dancing, ritual wailing, and feasting. Couples may choose to have a Christian marriage.

The corpse of a deceased Swazi undergoes a mortuary ritual. A widow may be expected to continue her husband's lineage by marrying one of her husband's brothers. This practice is known as the levirate *(ngena)*.

8 ● RELATIONSHIPS

The Swazi demand strict adherence to rules concerned with kinship and political hierarchy. These govern forms of greetings, body language, and gestures. Respect must be shown by youths to their elders, and by women to men. Ways that respect is demonstrated include lowering one's eyes, kneeling, and moving quietly.

Adults wear beads to designate social and marital status. A young woman gives beadwork to her sweetheart as a token of love. In a sense, the beadwork serves as a "love letter." Different bead patterns represent different stages in the courtship.

9 ● LIVING CONDITIONS

Most Swazis construct their own homes from rocks, logs, clay, and thatch. Those with sufficient funds hire builders and buy corrugated iron roofs, glass windows, and solid wood doors. In a traditional Swazi homestead, family members do not have chairs or beds. They sit and sleep on grass mats. They cook on an open fire in the hut or in the yard. Their tools and utensils are limited and often homemade.

Urban dwellers have better access to electricity and piped water than do those living in rural areas.

10 ● FAMILY LIFE

There are several forms of marriage in Swaziland. These include arranged marriages *(ukwendzisa)* and modern, Christian mar-

Jason Lauré

Swazis participating in the Umhlanga *(Reed Dance) in celebration of the Harvest Festival.*

riages. After marriage, a new bride goes to live with her husband and in-laws. The ordinary Swazi resides in a group of households called a homestead, or *umuti*. Each household *(indlu)* generally consists of one nuclear family (a man, his wife, and their children). Household members share agricultural tasks and eat from one kitchen. Sometimes the wife has a co-wife, or *inhlanti*.

11 ● CLOTHING

Swazis wear either traditional or modern-day clothing. Men's traditional clothing consists of a colorful cloth "skirt" covered by an *emajobo* (leather apron). Adornments on ceremonial occasions include the *lig-* *cebesha* (neckband), *umgaco* (ties), and *sagibo* (walking stick). Royalty wear *ligwalagwala* (red feathers). Women's traditional clothing consists of an *ilihhiya* (cloth). Married women cover their upper torsos and sometimes wear traditional "beehive" hairstyles. Single women sometimes wear only beads over their upper torsos, particularly on ceremonial occasions.

12 ● FOOD

Swazis cultivate corn, sorghum, beans, groundnuts (peanuts), and sweet potatoes for consumption. They also raise cattle, as well as smaller livestock. Mealie-meal (ground corn) serves as the primary food. It is accompanied by meat or chicken, and a variety of vegetables. Sometimes traditional Swazi beer is brewed.

For the ordinary Swazi, breakfast usually consists of tea, bread, and/or sour-milk porridge. Bread or leftovers are eaten for lunch. A typical dinner consists of porridge, vegetables, and meat.

13 ● EDUCATION

Children in Swaziland attend either secular schools operated by the Ministry of Education, or mission schools that convey Christian values. Schoolchildren do their lessons from siSwati textbooks in the lower grades, and English textbooks in the upper grades. Families must pay annual school fees.

14 ● CULTURAL HERITAGE

Swazis have inherited a rich tradition of music and dance. *SiBhaca* dance music has been adopted from the Xhosa-speaking people of South Africa. SiBhaca dance is performed by teams of men, and features stomping of feet in unisom while chanting rhythmic traditional chants. The SiBhaca dance often lasts two or three hours.

Women sing together as they work; men sing together as they pay tribute to their chiefs or kings. Special songs are performed at weddings, royal rituals, coming-of-age ceremonies, and national Independence Day festivities.

15 ● EMPLOYMENT

In modern-day Swaziland, people derive income from various agricultural and commercial activities. Rural Swazis divide tasks according to sex, age, and social status. Men construct house frames and cattle *kraals* (corrals). They plow, tend and milk cattle, sew skins, and cut shields. Women hoe, plant, and harvest crops. They also tend small livestock, braid ropes, weave mats and baskets, grind grain, and brew beer. Some men migrate within Swaziland and to South Africa in search of work.

Swaziland's mineral wealth, including iron ore, coal, diamonds, and asbestos, is mined for export. The industrial estate at Matsapha produces processed agricultural and forestry products, garments, textiles, and many light manufactured goods.

16 ● SPORTS

Soccer is popular throughout the country. In rural areas, both boys and girls play games with various sorts of balls. These are often homemade from twine or rubber.

17 ● RECREATION

In rural areas, people enjoy musical, news, and sports programs on battery-operated radios. In urban areas, where electricity is more widely available, some households have televisions.

Rural Swazi children are good at creating toys out of discarded items, such as tires, tin cans, wires, and corncobs. Boys build intricate, movable toy cars from rubber and metal scraps, and girls make dolls from corncobs.

18 ● CRAFTS AND HOBBIES

Pottery-making, using the coil technique, is a task assigned to women. Basket-weaving is also done by women. Woodcarving is used for functional items and utensils, such as meat dishes and spoons. Schools have encouraged the production of masks or sculptured figures for the tourist trade.

Swazi specialists make musical instruments to accompany singing and dancing. Traditional Swazi instruments include the *luvene* (hunting horn), *impalampala* (kudu bull horn), and *livenge* (a wind instrument made from a plant).

19 ● SOCIAL PROBLEMS

Social and economic changes, including labor migration and the growth of an educated elite, have produced new problems in modern-day Swaziland. These include an increase in crime and alcoholism—particularly on the outskirts of urban areas.

The traditional Swazi hierarchy, headed by the king and the royal family, is being challenged by new educated elites without hereditary privilege.

20 ● BIBLIOGRAPHY

Blauer, Ettagale, and Jason Lauré. *Swaziland*. "Enchantment of the World" Series. New York: Children's Press, 1996.

Booth, Alan R. *Swaziland: Tradition and Change in a Southern African Kingdom*. Boulder, Colo.: Westview, 1984.

Kuper, Hilda. *An African Aristocracy*. New York: Holmes & Meier, 1980 (orig. 1965).

Leigh, Nila K. *Learning to Swim in Swaziland: A Child's-Eye View of a Southern African Country*. New York: Scholastic, 1993.

WEBSITES

Internet Africa Ltd. [Online] Available http://www.africanet.com/africanet/country/swazi/, 1998.

World Travel Guide. Swaziland. [Online] Available http://www.wtgonline.com/country/sz/gen.html, 1998.

Sweden

The people of Sweden are called Swedes. Minorities include about 300,000 Finns in the north and approximately 20,000 Sami. For more information on the Finns, see the chapter on Finland in Volume 3; on the Sami, see the chapter on Norway in Volume 7.

Swedes

PRONUNCIATION: SWEEDS
LOCATION: Sweden
POPULATION: 8.8 million
LANGUAGE: Swedish; Sami; Finnish
RELIGION: Church of Sweden (Lutheran)

1 ● INTRODUCTION

Swedes live in Sweden, one of the countries that make up the region known as Scandanavia. (The other Scandinavian nations are Denmark, Finland, Iceland, and Norway.) The first written reference to the Swedes is by the Roman historian Tacitus, who called the Swedes "mighty in ships and arms" in AD 98. Sweden represented a major European power during the seventeenth century, with its territories including Finland (1000–1805), parts of Germany, and the Baltic States. Christianity was introduced during the ninth through the eleventh centuries. An age of territorial expansion during the 1500s and 1600s ended in defeat by Russia in 1709 and the loss of most overseas posses-

sions by the early nineteenth century. Norway was united with Sweden from 1814 to 1905.

In the twentieth century Sweden remained neutral in both world wars, serving as a haven (safe place) for refugees in World War II (1939–45). Carl XVI Gustaf has been king since 1973, though his duties and influence are limited to ceremonies.

2 ● LOCATION

Sweden is the largest country in Scandinavia and the fourth-largest in Europe. With a total area of 173,732 square miles (449,966 square kilometers), it is close in size to the state of California. It is one of the more sparsely populated countries, with only 55 people per square mile (21 people per square kilometer). It is bordered by Norway on the north and west, Denmark on the southeast, and the Gulf of Bothnia, the Baltic Sea, and Finland on the east. One-seventh of Sweden lies within the Arctic Circle, the "land of the midnight sun," where the sun never really sets for three months during the summer. The country has

SWEDES

0	100	200	300 Miles
0	100	200	300 Kilometers

Norwegian
Sea

Narvik
Kiruna

SWEDEN

Umeå

Trondheim

Gulf of Bothnia

NORWAY

Bergen
Gävle

Åland
Islands

Oslo

Stockholm

Gotland

North
Sea

Göteborg

Öland

Baltic Sea

DENMARK
København
(Copenhagen)

about 100,000 lakes and many rivers, and more than half its terrain is forested. Most of its 8.8 million people live in the south of the country.

The Swedes are a Scandinavian people descended from Germanic tribes who emigrated to the region in ancient times, displacing the indigenous Sami. Ethnic minorities include about 30,000 Swedish-speaking Finns living in the northeastern section of the country, and approximately 15,000 Sami, a traditionally nomadic group of reindeer herders who live in northern portions of Norway, Sweden, Finland, and Russia. Since World War II (1939–45), Sweden has also accepted immigrant work-

ers from Greece, Germany, Turkey, Great Britain, Poland, Italy, and the former Yugoslavia, as well as political refugees, mostly from the Middle East, Asia, and the Latin American countries of Chile and Argentina.

3 ● LANGUAGE

Swedish is a Germanic language closely related to Norwegian and Danish. There are also similarities between Swedish and English, and most Swedes speak English as a second language. The Sami have their own language, and there are also some Finnish speakers in the country.

EXAMPLES OF SWEDISH

English	Swedish	Pronunciation
hello	hej	HAY
goodbye	adjö	ah-YER
yes/no	ja/nej	YA/NAY
please	varsagod	var-shah-GUD
thank you	tack	TAHK
breakfast	rrukost	FROO-kohst
lunch	lunch	LOONSH
dinner	middag	MID-dahg
one	ett	AYN
two	två	TVAW
three	tre	TRAY
four	fyra	FEE-ra
five	fem	FEM
six	sex	SE
seven	sju	SHOO
eight	atta	AWT-tah
nine	nio	NEE-ah
ten	tio	TEE-eh

Popular boys' names that are distinctly Swedish are Anders, Bengt, Hans, Gunnar, Ake, and Lars, while girls are commonly named Margareta, Karin, Birgitta, Kerstin, and Ingrid.

4 ● FOLKLORE

Rural dwellers have traditionally believed in the existence of a variety of supernatural beings. Every province of Sweden has its own customs and local lore. For example, there is a legend about the difference between the lush, fertile land of Skåne in the south and the neighboring northern province of Småland, which is rocky and barren. While God was making Skåne so beautiful, the Devil supposedly sneaked past God and turned Småland into a harsh and desolate place. It was too late for God to change the land, but God was able to create its people and made them tough and resourceful enough to survive in their difficult environment.

Swedish folklore is also full of moral tales. One of the more popular, reflecting Sweden's deep egalitarianism, is called "Master Pär and Rag Jan's Boy."

Master Pär was a terribly rich landowner and Rag Jan was a dirt-poor farmer. Master Pär, however, was deeply dissatisfied because his wife had never been able to have children, so there was no one to inherit his wealth. Rag Jan, on the other hand, had several children and Master Pär envied the poor farmer terribly.

One night a strange traveler came to town and went to Master Pär's house asking if she could stay the night. Master Pär laughed and slammed the door in her face. Next she went to Rag Jan's, who, even though his wife had just given birth to another son, told her she was more than welcome. The strange traveler, who was something of a mystic, told Jan that in the morning he should go to Master Pär and ask him to be the godfather of his new son. Jan did so even though he knew Master Pär would sneer at the idea, which he did. "Never mind," said the strange woman,

"your new son will one day be heir to Master Pär's fortune: I have seen it in a vision." The only thing Jan had to do was to keep quiet about her plan.

Time passed and Master Pär continued to despair over not having an heir. Being rich, he thought that the solution would be to buy a child, so he went to Jan, remembering that strange day when Jan had suggested that he be the godfather to his new boy. He bought the boy and raised him for a year, but then his wife got pregnant and bore him a daughter. The boy and girl became inseparable friends, falling deeply in love. Then one day Rag Jan's wife forgot the strange woman's pleading to keep quiet and told a friend that it had been predicted that her son would one day inherit Master Pär's wealth. Well, Master Pär heard of this and had the boy sent off to the woods, to his sister's, to be killed. Years went by, and, through the help of the strange woman, the boy was not killed but raised by Master Pär's sister into a strong young man. When Master Pär found out, he again hatched a plot to have the boy killed, but, again through the workings of the strange woman, the boy was not only spared but became engaged to Master Pär's daughter. When Master Pär found out, he went into a rage and told the boy that the only way he could marry his daughter would be to travel to the end of the world and ask the giant that lived there why everything always went wrong for Master Pär.

The boy agreed to take the journey. Master Pär was happy because he knew (but the boy didn't) that the giant at the end of the world loved to eat Christians. As the boy journeyed to the end of the world, he passed three castles and met three kings, each of whom asked where he was going. "To the end of the world," the boy replied, "to ask the giant why everything always goes wrong for Master Pär." Each of the kings then asked him if he could ask the giant a question for him. The first wanted to know why the apples on one side of his apple tree grew red and on the other grew white; the second wanted to know why his spring had gone muddy; the third asked him to find out what had happened to his daughter. The boy happily told them all he would do the best he could.

When he got to the end of the world, he came to a river with a ferry operated by an ancient woman. The woman asked the young boy where he was going. When he told her, she too asked him to ask the giant a question. She wanted to know how long she would have to stay at the river. She had already been there for a hundred years.

Across the river, the young boy came to a mountain with a door leading into its heart. He went inside and came across a beautiful woman spinning golden thread. The woman asked the boy what he was doing there and when he told her, the woman told him that his journey was doomed: the giant would simply eat him up the minute he saw him. Then the woman had an idea and told the boy to hide. That night, when the giant fell asleep, the woman pretended to wake from a terrible dream, screaming. This woke the giant and he asked what was wrong. She told him that in her dream someone named Master Pär had asked her why things always went wrong for him. The giant, half asleep, said it was because he refused to accept the son-in-law the gods had chosen for

him. The woman then pretended to wake from three more dreams, each time asking the giant to solve one of the riddles. Then she pretended to awake one more time, this time asking how the ancient woman who operated the ferry could be relieved of her duty. The giant answered all the questions, and then the young boy jumped up from his hiding place and chopped off the giant's head.

When the boy and the woman got to the ferry, they told the ancient woman that they had found the answer to her question, but they would not tell her until they got across the river. When they landed, they told her that the next person who needed to get across could be forced to take her place if she said, "Now you must stay here as long as I have," while that person was in the ferry. The old woman shouted as the two ran off together that they should have told her that before getting out of the boat. All the kings were so grateful for the answers to their questions that they showered the young man with gifts, dressing him in the finest clothes and giving him the finest horse on which to ride the long journey home.

When he finally got to Master Pär's castle, Master Pär was quite surprised to see him alive and reluctantly agreed to allow the marriage. He was never happy, however, and became especially dissatisfied when his new son-in-law told him that he had left the giant's vast treasure of gold and jewelry behind after killing him. The treasure was still sitting there in the giant's mountain home. After a few years, the greed of Master Pär finally got the better of him, and he traveled to the end of the world to get the giant's treasure for himself. When he got to the ferry, the old woman told him to get in the boat and then said, "Now you must stay here as long as I have," and ran off cackling, leaving Master Pär to stare at the giant's unretrieved treasure, glistening in the mountain cave. He is sitting there still.

5 ● RELIGION

Sweden's state religion is Lutheranism, and about 90 percent of the population belongs to the Church of Sweden, the country's Lutheran church. In the past, all Swedes automatically became members of the church at birth but had the right to withdraw from it. As of January 1996, church membership is only achieved through baptism, as Sweden is currently negotiating a separation of church and state to be enacted by 2000. Although most people mark major life-cycle events such as baptism, confirmation, marriage, and death within the church, the majority do not attend services regularly. Of the 90-percent Lutheran population, only 10 percent attend church. Minority religions include Roman Catholicism, the Pentecostal Church, the Mission Covenant Church of Sweden, and the Greek Orthodox Church. In addition, there is a large concentration of Jews in Sweden, as well as a tremendous growth in the Islamic population.

6 ● MAJOR HOLIDAYS

Sweden's legal holidays are New Year's Day (January 1), Epiphany (January 6), Good Friday and Easter Monday (both in March or April), May Day (May 1), Ascension Day (May 31), Midsummer (June 23), All Souls' Day (November 3), and Christmas (December 25). At midnight on New Year's Eve (December 31), ship horns and factory sirens usher in the New Year and,

following a century-old tradition, Alfred Tennyson's poem, "Ring Out, Wild Bells," is read at an open-air museum in Stockholm and broadcast throughout the country. The feast of St. Knut on January 13 is the time when Christmas decorations are taken down. Shrove Tuesday, the last day before Lent begins, is traditionally observed by eating a bun filled with cream and marzipan. As Easter approaches, Swedes decorate twigs with colored feathers and place them in water to sprout new leaves in time for the holiday. Similar to Halloween rituals observed in the United States, young boys and girls dress up as the Easter Hag and visit their neighbors, from whom they receive small gifts.

Among the most important secular holidays is the Feast of Valborg, or Walpurgis Night, observed on April 30, which celebrates the coming of spring with bonfires and other festivities performed both publicly and privately. The Swedish flag is honored on June 6, a day on which all cities and towns fly flags and hold ceremonies in the flag's honor. Finally, the Summer Solstice is observed on June 21 and June 22 through the raising of the Maypole, around which celebrants dance, sing traditional songs, and eat.

7 ● RITES OF PASSAGE

Modern Swedish children can expect to spend a lot of time in well-kept day care centers. Most parents, whether married or not, both work outside the home, requiring children to spend their early years in day care. Once in school, the children can look forward to spending their after-school hours in an expanded day care. Swedish children also have legal protections unheard of in other countries. There is a government office specifically designed to serve children's interests, and it is against the law for parents to hit their children.

8 ● RELATIONSHIPS

The Swedish character is influenced by the harsh weather. During warm months, Swedes love to spend time outdoors, picnicking with friends in the country, or having a meal at a sidewalk cafe in the city. In the winter, most socializing comes to an end as Swedes generally retreat to their homes, waiting out the long, dark winter. Swedes tend to be reserved in public and in interpersonal relations. They do not usually touch others when communicating, as it is considered poor manners.

9 ● LIVING CONDITIONS

Except for brick-and-clay farm houses in southern Sweden, most dwellings were traditionally built of wood. In the past, the style of rural dwellings varied by region. Contemporary housing is basically similar throughout the country, and it features building materials and styles similar to those in the United States. Many empty country houses are now used as summer homes. Fewer than 50 percent of Swedes live in detached single homes, and about one-third live in or near the country's three largest cities.

Sweden's extensive system of social insurance pays for medical and dental care. The nation's infant mortality rate—6 deaths for every 1,000 live births—is one of the lowest in the world. Maternity leave with pay is granted one month before the expected birth of a child, with twelve additional months after the child is born, which can be taken by either parent or split between them. This legitimate leave of absence is termed "parental leave," as it can be chosen by either mother or father. However, 90 percent of parental leave is taken only by the mother, as 50 percent of Swedish fathers do not take even a single day off. The average life expectancy in Sweden is seventy-seven years for men and eighty-one years for women.

10 ● FAMILY LIFE

Most Swedish families have only one or two children. During the past twenty years, it has become so common for unmarried couples to live together that the people have coined a name for this arrangement: *sambo* (*sam* means together; *bo* means live). In 1988 the legal rights of persons involved in such relationships were expanded, making them almost the legal equal of married spouses. Nevertheless, sambo relationships often lead to marriage. Sweden's divorce rate has doubled since 1960. The older Swedish generation views the husband's role as that of the breadwinner, and still relegates the wife to domestic tasks within the home. However, as in the United States, the younger Swedish generation considers marriage more as a partnership with shared responsibilities, since both spouses work. Swedish women are guaranteed equal rights under the law, and 82 percent work outside the home—the highest rate in Europe. Many women hold upper-level government positions, including positions in parliament and the governing cabinet. Almost half of all working women have children under the age of sixteen.

The elderly Swede enjoys generous social benefits from the state and, usually, does not live with a younger relative, as used to be the norm. As in most industrialized countries, the extended family has become less central to life in Sweden as children move in pursuit of careers, independence, and wealth. More than 90 percent of Swedes over sixty-five live independently outside of retirement homes, with medical care brought to them if they are unable to get around easily.

11 ● CLOTHING

Modern, Western-style clothing is worn in Sweden. As in the United States, the Swedes' casual wear is typically slacks, shorts, and T-shirts. Likewise, suits are worn by both men and women in most places of business, and tuxedos and evening gowns are worn at formal affairs

Swedish folk costumes, which were introduced as late as the 1890s as a means of glorifying the cultural richness of the nation, are worn for special festivals such as Midsummer's Eve. They consist of white blouses, vests, and long dark skirts (often worn with aprons) for women, and white shirts, vests, dark knee-length breeches, and white hose for men. Only a small segment of the population even owns such a costume, and the costumes vary dramatically from region to region.

12 ● FOOD

The Swedes, heavily influenced by the French, use rich sauces in their food. The Swedish name for the open-faced sandwich meal enjoyed throughout Scandinavia— *smörgåsbord* (SMUR-gawss-boord)—is the

Recipe

Rose Hip Soup

Ingredients

1½ to 2 cups dried rose hips (available at health food stores)
1½ quarts water
¼–½ cup sugar
1 Tablespoon potato starch (cornstarch may be substituted)

Directions

1. Rinse the rose hips and lightly crush them. Put them in a saucepan with the water. Heat to boiling.
2. Simmer until rose hips are tender.
3. Transfer to a blender or food processor and purée. There should be about 1¼ quarts of liquid; if there is less, add water.
4. Pour puréed rose hips back into the saucepan and add the sugar. Stir and cook over medium heat.
5. Dissolve the potato starch in a small amount of cold water. Stir into soup slowly. Remove from heat just when is begins to boil. Chill before serving.
6. Serve cold with ice cream or whipped cream. Top with slivered almonds or corn flakes.

one by which this buffet meal is known in the United States. In Sweden it commonly includes herring, smoked eel, roast beef, tongue, jellied fish, boiled potatoes, and cheese. Favorite hot dishes include meatballs *(köttbulla;* CHURT-boolar*)* served with lingonberry jam *(lingonsylt;* LING-onn-seelt*),* fried meat, potatoes, and eggs; and *Janssons frestelse* (YAHN-sons FREH-stehl-seh), a layered potato dish with onions and cream, topped with anchovies. The

Swedes love fish, especially salmon, which is typically smoked, marinated, or cured with dill and salt. Fresh fruits and vegetables, including all kinds of berries, are also very popular. Favorite beverages include milk, *lättöl* (LETT-url; a type of beer with almost no alcohol), and strong coffee.

Ceremonial foods include salt salmon on Good Friday, and roasted lamb on Easter Eve. At Christmas, an almond is placed in the rice pudding. Before serving themselves, each person has to make up a short rhyme. The one who gets the portion with the almond will marry within the year.

Sweden's best known contributions to world cuisine are Swedish meatballs and, of course, the smörgåsbord. Less well known is rose hip soup, a sweet, cold soup high in vitamin C, traditionally served during the long winter months when fruits are scarce. It is usually served cold with whipped cream or ice cream and topped with almond slivers or crushed corn flakes.

13 ● EDUCATION

Almost all Swedes can read and write. School is required between the ages of seven and seventeen. During the first nine years, students attend a "comprehensive school" where they study a variety of subjects. Grades one through three are called the "junior" grades, four through six the "middle" grades, and seven through nine the "senior" grades. There is a three-week Christmas vacation, and a summer vacation that extends from early June to late August. Free hot lunches are provided to all students. English is taught as a second language from the third grade on, and crafts such as woodworking and textile-making are also part of the curriculum. While immigrant children from countries such as Germany and Turkey receive education in their own language a few hours each day, there are also special English classes for these students.

Beginning in the seventh year, instruction varies based on students' interests and abilities. About 30 percent choose the college-preparatory curriculum, while others opt for more vocationally-oriented training. Swedes maintain the Scandinavian tradition of giving ceremonial white hats to secondary school graduates. Sweden has six universities, located in Stockholm, Linköping, Uppsala, Lund, and Umeå.

14 ● CULTURAL HERITAGE

Swedes take an intense interest in their cultural heritage, devoting a large part of their public funds to institutions such as museums, libraries, theaters, and galleries. The arts receive strong support from the government in Sweden. An example of the intense Swedish interest in art is the fact that Stockholm's subway system is filled with public art and has been called the world's longest art gallery.

Performers in Sweden enjoy a level of job security unknown in most other countries, including the United States. They are hired by the year, drawing a regular salary and receiving pension, insurance, and vacation benefits. However, even the most successful Swedish performers do not receive the extremely high levels of pay accorded to "superstars" in some other countries, particularly the United States.

Sweden's best-known writer was August Strindberg, who wrote novels, short stories, essays, and plays that influenced the course of modern drama. Selma Lagerlof, the first Swede to win the Nobel Prize, is known for both her novels and her children's classic, *The Wonderful Adventures of Nils.* Another world-famous Swedish children's author is Astrid Lindgren, creator of the Pippi Long-stocking books.

In the visual arts, prominent Swedish names include the sculptor Carl Milles and the jewelry maker Sigurd Persson. The Swedish film industry has gained a world-wide audience for its films, especially those of its director Ingmar Bergman, whose internationally known films include *The Seventh Seal, Persona*, and *Fanny and Alexander.* Famous Swedish film stars include Ingrid Bergman and Max von Sydow. The creator of the Nobel Prize itself was a Swede—Alfred Nobel, the inventor of dynamite.

15 ● EMPLOYMENT

Swedes entering the work force, like people in most industrialized countries, face bright prospects. Sweden has a stable, growing economy and is a world leader in engineering and science. Swedes take great pride in their jobs (professions are listed with names in the phone book), and Swedish-made products are world-renowned for their quality and durability. This is especially true of the automobiles, the Volvo and the Saab, which are considered two of the finest-made cars in the world.

Sweden's labor force is divided almost equally between men and women. About 67 percent are employed in the service sector,

31 percent in industry, and 2 percent in agriculture. Unemployment in Sweden has been low compared to other European countries (under 5 percent in 1992) but is rising due to cuts in defense spending and government employment. About 85 percent of the Swedish work force is unionized. The minimum age for employment is sixteen; persons under that age may be hired during school vacations for easy jobs that last five days or less.

There are extensive worker training programs in Sweden, provided by both government and industry. These programs help train unemployed workers for new jobs, and train current workers for better jobs or to prepare them for new technology.

Though Sweden has some of the highest taxes in the world, it generously pays a pension that is two-thirds of the worker's pre-retirement salary. Swedish retirees enjoy other benefits, such as health insurance and half-priced prescriptions.

16 ● SPORTS

There are about 40,000 sports clubs throughout Sweden. The most popular sport is soccer (called *fotboll;* FOOT-boll). Favorite winter sports include cross-country and downhill skiing, and long-distance skating. Popular water sports include swimming, rowing, and sailing, and many Swedes also enjoy cycling. Major annual events for amateur athletes include the Vasa cross-country ski race, the Vace, the Vansbro swim meet, and the Liding the Swedish tennis team won the Davis Cup for the fourth time. Outstanding Swedish athletes include alpine skier Ingemar Stenmark, and tennis great Björn Borg.

17 ● RECREATION

Many of the Swedes' leisure hours are devoted to outdoor activities that enable them to enjoy their country's beautiful natural scenery. It is common to retreat to rural areas during weekends and vacations. The summer cottage by the lake is a common sight. Altogether there are about 600,000 summer homes in Sweden, many in abandoned rural areas. The islands near Stockholm are especially popular sites for these retreats. In recent years, it has also become popular to take winter vacations in Mediterranean resort areas. Walking is a favorite pastime in Sweden, and marked walking paths can be found throughout the country. Sailing on Sweden's rivers and lakes is also very popular: about one in every five households owns a boat.

18 ● CRAFTS AND HOBBIES

The Swedes are known for their high-quality handicrafts. Handmade utensils have been produced since the beginning of the nineteenth century; the primary textiles are wool and flax. Swedish crystal and glass—of which 90 percent is produced at the Orrefors factory—are famous worldwide, and half of the country's production is exported, much of it to the United States. The Dalarna region is known for its distinctive wooden horses with their brightly painted designs. Folk influences are evident in modern Swedish ceramics, woodwork, textiles, furniture, silver, and other products.

19 ● SOCIAL PROBLEMS

Like several neighboring countries, Sweden has a high rate of alcoholism. Organizations devoted to helping people deal with this problem have about 6,000 local chapters altogether. Another—and possibly related—problem is absenteeism from work, which rose sharply in the late 1980s. One of out every four workers calls in sick on any given day. There has also been some discontent with the high taxes necessary to fund Sweden's extensive network of social services.

A relatively new and sweeping social problem in Sweden is that of racism. A neo-Nazi group similar to the "skinheads" of the United States is VAM ("Vit Ariskt Motstand" or "White Aryan Resistance"), which in recent years has experienced an increase in membership.

20 ● BIBLIOGRAPHY

Alderton, Mary. *Sweden. Blue Guide.* New York: Norton, 1995.

Gall, Timothy, and Susan Gall, eds. *Junior Worldmark Encyclopedia of the Nations.* Detroit: UXL, 1996.

Gan, Delice. *Sweden.* New York: Marshall Cavendish, 1992.

Gerholm, Lena. "Swedes." In *Encyclopedia of World Cultures* (*Europe*). Boston: G. K. Hall, 1992.

Hintz, Martin. *Sweden.* "Enchantment of the World" Series. Chicago: Children's Press, 1994.

Keeler, Stephen, and Chris Fairclough. *We Live in Sweden.* New York: Bookwright Press, 1985.

Sweden in Pictures. Minneapolis, Minn.: Lerner Publications Co., 1990.

WEBSITES

Embassy of Sweden, Washington, D.C. [Online] Available http://www.swedenemb.org/, 1998.

Swedish Travel & Tourism Council. [Online] Available http://www.gosweden.org/, 1998.

World Travel Guide. Sweden. [Online] Available http://www.wtgonline.com/country/se/gen.html, 1998.

Switzerland

The people of Switzerland are called Swiss. The Swiss trace their ancestry to Germany, France, and Italy.

Swiss

PRONUNCIATION: SWIS
LOCATION: Switzerland
POPULATION: About 7 million
LANGUAGE: Schwyzerdütsch (Swiss-German dialect); French; Italian; Romansh; English
RELIGION: Protestantism; Roman Catholicism

1 ● INTRODUCTION

Switzerland is located at the crossroads of Europe. Although a small country, it is the meeting point for three of Europe's major cultures—German, French and Italian. It is a country known for its stability, multiculturalism, and prosperity.

Archeological evidence shows that the area that is now Switzerland was inhabited as early as 40,000 BC. The development of modern Switzerland can be traced back to a confederation (loose political grouping) of several Alpine valley communities and states in the Middle Ages. These original communities were called cantons, and today Switzerland's twenty-six provinces are called by the same name. Swiss history is unique in Europe since the Swiss never had a monarchy. Instead, the different members of the confederation governed political affairs. In today's political system, many powers are still left in the hands of the cantons.

Switzerland's present boundaries were fixed in 1815 at the Congress of Vienna. Switzerland was neutral (refused to take sides) in World War I (1914–1918) and World War II (1939–1945). Its neutral stance has also kept it from joining the United Nations.

The Swiss live in a democracy where the average citizen often has greater influence than in other countries. A unique example of direct democracy found in parts of Switzerland is the Landsgemeinde (People's Assembly). Citizens gather under the open sky on a Sunday in spring to pass laws and elect officials by a show of hands.

SWISS

0   100   200   300 Miles

0   100   200   300 Kilometers

principal rivers, the Rhine and the Rhone, have their sources in the Swiss Alps.

Switzerland's population of almost 7 million people is very diverse. It is composed of four major ethnic groups: German, French, Italian, and Romansh.

3 ● LANGUAGE

Switzerland has four national languages. Speakers of Schwyzerdütsch (the German dialects spoken in Switzerland), account for about two-thirds of all Swiss. Another 18 percent speak French, about 10 percent—mostly in the Ticino region—speak Italian, and roughly 1 percent speak Romansh, a dialect spoken mostly in the Grison region. The remainder of the population consists of foreign workers who speak the languages of their homelands. Most native Swiss are bi- or multi-lingual, and many speak English.

2 ● LOCATION

Switzerland is one of Europe's smallest countries in terms of both territory and population. It is roughly equal in size to the combined area of Massachusetts, Connecticut, and Rhode Island. Although it is a place of contrasts—of plains, lakes, rivers and mountains—approximately 70 percent of the country is covered by mountains.

Switzerland's three natural geographic regions are the Jura Mountains in the northwest, the Alps in the south, and the central plateau, or Mittelland. This central plateau contains all of the larger towns and most major cities.

The most famous of the Swiss Alps is the Matterhorn, rising 14,692 feet (4,478 meters) above sea level. Two of Europe's

4 ● FOLKLORE

The national hero of Swiss legend is William Tell, supposed to have lived in the early 1300s. He was forced to shoot an apple off his son's head as punishment for disobeying the imperial governor Gessler. Tell later escaped from his captors to slay the tyrant. This legend inspired popular ballads during the fifteenth century. It has also been made famous by the overture to Italian composer Gioacchino Rossini's (1792–1868) opera *Guillaume Tell* (1829), which English-speaking audiences are familiar with as the *William Tell* overture.

The Rütli Schwur (Rutli Oath) is another powerful symbol in Swiss folklore. This oath refers to an agreement made in the Rutli meadow between several Swiss valley communities in the Middle Ages. Together they created an alliance for common protection and defense. Although historians question whether or not this event actually took place, for many it symbolizes Swiss freedom and democracy. During World War II when Switzerland was surrounded by Nazi Germany, the Swiss army commander, General Guisan, gathered his officers on the Rutli meadow as a symbol of Swiss determination to fight for their freedom.

5 ● RELIGION

Switzerland is evenly divided between Protestants and Roman Catholics (48 percent versus 49 percent). The mostly German-speaking cantons, or provinces, are divided nearly equally between the two religious affiliations. Catholicism is the major religion of the French-speaking cantons and the Italian-speaking canton of Ticino. Throughout Switzerland there are both Protestant and Catholic youth organizations, labor unions, and women's associations. In addition, the Swiss political parties have been shaped by the religious differences of the past.

Switzerland's continuing close ties with the Catholic Church can still be seen today in the Swiss Guards at the Vatican. They once protected the Pope but now serve as an honor guard with their colorful uniforms and shiny helmets.

6 ● MAJOR HOLIDAYS

Switzerland's legal holidays are New Year's Day (January 1), Good Friday and Easter Monday (in March or April), Ascension Day and Whitmonday (in April or May), Bundesfeier (which resembles the American Fourth of July and occurs on August 1), and Christmas (December 25). The German-speaking Swiss mark the seasons and many religious days with festivals, which vary with each canton (province) and commune (city or town). Altogether, over one hundred different festivals—pagan, Christian, and patriotic—are celebrated in Switzerland. The most famous celebration is Basel's Fastnacht, or carnival. Marking the final days before Lent, it is similar to the Mardi Gras festivities held in New Orleans. For three days, masked and costumed merrymakers parade through streets filled with decorative floats while the strains of pipe-and-drum bands are heard.

7 ● RITES OF PASSAGE

In Switzerland many rites of passage are similar to those found in the United States. These include religious rituals such as baptism and first communion and family events such as births, deaths, and marriages.

For men, one of the most important aspects of life in Switzerland is military service. All male citizens serve compulsory periods of military duty between the ages of twenty and fifty. They keep all of their equipment, including weapon and ammunition, at home. Swiss military duty may be considered a rite of passage because serving in the army is seen as a sign of true citizenship. However, women are not required to perform military service, and many women criticize their exclusion from the army.

8 ● RELATIONSHIPS

The Swiss are known for their tolerance, politeness, and independence. Relationships among the Swiss reflect the country's diversity of languages, religions, and regions. A number of stereotypes exist between the various regions. An example of this is the Röstigraben—the ongoing tension between the French- and German-speaking parts of Switzerland. The German-speaking Swiss see themselves as hard working and efficient. They see their French-speaking countrymen as easy-going and friendly. However, the French-speaking Swiss tend to see the German speakers as arrogant, pushy, and too serious.

A handshake is the normal greeting between men and women unless one is very familiar with the person. In this case, a triple kiss on each cheek is appropriate. This consists of first one kiss on one cheek, then one on the next cheek, and finally back to the first cheek. Two men greet each other by shaking hands. It is customary to greet and say good-bye to a person using their name. The Swiss use formal forms of address both in German (*Sie* rather than *du*) and in French (*vous* rather than *tu*). Formal speech is used in less intimate situations, such as in business settings.

9 ● LIVING CONDITIONS

The Swiss enjoy an impressive standard of living. Those living in the Alpine or forest regions have traditionally lived in wooden houses with shingled or tiled roofs and carved gables. Corners and roofs have often been reinforced with stone. Kitchens have been encased in stone or masonry to prevent fires. Today, fewer houses of this type are constructed. Even in remote rural areas, newer houses are commonly of brick or block. However, mountain chalets (country houses) built by city-dwellers as vacation homes often imitate the older rural styles. In general, most Swiss live in apartments rather than owning their own houses.

10 ● FAMILY LIFE

Most Swiss women today prefer to have no more than one or two children, and an increasing number of people choose to remain single. Women who marry do so at a later age than their mothers did and also have their children later. In general, the German-speaking Swiss tend to marry among themselves.

The status of Swiss women is below that of women in most other European countries. They have only had suffrage (the right to vote) since 1971. By law, a woman has traditionally needed her husband's permission to get a job, open a bank account, or run for political office. Although Swiss women gained their political equality late, they have been catching up quickly. Today they fill 15 percent of all elected posts, a figure slightly above the European average.

11 ● CLOTHING

Western-style clothing is the norm. However, traditional costumes can still be seen at local festivities and parades. Many display the Swiss art of fine embroidery. Herdsmen in the Gruyère region wear a short blue jacket of cloth or canvas called a *bredzon* with sleeves gathered at the shoulders. On special occasions, women in this region wear silk aprons, long-sleeved jackets, and straw hats with ribbons hanging from the brim. Other traditional women's costumes include gold lace caps in St. Gallen and dresses with silver ornaments in Unterwalden. Traditional male dress common to many Alpine areas are the leather shorts called *lederhosen*, often worn with sturdy leather boots.

12 ●FOOD

Swiss cuisine combines the culinary traditions of Germany, France, and Italy. It varies by region. Throughout the land, however, cheese is king. The Swiss have been making cheese for at least 2,000 years. The hole-filled Emmentaler, which is popularly called "Swiss cheese," is only one of hundreds of varieties produced in Switzerland. The country's most typical national dish is fondue, melted Emmentaler or Gruyère cheese in which pieces of bread are dipped, using long forks. A recipe follows.

Also popular is another melted-cheese dish called *raclette*. A quarter or half a wheel of cheese (a big, round slab) is melted in front of an open fire. Pieces of it are scraped off onto the diners' plates with a special knife. The cheese is traditionally eaten with potatoes, pickled onions or other vegetables, and dark bread.

A popular dish in German-speaking regions is *rösti*, hash-browned potatoes mixed with herbs, bacon, or cheese. Typical dishes in the Italian-speaking Ticino region are a potato pasta called *gnocchi*; *risotto*, a rice dish; and *polenta*, which is made from cornmeal. French specialties such as steaks, organ meats, and wine-flavored meat stews are prevalent in French-speaking parts of the country. Besides cheese, the other principal food for which the Swiss are known is chocolate.

13 ●EDUCATION

Education at all levels is the responsibility of the cantons, or provinces. Thus Switzer-

---

Recipe

Cheese Fondue

Ingredients

1 clove garlic
2 cups white wine or white grape juice
¾ pound Swiss cheese, cut into small cubes
¾ Gruyere cheese, cut into small cubes
4 Tablespoons flour
4 Tablespoons kirsch (cherry liqueur)
Crusty French bread and apple slices

Procedure

1. Cut the clove of garlic in half. Rub the inside of an electric fondue pot with the cut side of the garlic clove.
2. Heat the fondue pot to medium-high, and pour in the wine or white grape juice. Heat the liquid until it begins to bubble.
3. Place the cubes of cheese in a large plastic bag with the flour. Seal the bag and shake well to coat the cheese with the flour.
4. Add the cheese, a few cubes at a time, to the simmering liquid. Stir constantly in a figure-eight pattern until all the cheese is melted. Don't rush this process or the cheese will become stringy.
5. Add kirsch and stir until blended.
6. Cut the bread into bite-size cubes.

To serve, spear cubes of bread and apple slices, one at a time, with long-handled forks. Dip into melted cheese and enjoy!

Adapted from *Recipes from Around the World.* Howard County, Md.: Foreign-Born Information and Referral Network, 1993, p. 8.)

Susan D. Rock

Swiss choir group singing, Rigi, Switzerland. At their many festivals, the Swiss still enjoy traditional activities, including dancing and yodeling.

land actually has twenty-six different educational systems. They have varying types of schools, curricula, length of study, and teachers' salaries. However, all require either eight or nine years of schooling beginning at age six or seven. In secondary school those students entering an academic track take a course of instruction to prepare them for university study. Students in a vocational program continue to take classes while also entering into an apprenticeship. Afterward students receive certification in a specific trade and are ready to enter the work force. Post-secondary education is offered at nine universities and two federal institutes of technology at Zurich and Lausanne.

14 ● CULTURAL HERITAGE

Switzerland's cultural achievements have been wide-ranging and significant. Swiss who have made significant achievements in the arts during the late nineteenth and twentieth centuries include playwright Friedrich Dürrenmatt, novelists Gottfried Keller and Max Frisch, sculptor Alberto Giacometti, architect Le Corbusier, and painter Paul Klee. Also well known are psychologist Carl Jung and child psychologist Jean Piaget.

Switzerland has also made a unique contribution to world culture by providing a neutral refuge for leading intellectuals fleeing their own countries for political or other reasons. Distinguished emigrés (emigrants) welcomed by the Swiss include authors Thomas Mann, James Joyce, and Alexander Solzhenitsyn, film star Charlie Chaplin, scientist Albert Einstein, philosopher Friedrich Nietzsche, and musician Richard Wagner.

15 ● EMPLOYMENT

The percentage of Swiss people engaged in agriculture has declined sharply since the nineteenth century. Today fewer than 6 percent of the Swiss are farmers. Almost a third of Switzerland's labor force is employed in the machinery, electronics, and metal industries. The chemical, pharmaceutical, and textile industries are also major employers. One traditional type of labor for which the Swiss are famous is watchmaking. Today Switzerland produces over seventy million watches and watch parts annually. More than half the work force is employed in service jobs. Tourism and banking are among the most important employers.

There are relatively few labor strikes in Switzerland due to special agreements called "industrial peace treaties." Employers and employees agree to cooperate with each other, and strikes and lockouts are forbidden.

Many young Swiss spend a period of apprenticeship outside the country before entering the labor force. A unique Swiss practice is the *Welschlandjahr*. Young Swiss from the German-speaking region spend time in the French-speaking area in order to learn French and become familiar with the way of life there.

16 ● SPORTS

Both summer and winter sports are extremely popular among the Swiss. The country's Alpine peaks provide a setting for skiing, bobsledding, tobogganing, mountain walking, and climbing. After skiing, ice skating is Switzerland's favorite winter sport. Summer activities include tennis, hiking, golf, cycling, fishing, and a variety of water sports. Two especially popular sports are handball and soccer.

Traditional Swiss sports are still enjoyed at festivals. These include the baseball-like *Hornussen,* or farmer's tennis, and stone-putting *(Steinstossen),* where the object is to throw a stone weighing 184 pounds (80 kilograms) as far as possible. In Swiss wrestling *(Schwingen),* each wrestler wears a pair of canvas-like shorts over his pants and tries to throw his opponent to the ground by grabbing hold of these shorts.

17 ● RECREATION

Relaxing after hours is important to the Swiss, who have one of the longest work days in Europe (usually 8:00 AM to 5:00 PM). Much of their recreation is family oriented, and they often entertain at home rather than going out. A favorite leisure-time activity is simply reading the newspaper, either at home or at a cafe. A card game called Jass is extremely popular. It is played with thirty-six cards according to rules that vary from region to region. Concerts and the theater are also enjoyed by many Swiss. The youth scene is dominated by dancing and parties, with a subculture centered around techno music.

At their many festivals, the Swiss still enjoy traditional activities, including dancing and yodeling. Each region of Switzerland has its own festivals and special events.

18 ● CRAFTS AND HOBBIES

Switzerland's traditional decorative arts include weaving, embroidery, dressmaking *(Frauentracht),* wood carving, and painting. A unique form of Swiss folk art is *Senntumsmalerei,* or herd-painting. It originated among Alpine dairy farmers who carved and painted farm implements as far back as the early eighteenth century. There are several typical forms of Senntumsmalerei. *Fahreimebödeli* are wooden pails with decorated bases. *Sennenstreifen* are long boards or strips of paper picturing cattle drives to the high Alpine pastures. *Wächterbild* are large-scale paintings of cow herders traditionally found on window shutters.

19 ● SOCIAL PROBLEMS

The influx of foreign, or "guest," workers *(Gastarbeiter)* from southern Europe and north Africa since World War II has produced a fear of *Übezfremdung* (over-foreignization). Anti-immigrant feeling subjects *Ausländers* (foreigners) to discrimination and social isolation.

The problems of youth are another area of concern, especially drug abuse. Switzerland has the highest instance of drug abuse and AIDS in Europe. Approximately 20 percent of youth between the ages fifteen and twenty-four have used hard drugs.

Another major challenge facing the Swiss is the debate over greater cooperation and unity with the other countries of Europe, an issue known as "European integration." Fears over European integration have raised concern about the preservation of Switzerland's neutrality and democratic institutions.

20 ● BIBLIOGRAPHY

Bouvier, N., G. Craig, and L. Gossman. *Geneva, Zurich, Basel: History, Culture & National Identity.* Princeton, N.J.: Princeton University Press, 1994.

Hilowitz, Janet. *Switzerland in Perspective.* Westport, Conn.: Greenwood Press, 1990.

Levy, Patricia. *Switzerland.* New York: Marshall Cavendish, 1994.

Recipes from Around the World. Howard County, Md.: Foreign-Born Information and Referral Network, 1993.

WEBSITES

Embassy of Switzerland, Washington, D.C. [Online] Available http://www.swissemb.org/, 1998.

Switzerland Tourism North America. [Online] Available http://www.switzerlandtourism.com, 1998.

World Travel Guide. Switzerland. [Online] Available http://www.wtgonline.com/country/ch/gen.html, 1998.

Syria

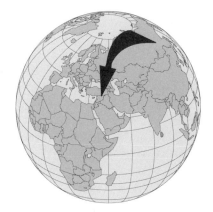

The people of Syria are called Syrians. The Druze, about 8 percent of the population, are both a religious and an ethnic group.

Syrians

PRONUNCIATION: SEER-ee-uhns

LOCATION: Syria

POPULATION: Over 13 million

LANGUAGE: Arabic (official); French; English

RELIGION: Islam (Sunni, Alawi); Christianity; Druze; Judaism; Baha'i

1 ● INTRODUCTION

Syrians live in the Syrian Arab Republic, more commonly known as Syria. It is a land that has been inhabited for more than 7,000 years. The fertile land of Syria lies at the crossroads of great trade routes between the East and West. It is also the site of many holy places in Judaism, Christianity, and Islam. Because of these advantages, it has been invaded, conquered, and occupied by many different peoples over its long history. These groups include the Egyptians, Babylonians, Persians, Greeks, Romans, Arabs, European Crusaders, Mongols from Central Asia, Turks, British, and French.

In 1946, the French gave up control over Syria, and the Syrian Arab Republic was created.

2 ● LOCATION

The Syrian Arab Republic is a small country located on the eastern edge of the Mediterranean Sea. With a total area of 71,500 square miles (85,180 square kilometers), Syria is slightly larger than the state of North Dakota. Two-thirds of Syria is desert; the other third is part of the Fertile Crescent along the Mediterranean coast. About 80 percent of the population lives in that fertile region.

The total population of Syria is a little over 13 million. Half the people live in cities, 4 million in Damascus alone.

3 ● LANGUAGE

Arabic is the official language of the Syrian Arab Republic and the language spoken by nearly all Syrians. French is the second-most-common language. However, it has started to be rivaled by English.

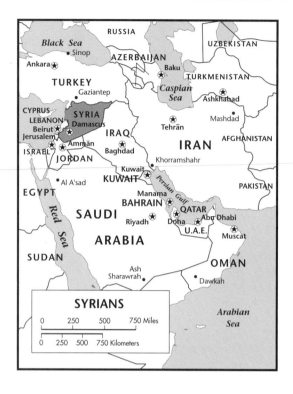

SYRIANS

0   250   500   750 Miles

0   250   500   750 Kilometers

At least half of Syria's men and boys are named *Muhammad*. (They often use their middle names to distinguish themselves from each other).

4 ● FOLKLORE

Syrians are great believers in fate and frequently resign themselves to it. They also love proverbs. The following are two examples: "One who has no good for his family has no good for anyone," and "Where there are no people, there is Hell."

One of Syria's heroes is Queen Zenobia of the ancient city of Palmyra who took control in AD 267 when her husband and her son were both assassinated. Queen Zenobia led her troops in battle against the Romans. When a Syrian man tells a woman that she is incapable of doing something, she often retorts, "What about our Queen Zenobia?" This is supposed to remind him of a woman's ability to meet a great challenge.

5 ● RELIGION

The majority religion in Syria is Islam: 85 percent of the population is Muslim (most are of the Sunni sect, the rest are Alawi). Other groups include Christians (mostly Roman Catholic or Eastern Orthodox), Druze, Jews, Baha'is, and others.

The Islamic religion has five "pillars," or practices, that must be observed by all Muslims: (1) praying five times a day; (2) giving alms, or *zakat,* to the poor; (3) fasting during the month of *Ramadan;* (4) making the pilgrimage, or *hajj,* to Mecca; and (5) reciting the *shahada (ashhadu an la illah ila Allah wa ashhadu in Muhammadu rasul Allah),* which means "I witness that there is

Oddly, Syrians do not use standard Arabic numerals. Instead they use numerals that came to them from India. "Hello" in Arabic is *marhaba* or *ahlan,* to which one replies, *marhabtayn* or *ahlayn.* Other common greetings are *As-salam alaykum* (Peace be with you), with the reply of *Walaykum as-salam* (and to you peace). *Maassalama* means "goodbye." "Thank you" is *Shukran,* and "You're welcome" is *Afwan.* "Yes" is *naam,* and "no" is *laa.* The numbers one to ten in Arabic are: *wahad, ithnayn, thalatha, arbaa, khamsa, sita, saba, thamanya, tisa,* and *ashara.*

Ice cream is called *booza,* and fruity soft drinks are known as *gazooza.* All other soft drinks are called cola.

no god but Allah and that Muhammad is the prophet of Allah."

6 ● MAJOR HOLIDAYS

Muslim holidays, Christmas and Easter (both the Western and Orthodox dates), and the Western New Year (January 1) are official days off in Syria. There are also many political holidays, celebrated with fireworks, parades, military air shows, and speeches. Some of these are Union Day (February 22), Revolution Day/Women's Day (March 8), Arab League Day (March 22), Evacuation Day (commemorating Syrian independence, April 17), and Martyr's Day (May 6).

Most businesses and services are closed on Friday, the Islamic day of rest. The main Muslim holidays are *Eid al-Fitr,* a three-day festival at the end of *Ramadan; Eid al-Adha,* a three-day feast of sacrifice at the end of the month of pilgrimage to Mecca (known as the *hajj*), when families who can afford it slaughter a lamb and share the meat with poorer Muslims; the First of *Muharram,* or the Muslim New Year; *Mawlid An-Nabawi,* the prophet Muhammad's birthday; and *Eid Al-Isra wa Al-Miraj,* a feast celebrating Muhammad's legendary nocturnal visit to heaven.

7 ● RITES OF PASSAGE

Weddings are a major social event and rite of passage. The actual exchange of vows often takes place a few days or weeks before the wedding reception. In the presence of a religious leader, a marriage contract is signed before witnesses. A *mahr* (dowry) is paid by the groom's family to the bride's family.

Children live at home until marriage. Sons might bring their wives to live with their families. Upon the death of one parent, an adult child (usually a son) is required to take care of the surviving parent until death.

After a death, there are three days of mourning. Friends, relatives, and neighbors visit the family of the deceased. Close women relatives wear black for many months. Later they can start wearing half black and half white. Traditionally, it can be up to a year before the women can wear colors again.

8 ● RELATIONSHIPS

Syrians are often aggressive in public. They cut in line, bump into people without apologizing, and honk their car horns constantly. Haggling over prices is a way of life. Punctuality is not considered important. Both men and women are very affectionate with others of the same sex. They may touch, hold hands, or even kiss their friends on the mouth in public. This is not considered sexual behavior.

Syrians stand close together, talk loudly, and use vigorous hand gestures. A downward nod of the head to one side means "Yes." Brushing open palms together quickly as if to brush off dirt means "I'm finished with it (or you)." Patting the hand over the heart when meeting someone expresses affection for that person.

9 ● LIVING CONDITIONS

Syria is not a wealthy country; most people have a mediocre standard of living at best. City dwellers live in apartments. Those who are wealthy enough build villas or large vacation homes in the mountains or on the sea coast.

Villagers live in small, one- to three-room houses with a small courtyard. The older ones are made of adobe bricks and plaster. The central point of the house is the front door. It is often huge and painted with multicolored geometric patterns. The interiors of most Syrian homes are ornate and highly decorated. A favorite Syrian decoration is a massive crystal chandelier that can be seen from outside the house.

10 ● FAMILY LIFE

Children live with their parents until they marry and sometimes after. There are no nursing homes in Syria; the elderly are cared for at home by their families. Children are sometimes punished harshly. However, children and parents show a great deal of affection for each other. Arranged marriages are still common. First cousins are the preferred match. Divorce is rare. When a divorce is granted, the father usually gets custody of the children. Women are constitutionally guaranteed equal rights. In reality, however, traditional duties and expectations usually keep them from enjoying those rights.

11 ● CLOTHING

Syrians wear a mix of traditional Arab and Western-style clothing. However, casual Western clothes such as jeans, T-shirts, and running shoes are rarely seen. Both men and women cover their legs to at least below the knee. Their arms are covered to below the elbow. Neither men nor women wear shorts. Middle- and upper-class women, especially younger ones, are flashy dressers. They like

bright colors, lots of jewelry and make-up, high-heeled shoes, and "big hair." Young men have very short, closely cropped hair and also dress stylishly.

12 ● FOOD

Syrians eat typical Middle Eastern food. Common dishes include *hummus* (a ground chickpea paste), *falafel* (fried, ground chickpeas), and *shish kebab* (lamb chunks on skewers). A special Syrian dish is *farooj*, roasted chicken with chilies and onions. In general, Syrians love their food either very sweet or very sour. Common basic ingredients in Syrian food include lamb, chicken, chickpeas, eggplant, rice, *burghul* (cracked wheat), olives, and yogurt. Syrians drink their coffee *(qahwa)* strong and sweet; tea *(shay)* is also drunk frequently.

Stuffed grape leaves are a common dish in Syria, as elsewhere in the Middle East. Leaves are picked off the vine, washed, and dipped briefly in boiling water. Each leaf is laid out on a flat surface. A mixture of rice, margarine, spices, and ground meat is prepared. A small portion of the filling is laid in a straight line across the bottom of the leaf. The leaf is then rolled up over the rice mixture. The stuffed grape leaves are set in a pot and covered with water, salt, and tomato sauce. They are cooked on the stovetop until tender, about one-half hour.

Meals in Syria last a long time, two to three hours or more. Most food is eaten by hand or scooped up with flatbread.

13 ● EDUCATION

Schooling is required for six years. Schoolchildren wear green, military-style uniforms and attend school six days a week. In high

A Syrian marketing chicken. Most Syrian food uses some combination of the same basic ingredients: lamb, chicken, chickpeas and other dried beans, eggplant, rice, cracked wheat, olives, yogurt, cheese, garlic, and olive oil.

school, students must study either English or French for two years. Higher education is paid for by the government at the four Syrian universities. These universities, however, are overcrowded and use outdated teaching methods. Thus, those who can afford it study abroad.

14 ● CULTURAL HERITAGE

Syria's literary heritage includes mostly theologians, philosophers, and scientists. Jacob of Edessa (late seventh century AD) is best known for his *Syriac Grammar*. The philosopher Bar Hebraeus (mid-thirteenth century AD) wrote on logic, physics, mathematics, and astronomy.

The Arabic poetry tradition remains strong in Syria. Ali Ahmad Said (1930–), pen-named Adunis, is an influential Syrian poet. He was exiled to Beirut in 1956 and still lives there. A popular contemporary woman writer is Ghada al-Samman, who also lives in Beirut.

The 'oud is a popular musical instrument. An ancient stringed instrument, it is an ancestor of the European lute.

The Islamic ban on depicting the human form has greatly shaped Muslim visual art.

This art finds its greatest expression in mosques.

15 ● EMPLOYMENT

Engineering graduates must work for a government agency for five years. Otherwise, however, most Syrians may work at any job they can find. All jobs pay low wages, so almost all Syrians work two or three jobs. Unemployment was high in the 1970s and 1980s and remains a serious problem. One out of five workers is employed by the government. Many work in unnecessary jobs created mostly to reduce unemployment. Fewer than 10 percent of Syrian women work outside the home. There is a large standing army, which employs a number of young men.

16 ● SPORTS

Syrians enjoy soccer as a spectator sport. They also play the game in friendly street competitions. One can regularly spot boys playing soccer in open fields, school playgrounds, or anywhere there is enough space for a game. Martial arts are very popular. Syrians also enjoying swimming, tennis, track meets, and ping-pong tournaments. There are soccer and basketball teams, and camel racing is a popular spectator sport.

17 ● RECREATION

Eating and socializing are the main forms of entertainment. Some public activities are considered socially unacceptable for women. Men sit for hours in all-male teahouses drinking tea or Turkish coffee. They smoke water-pipes, talk, and sometimes play a favorite board game—a Turkish form of backgammon. Young men often hang out in the streets. If they have cars, they cruise the streets. On Fridays, the Islamic day of rest, Syrians with cars often drive to mountain resorts. There they eat, talk, and take strolls.

Cinemas show American and Asian action films that are popular with young men. Wealthy Syrians own VCRs and like to rent videos. All Syrians enjoy concerts, from jazz to classical. They especially love parties. At celebrations men and women, either separately or together, perform the *dabka,* a line dance. It is performed to the music of a band or a hand-held drum called a *tabla.* A leader guides the dancers by shouting out moves as he or she dances in front of them.

There is a well-attended international folk music and dance festival every September in an ancient Roman amphitheater in Busra.

18 ● CRAFTS AND HOBBIES

Syrian crafts include jewelry-making, inlaid woodworking, glass-blowing, weaving, and embroidery. Textiles include clothing, tablecloths, pillow covers, and carpets. A special brocaded fabric called "damask" is named for the city of Damascus. Modern damask is still woven by hand.

Syria is known for an *alum* charm that is supposed to ward off evil. The charm is blue and triangular. It is adorned with strands of beads and a symbolic blue hand that protects its owner. Taxis and buses have the charms hanging from their rearview mirrors.

19 ● SOCIAL PROBLEMS

A struggling economy, high unemployment, and a low standard of living make life difficult for most Syrians. Many of the brightest students go abroad to study and never return. Social status is associated with skin color, with the lightest-skinned people at the top and the darkest-skinned at the bottom.

20 ● BIBLIOGRAPHY

Beaton, M. *Syria.* Chicago: Children's Press, 1988.

Mulloy, Martin. *Syria.* New York: Chelsea House, 1988.

Roberts, David. *The Ba'th and the Creation of Modern Syria.* New York: St. Martin's, 1987.

South, Coleman. Cultures of the World: Syria. New York: Marshall Cavendish, 1995.

WEBSITES

ArabNet. [Online] Available http://www.arab.net/syria/syria_contents.html, 1998.

World Travel Guide. Syria. [Online] Available http://www.wtgonline.com/country/sy/gen.html, 1998.

Druze

PRONUNCIATION: DROOZ
LOCATION: Lebanon; Syria; Israel; Jordan
POPULATION: Under 1 million
LANGUAGE: Arabic
RELIGION: Secret Druze faith (Muhwahhidun)

1 ● INTRODUCTION

The Druze are both a religious and an ethnic group. The group originated in Cairo, Egypt, in AD 1009–10. They then spread to the mountains of southern Lebanon and beyond. The Druze faith grew out of the Ismaili sect of Shi'ah Islam. However, disil-lusioned with the Ismailis, the Druze turned to Caliph al-Hakim of Egypt as their deliverer.

Persecution of the Druze began early in their history. Their earliest leaders were forced into hiding, and many Druze were murdered. The survivors in southern Lebanon and Syria became secretive in order to survive. For the most part, no new converts have been accepted by the Druze since AD 1043. One must be born a Druze; no one can become one by choice.

Today, the Syrian Druze community is growing, as many have fled the former Druze center in war-torn Lebanon.

2 ● LOCATION

The total Druze population throughout the world is probably under 1 million. Approximately 900,000 live in Lebanon, Syria, Israel, and Jordan. The largest communities outside the Middle East are in North and South America. There are smaller groups in Australia, West Africa, and Western Europe.

Most Druze are still hardy, independent farmers living in mountain villages of less than 10,000 people. All Druze villages are located on hills or mountains, primarily for purposes of defense. In Lebanon, most Druze have olive groves and fruit orchards. In southern Syria, they are more likely to be wheat farmers.

3 ● LANGUAGE

The Druze speak Arabic, with some distinguishing features. For example, they have kept the *qaf,* the strong guttural *k* sound of classical Arabic. (It has been dropped or changed to a *j* or hard *g* sound in other Arabic dialects.) They have also retained the *dad,* a soft *d* sound that has been lost in other Arabic dialects.

Today most Druze children are given names that are common to Christians and Muslims, such as *Samir, Salim, Fu'ad,* or *Fawzi* for boys.

4 ● FOLKLORE

The Druze believe that the number of souls of believers and nonbelievers was fixed at Creation. Thus, every time a Druze dies, another Druze is born. The soul of the deceased immediately enters the body of the newborn.

5 ● RELIGION

Because the Druze faith is surrounded by secrecy, few of their beliefs are known to the world. However, it is known that they believe in one God.

In every community, only a few Druze of each generation learn all the details of their faith. The rest are called the *juhhal,* or "noninitiated." They are given a simplified outline of the faith to follow.

The initiated, called `*uqqal,* or "enlightened," are put through rigorous tests. Once initiated, they wear a heavy white turban. They never wear bright colors, swear or use obscene language, drink alcohol, or smoke. At religious services, the juhhal attend only the first part of the service, where community affairs are discussed. Then they leave so the `uqqal can engage in prayer, study, and meditation.

The Druze believe that prayer and ritual are unnecessary when true knowledge of God's unity is gained. They consider prayer

to be a constant state of being, rather than something one does at certain times of day.

Women have been included in the `uqqal since the beginning of the Druze movement.

The Druze have shrines that they visit frequently, called *mazar* or *maqam,* located on the tops or sides of hills and mountains. At the tomb of the holy man or woman to whom the shrine is dedicated, the Druze pray quietly, leave small gifts of food and money, and take away small pieces of colored cloth as tokens of divine blessing to be kept in their homes or in the family car. Some families come for extended stays to sacrifice animals in the fulfillment of a vow. Others just have picnics or spend a quiet weekend there.

6 ● MAJOR HOLIDAYS

Religious observance of holy days is not important to the Druze. However, annual religious festivals do attract thousands of Druze to the shrines of certain holy men and women, such as al-Nabi Shuayb. There is also an annual pilgrimage to the alleged burial place of Jethro, Moses' father-in-law, near the Horns of Hittim in Galilee.

7 ● RITES OF PASSAGE

Unlike Muslims and Jews, the Druze do not practice circumcision of males.

Weddings are small gatherings. However, they can be extravagant, depending on the wealth of the family.

Funerals are huge community events; people from all over attend. Funeral arrangements are made immediately after death. The ceremony is held the next day at the latest. The body is washed and dressed in the finest clothes available. It is buried above ground level just outside the village. Every Druze village has a *mawqaf*, or "stopping place." This is a small cement or stone amphitheater with rows of seats. Hundreds, even thousands, can gather there to honor and remember a deceased person and give condolences to the family.

8 ● RELATIONSHIPS

Among themselves (and others they feel they can trust), the Druze are extremely hospitable and generous. Almost all Druze villages have one or more *mudafat*, guest houses where visitors can stay.

The Druze look after the less fortunate in their community. There is no such thing as a Druze beggar. If an extended family cannot support one of its members, the rest of the community will help out.

9 ● LIVING CONDITIONS

Most Druze still live in small villages. Some villages have electricity and telephone service; others do not. Almost all villages now have regular bus and taxi service to major nearby cities.

10 ● FAMILY LIFE

The most important factor in Druze family life is a woman's honor *(ird)*. For this reason, women are very restricted socially, even though they have equal rights politically and religiously. Marriages are almost always arranged by the family. Marriage partners usually come from the same village and often from the same extended family (including first cousins). The groom pays the bride's family a dowry. Polygamy (having more than one spouse) is forbidden, as is marriage to a non-Druze.

The Druze prefer sons to daughters, particularly for the firstborn child. They will continue to have children until a son is born. The average family has five or six children, but Druze families can be as large as ten to twelve children.

Divorce is difficult to obtain, but women as well as men can initiate the proceedings. The failure of a woman to bear children (particularly sons) is a frequent cause for divorce.

11 ● CLOTHING

Druze living in small villages still wear traditional clothing. Women wear a blue or black peasant dress with a gauzy white head covering called a *mandil*. They wear red slipperlike shoes. The `uqqal (initiated) wear baggy pants that are tight at the ankle. *Juhhal* (uninitiated) men wear the common Arab head scarf, the *keffiyeh*. The `uqqal wear heavy white turbans. Most Druze men have large moustaches with waxed tips.

12 ● FOOD

Most Druze families grow their own fruit and vegetables and bake their own bread. They eat a mostly vegetarian diet, with meat only on special occasions. Typical foods include olives; mountain bread (paper-thin, round, unleavened bread); yogurt; chickpeas flavored with onions, garlic, and tahini (sesame paste); and bulghur (cracked wheat). Salad is made of tomatoes, cucumber, parsley, and other herbs, with olive oil and lemon juice. Meats include lamb, kid (young goat's meat), chicken, and beef.

13 ● EDUCATION

Among the younger generation of Druze (under age twenty-five), literacy is almost universal. Most girls traditionally stopped their formal schooling after six years of basic elementary education. Today more girls attend secondary school, and some even go on to university or professional training (as nurses or teachers, for example).

14 ● CULTURAL HERITAGE

Druze poetry does not have any love songs. Instead, it focuses on themes such as the love of God and of one's native countryside. Druze writers include poet Samih al-Qasim and Shaqib Arslan, known as "the prince of eloquence" *(amir al-bayan)*. Among classical musicians, pianist Diana Taqi al-Din is a Druze. A well-known performer of traditional Middle Eastern music was singer and composer Farid al-Atrash (1916–76).

15 ● EMPLOYMENT

The Druze were traditionally farmers. Now they can now be found in all areas of business. These include banking, trade, retail, and transportation services. Druze women rarely work outside the home.

16 ● SPORTS

The Druze enjoy most popular sports, including hunting, fishing, soccer, basketball, tennis, volleyball, water skiing, and water polo.

17 ● RECREATION

Druze families often enjoy picnics at religious shrines on mountaintops and hillsides. They may spend an entire weekend at these sites, relaxing in the quiet atmosphere.

18 ● CRAFTS AND HOBBIES

The Druze are known for their weaving, carpet-making, and basketry.

19 ● SOCIAL PROBLEMS

Because they are such a close-knit society, the Druze have very few social problems. Living in small mountain villages, the Druze have learned to take care of their own. However, they have suffered almost constant persecution from outsiders.

20 ● BIBLIOGRAPHY.

Betts, Robert Brenton. *The Druze*. New Haven, Conn.: Yale University Press, 1988.

Makarem, Sami Nasib. *The Druze Faith*. Delmar, N.Y.: Caravan Books, 1974.

WEBSITES

ArabNet. [Online] Available http://www.arab.net/syria/syria_contents.html, 1998.

World Travel Guide. Syria. [Online] Available http://www.wtgonline.com/country/sy/gen.html, 1998.

Glossary

aboriginal: The first known inhabitants of a country.

adobe: A brick made from sun-dried heavy clay mixed with straw, used in building houses.

Altaic language family: A family of languages spoken in portions of northern and eastern Europe, and nearly the whole of northern and central Asia, together with some other regions.

Amerindian: A contraction of the two words, American Indian. It describes native peoples of North, South, or Central America.

Anglican: Pertaining to or connected with the Church of England.

animism: The belief that natural objects and phenomena have souls or innate spiritual powers.

apartheid: The past governmental policy in the Republic of South Africa of separating the races in society.

arable land: Land that can be cultivated by plowing and used for growing crops.

archipelago: Any body of water abounding with islands, or the islands themselves collectively.

Austronesian language: A family of languages which includes practically all the languages of the Pacific Islands—Indonesian, Melanesian, Polynesian, and Micronesian sub-families.

average life expectancy: In any given society, the average age attained by persons at the time of death.

Baha'i: The follower of a religious sect founded by Mirza Husayn Ali in Iran in 1863.

Baltic states: The three formerly communist countries of Estonia, Latvia, and Lithuania that border on the Baltic Sea.

Bantu language group: A name applied to the languages spoken in central and south Africa.

Baptist: A member of a Protestant denomination that practices adult baptism by complete immersion in water.

barren land: Unproductive land, partly or entirely treeless.

barter: Trade practice where merchandise is exchanged directly for other merchandise or services without use of money.

Berber: a member of one of the Afroasiatic peoples of northern Africa.

Brahman: A member (by heredity) of the highest caste among the Hindus, usually assigned to the priesthood.

bride wealth (bride price): Fee, in money or goods, paid by a prospective groom (and his family) to the bride's family.

Buddhism: A religious system common in India and eastern Asia. Founded by Siddhartha Gautama (c.563–c.483 BC), Buddhism asserts that suffering is an inescapable part of life. Deliverance can only be achieved through the practice of charity, temperance, justice, honesty, and truth.

Byzantine Empire: An empire centered in the city of Byzantium, now Istanbul in present-day Turkey.

cassava: The name of several species of stout herbs, extensively cultivated for food.

caste system: Heriditary social classes into which the Hindus are rigidly separated according to the religious law of Brahmanism. Privileges and limitations of each caste are passed down from parents to children.

Caucasian: The white race of human beings, as determined by genealogy and physical features.

census: An official counting of the inhabitants of a state or country with details of sex and age, family, occupation, possessions, etc.

Christianity: The religion founded by Jesus Christ, based on the Bible as holy scripture.

Church of England: The national and established church in England.

civil rights: The privileges of all individuals to be treated as equals under the laws of their country; specifically, the rights given by certain amendments to the U.S. Constitution.

coastal plain: A fairly level area of land along the coast of a land mass.

coca: A shrub native to South America, the leaves of which produce organic compounds that are used in the production of cocaine.

colonial period: The period of time when a country forms colonies in and extends control over a foreign area.

colonist: Any member of a colony or one who helps settle a new colony.

colony: A group of people who settle in a new area far from their original country, but still under the jurisdiction of that country. Also refers to the newly settled area itself.

commonwealth: A free association of sovereign independent states that has no charter, treaty, or constitution. The association promotes cooperation, consultation, and mutual assistance among members.

communism: A form of government whose system requires common ownership of property for the use of all citizens. Prices on goods and services are usually set by the government, and all profits are shared equally by everyone. Also, communism refers directly to the official doctrine of the former Soviet Union.

compulsory education: The mandatory requirement for children to attend school until they have reached a certain age or grade level.

Confucianism: The system of ethics and politics taught by the Chinese philosopher Confucius.

constitution: The written laws and basic rights of citizens of a country or members of an organized group.

copra: The dried meat of the coconut.

cordillera: A continuous ridge, range, or chain of mountains.

coup d'ètat (coup): A sudden, violent overthrow of a government or its leader.

cuisine: A particular style of preparing food, especially when referring to the cooking of a particular country or ethnic group.

Cushitic language group: A group of languages that are spoken in Ethiopia and other areas of eastern Africa.

Cyrillic alphabet: An alphabet invented by Cyril and Methodius in the ninth century as an alphabet that was easier for the copyist to write. The Russian alphabet is a slight modification of it.

deity: A being with the attributes, nature, and essence of a god; a divinity.

desegregation: The act of removing restrictions on people of a particular race that keep them socially, economically, and, sometimes, physically, separate from other groups.

desertification: The process of becoming a desert as a result of climatic changes, land mismanagement, or both.

Dewali (Deepavali, Divali): The Hindu Festival of Lights, when Lakshmi, goddess of good fortune, is said to visit the homes of humans. The four- or five-day festival occurs in October or November.

dialect: One of a number of regional or related modes of speech regarded as descending from a common origin.

dowry: The sum of the property or money that a bride brings to her groom at their marriage.

Druze: A member of a Muslim sect based in Syria, living chiefly in the mountain regions of Lebanon.

dynasty: A family line of sovereigns who rule in succession, and the time during which they reign.

Eastern Orthodox: The outgrowth of the original Eastern Church of the Eastern Roman Empire, consisting of eastern Europe, western Asia, and Egypt.

Eid al-Adha: The Muslim holiday that celebrates the end of the special pilgrimage season (hajj) to the city of Mecca in Saudi Arabia.

Eid al-Fitr: The Muslim holiday that begins just after the end of the month of Ramadan and is celebrated with three or four days of feasting.

emigration: Moving from one country or region to another for the purpose of residence.

empire: A group of territories ruled by one sovereign or supreme ruler. Also, the period of time under that rule.

Episcopal: Belonging to or vested in bishops or prelates; characteristic of or pertaining to a bishop or bishops.

exports: Goods sold to foreign buyers.

Finno-Ugric language group: A subfamily of languages spoken in northeastern Europe, including Finnish, Hungarian, Estonian, and Lapp.

fjord: A deep indentation of the land forming a comparatively narrow arm of the sea with more or less steep slopes or cliffs on each side.

folk religion: A religion with origins and traditions among the common people of a nation or region that is relevant to their particular life-style.

Former Soviet Union: Refers to the republics that were once part of a large nation called the Union of Soviet Socialists Republics (USSR). The USSR was commonly called the Soviet Union. It included the 12 republics: Russia, Ukraine, Belarus, Moldova, Armenia, Azerbaijan, Uzbekistan, Turkmenistan, Tajikistan, Kazakhstan, Kyrgizstan, and Georgia. Sometimes the Baltic republics of Estonia, Latvia, and Lithuania are also included.

fundamentalist: A person who holds religious beliefs based on the complete acceptance of the words of holy scriptures as the truth.

Germanic language group: A large branch of the Indo-European family of languages including German itself, the Scandinavian languages, Dutch, Yiddish, Modern English, Modern Scottish, Afrikaans, and others. The group also includes extinct languages such as Gothic, Old High German, Old Saxon, Old English, Middle English, and the like.

Greek Orthodox: The official church of Greece, a self-governing branch of the Orthodox Eastern Church.

guerrilla: A member of a small radical military organization that uses unconventional tactics to take their enemies by surprise.

hajj: A religious journey made by Muslims to the holy city of Mecca in Saudi Arabia.

Holi: A Hindu festival of processions and merriment lasting three to ten days that marks the end of the lunar year in February or March.

Holocaust: The mass slaughter of European civilians, the vast majority of whom were Jews, by the Nazis during World War II.

Holy Roman Empire: A kingdom consisting of a loose union of German and Italian territories that existed from around the ninth century until 1806.

homeland: A region or area set aside to be a state for a people of a particular national, cultural, or racial origin.

homogeneous: Of the same kind or nature, often used in reference to a whole.

Horn of Africa: The Horn of Africa comprises Djibouti, Eritrea, Ethiopia, Somalia, and Sudan.

human rights issues: Any matters involving people's basic rights which are in question or thought to be abused.

immigration: The act or process of passing or entering into another country for the purpose of permanent residence.

imports: Goods purchased from foreign suppliers.

indigenous: Born or originating in a particular place or country; native to a particular region or area.

Indo-Aryan language group: The group that includes the languages of India; also called Indo-European language group.

Indo-European language family: The group that includes the languages of India and much of Europe and southwestern Asia.

Islam: The religious system of Muhammad, practiced by Muslims and based on a belief in Allah as the supreme being and Muhammed as his prophet. Islam also refers to those nations in which it is the primary religion. There are two major sects: Sunni and Shia (or Shiite). The main difference between the two sects is in their belief in who follows Muhammad, founder of Islam, as the religious leader.

Judaism: The religious system of the Jews, based on the Old Testament as revealed to Moses and characterized by a belief in one God and adherence to the laws of scripture and rabbinic traditions.

khan: A sovereign, or ruler, in central Asia.

khanate: A kingdom ruled by a khan, or man of rank.

literacy: The ability to read and write.

Maghreb states: Refers to Algeria, Morocco, and Tunisia; sometimes includes Libya and Mauritania.

maize: Another name (Spanish or British) for corn or the color of ripe corn.

manioc: The cassava plant or its product. Manioc is a very important food-staple in tropical America.

matrilineal (descent): Descending from, or tracing descent through, the maternal, or mother's, family line.

Mayan language family: The languages of the Central American Indians, further divided into two subgroups: the Maya and the Huastek.

mean temperature: The air temperature unit measured by the National Weather Service by adding the maximum and minimum daily temperatures together and diving the sum by 2.

Mecca: A city in Saudi Arabia; a destination of Muslims in the Islamic world.

mestizo: The offspring of a person of mixed blood; especially, a person of mixed Spanish and American Indian parentage.

millet: A cereal grass whose small grain is used for food in Europe and Asia.

monarchy: Government by a sovereign, such as a king or queen.

Mongol: One of an Asiatic race chiefly resident in Mongolia, a region north of China proper and south of Siberia.

Moors: One of the Arab tribes that conquered Spain in the eighth century.

Moslem *see* **Muslim.**

mosque: An Islam place of worship and the organization with which it is connected.

Muhammad (or Muhammed or Mahomet): An Arabian prophet (AD 570–632), known as the "Prophet of Allah" who founded the religion of Islam in 622, and wrote the Koran, (also spelled Quran) the scripture of Islam.

mulatto: One who is the offspring of parents one of whom is white and the other is black.

Muslim: A follower of Muhammad in the religion of Islam.

Muslim New Year: A Muslim holiday also called Nawruz. In some countries Muharram 1, which is the first month of the Islamic year, is observed as a holiday, in other places the new year is observed on Sha'ban, the eighth month of the year. This practice apparently stems from pagan Arab times. Shab-i-Bharat, a national holiday in Bangladesh on this day, is held by many to be the occasion when God ordains all actions in the coming year.

mystic: Person who believes he or she can gain spiritual knowledge through processes like meditation that are not easily explained by reasoning or rational thinking.

nationalism: National spirit or aspirations; desire for national unity, independence, or prosperity.

oasis: Fertile spot in the midst of a desert or wasteland.

official language: The language in which the business of a country and its government is conducted.

Ottoman Empire: A Turkish empire that existed from about 1603 until 1918, and included lands around the Mediterranean, Black, and Caspian seas.

patriarchal system: A social system in which the head of the family or tribe is the father or oldest male. Ancestry is determined and traced through the male members of the tribe.

patrilineal (descent): Descending from, or tracing descent through, the paternal, or father's, family line.

pilgrimage: religious journey, usually to a holy place.

plantain: Tropical plant with fruit that looks like bananas, but that must be cooked before eating.

Protestant: A member of one of the Christian bodies that descended from the Reformation of the sixteenth century.

pulses: Beans, peas, or lentils.

Ramadan: The ninth month of the Muslim calender. The entire month commemorates the period in which the Prophet Muhammad is said to have recieved divine revelation and is observed by a strict fast from sunrise to sundown.

Rastafarian: A member of a Jamaican cult begun in 1930 that is partly religious and partly political.

refugee: Person who, in times of persecution or political commotion, flees to a foreign country for safety.

revolution: A complete change in a government or society, such as in an overthrow of the government by the people.

Roman alphabet: Alphabet of the ancient Romans from which alphabets of most modern European languages, including English, are derived.

Roman Catholic Church: Christian church headed by the pope or Bishop of Rome.

Russian Orthodox: The arm of the Eastern Orthodox Church that was the official church of Russia under the tsars.

Sahelian zone: Eight countries make up this dry desert zone in Africa: Burkina Faso, Chad, Gambia, Mali, Mauritania, Niger, Senegal, and the Cape Verde Islands.

savanna: A treeless or near treeless grassland or plain.

segregation: The enforced separation of a racial or religious group from other groups, compelling them to live and go to school separately from the rest of society.

Seventh-day Adventist: One who believes in the second coming of Christ to establish a personal reign upon the earth.

shamanism: A religion in which shamans (priests or medicine men) are believed to influence spirits.

shantytown: An urban settlement of people in inadequate houses.

Shia Muslim *see* Islam.

Shiites *see* Islam.

Shintoism: The system of nature- and hero-worship that forms the native religion of Japan.

sierra: A chain of hills or mountains.

Sikh: A member of a community of India, founded around 1500 and based on the principles of monotheism (belief in one god) and human brotherhood.

Sino-Tibetan language family: The family of languages spoken in eastern Asia, including China, Thailand, Tibet, and Myanmar.

slash-and-burn agriculture: A hasty and sometimes temporary way of clearing land to make it available for agriculture by cutting down trees and burning them; also known as swidden agriculture.

slave trade: The transportation of black Africans beginning in the 1700s to other countries to be sold as slaves—people owned as property and compelled to work for their owners at no pay.

Slavic languages: A major subgroup of the Indo-European language family. It is further subdivided into West Slavic (including Polish, Czech, Slovak and Serbian), South Slavic (including Bulgarian, Serbo-Croatian, Slovene, and Old Church Slavonic), and East Slavic (including Russian Ukrainian and Byelorussian).

sorghum: Plant grown for its valuable uses, such as for grain, syrup, or fodder.

Southeast Asia: The region in Asia that consists of the Malay Archipelago, the Malay Peninsula, and Indochina.

Soviet Union *see* **Former Soviet Union.**

subcontinent: A large subdivision of a continent.

subsistence farming: Farming that provides only the minimum food goods necessary for the continuation of the farm family.

Sudanic language group: A related group of languages spoken in various areas of northern Africa, including Yoruba, Mandingo, and Tshi.

Sufi: A Muslim mystic who believes that God alone exists, there can be no real difference between good and evil, that the soul exists within the body as in a cage, so death should be the chief object of desire.

sultan: A king of a Muslim state.

Sunni Muslim *see* Islam.

Taoism: The doctrine of Lao-Tzu, an ancient Chinese philosopher (c.500 BC) as laid down by him in the *Tao-te-ching.*

Third World: A term used to describe less developed countries; as of the mid-1990s, it is being replaced by the United Nations designation Less Developed Countries, or LDC.

treaty: A negotiated agreement between two governments.

tribal system: A social community in which people are organized into groups or clans descended from common ancestors and sharing customs and languages.

tundra: A nearly level treeless area whose climate and vegetation are characteristically arctic due to its northern position; the subsoil is permanently frozen.

untouchables: In India, members of the lowest caste in the caste system, a hereditary social class system. They were considered unworthy to touch members of higher castes.

Union of the Soviet Socialist Republics *see* Former Soviet Union.

veldt: A grassland in South Africa.

Western nations: General term used to describe democratic, capitalist countries, including the United States, Canada, and western European countries.

Zoroastrianism: The system of religious doctrine taught by Zoroaster and his followers in the Avesta; the religion prevalent in Persia until its overthrow by the Muslims in the seventh century.

Index

All culture groups and countries included in this encyclopedia are included in this index. Selected regions, alternate groups names, and historical country names are cross-referenced. Country chapter titles are in boldface; volume numbers appear in brackets, with page number following.